II1032222

Walking with God
Day by Day

OTHER CROSSWAY BOOKS BY
MARTYN LLOYD-JONES

Alive in Christ
The Cross
The Kingdom of God
My Soul Magnifies the Lord
Out of the Depths
Revival
True Happiness
Truth Unchanged, Unchanging
Why Does God Allow War?
(originally *Why Does God Allow Suffering?*)

GREAT DOCTRINES OF THE BIBLE
Volume 1: *God the Father, God the Son*
Volume 2: *God the Holy Spirit*
Volume 3: *The Church and Last Things*
(also available in one volume: *Great Doctrines of the Bible)*

LIFE IN CHRIST: STUDIES IN 1 JOHN
Volume 1: *Fellowship with God*
Volume 2: *Walking with God*
Volume 3: *Children of God*
Volume 4: *The Love of God*
Volume 5: *Life in God*
(also available in one volume: *Life in Christ*)

STUDIES IN THE BOOK OF ACTS
Volume 1: *Authentic Christianity*
Volume 2: *Courageous Christianity*
Volume 3: *Victorious Christianity*

STUDIES IN JOHN 17
Volume 1: *Saved in Eternity*
Volume 2: *Safe in the World*
Volume 3: *Sanctified Through the Truth*
Volume 4: *Growing in the Spirit*
(also available in one volume: *The Assurance of Our Salvation*)

365 DAILY DEVOTIONAL SELECTIONS

WALKING WITH GOD

Day by Day

❧

MARTYN LLOYD-JONES

ROBERT BACKHOUSE, EDITOR

CROSSWAY BOOKS
WHEATON, ILLINOIS

Walking with God Day by Day

Copyright © 2003 by Good News Publishers

Published by Crossway Books
        a publishing ministry of Good News Publishers
        1300 Crescent Street
        Wheaton, Illinois 60187

All rights reserved. No part of this publication may be reproduced, stored in a retrieval system or transmitted in any form by any means, electronic, mechanical, photocopy, recording or otherwise, without the prior permission of the publisher, except as provided by USA copyright law.

Cover design: David LaPlaca

Cover photo: Getty Images

First printing, 2003

Printed in the United States of America

Note: *Why Does God Allow War?* has also been published as *Why Does God Allow Suffering?*

All Scripture quotations are taken from the King James Version.

Library of Congress Cataloging-in-Publication Data
Lloyd-Jones, David Martyn.
   Walking with God day by day : 365 daily devotional selections /
Martyn Lloyd-Jones ; Robert Backhouse, editor.
     p. cm.
   ISBN 13: 978-1-58134-516-2 (alk. paper)
   ISBN 10: 1-58134-516-X
   1.Devotional calendars. I. Backhouse, Robert. II. Title.
BV4811.L56   2003
242'.2—dc21   2003006384

LB		18	17	16	15	14	13	12	11	10	09
15	14	13	12	11	10	9	8	7	6	5	4

CONTENTS

PUBLISHER'S FOREWORD

It is impossible to grow spiritually without spending time in God's Word, the Holy Bible. Hearing Scripture on Sundays and occasionally in between is not enough—we need to feed on it regularly for ourselves.

Godly pastors and authors can greatly assist us in such an endeavor. One of these, Martyn Lloyd-Jones (1899-1981), minister of Westminster Chapel in London for thirty years, was one of the twentieth century's leading voices in evangelical doctrine and preaching. His numerous books (many of them published after his home-going) have brought profound spiritual encouragement to literally millions of readers around the world over the years.

Lloyd-Jones had been perhaps the most distinguished medical doctor in all of England. Early in his career, however, he left the medical profession to pursue a "higher calling," namely, the "cure of souls." He is noted for his penetrating diagnosis of the human condition and his persuasive proclamation of the Gospel as the only sufficient answer. This present volume is a valuable continuation of that ministry.

Walking with God Day by Day is a daily devotional sharing short excerpts from many of Dr. Lloyd-Jones's books. The selections are encouraging, enlightening, and challenging. All who use this volume will acquire a greater grasp of biblical truth (concerning salvation, the Gospel, revival, the kingdom of God, knowing God, the victory of faith, and much more) and will learn how to grow closer to Christ with increasing faith.

It is our prayer that these brief readings from the works of Dr. Martyn Lloyd-Jones will nurture and equip you in your walk with Christ.

The Publisher

January

NEW LIFE IN THE SPIRIT

FROM

God the Holy Spirit

NAMES OF THE HOLY SPIRIT

The Spirit of the Lord GOD is upon me.

ISAIAH 61:1

The best way to approach the doctrine of the Holy Spirit is to notice the names or the descriptive titles given to this blessed Person.

First of all, there are the many names that relate Him to the Father. Let me enumerate some of them: "the Spirit of God" (Genesis 1:2); "the Spirit of the Lord" (Luke 4:18); "the Spirit of our God" (1 Corinthians 6:11). Another is "the Spirit of the Lord GOD," which is in Isaiah 61:1. Our Lord speaks, in Matthew 10:20, of "the Spirit of your Father," while Paul refers to "the Spirit of the living God" (2 Corinthians 3:3). "My Spirit," says God in Genesis 6:3, and the psalmist asks, "Whither shall I go from thy spirit?" (Psalm 139:7). He is referred to as His Spirit—God's Spirit—in Numbers 11:29; and Paul, in Romans 8:11, uses the phrase "the Spirit of him [God the Father] that raised up Jesus from the dead." All these are descriptive titles referring to the Holy Spirit in terms of His relationship to the Father.

In the second group are the titles that relate the Holy Spirit to the Son. First, "If any man have not the Spirit of Christ, he is none of his" (Romans 8:9), which is a most important phrase. The word "Spirit" here refers to the Holy Spirit. In Philippians 1:19, Paul speaks about "the Spirit of Jesus Christ," and in Galatians 4:6 he says, "God hath sent forth the Spirit of his Son." Finally He is referred to as "the Spirit of the Lord" (Acts 5:9).

The third group comprises the direct or personal titles, and first and foremost here, of course, is the name *Holy Spirit* or *Holy Ghost*. Some people are confused by those two terms, but they mean exactly the same thing. The English language is a hybrid that has borrowed from other languages, and "Ghost" is an old Anglo-Saxon word, while "Spirit" is derived from the Latin *spiritus*.

❧ A THOUGHT TO PONDER ❧
Notice the names or the descriptive titles given to the Holy Spirit.

WHY IS THE HOLY SPIRIT CALLED HOLY?

But ye have an unction from the Holy One.
1 JOHN 2:20

Why is the Holy Spirit called holy? Surely, the explanation is that it is His special work to produce holiness and order in all that He does in the application of Christ's work of salvation. His objective is to produce holiness, and He does that in nature and creation, as well as in human beings. But His ultimate work is to make us a holy people, holy as the children of God. It is also probable that He is described as the Holy Spirit in order to differentiate Him from the other spirits—the evil spirits. That is why we are told to test the spirits and to prove them and to know whether they are of God or not (1 John 4:1).

Then the next great question is the personality or the personhood of the Spirit. The personhood of the Holy Spirit is not only forgotten by those whom we describe as liberals or modernists in their theology, but we ourselves are often guilty of precisely the same thing. I have heard most orthodox people referring to the Holy Spirit and His work as "it" and "its" influence and so on, as if the Holy Spirit were nothing but an influence or a power. And hymns, too, frequently make the same mistake. There is a confusion about the Holy Spirit, and I am sure there is a sense in which many of us find it a little more difficult to conceive of the third person in the blessed Holy Trinity than to conceive of the Father or the Son.

Why is there this tendency to think of Him as a force or an influence or an emanation? There are a number of answers to that question, but they are not good reasons. His work seems to be impersonal because it is a kind of mystical and secret work. He produces graces and fruits; He gives us gifts, and He gives us various powers. And because of that, we tend to think of Him as if He were some influence. I am sure that this is a great part of the explanation.

❧ A THOUGHT TO PONDER ❧
His special work is to produce holiness.

From *God the Holy Spirit*, p. 8.

THE PERSONALITY OF THE HOLY SPIRIT

The grace of the Lord Jesus Christ, and the love of God, and the
communion of the Holy Ghost . . .

2 CORINTHIANS 13:14

The Holy Spirit is identified with the Father and the Son in such a way as to indicate personality.

There are two great arguments here. The first is the baptismal formula: "baptizing them in the name of the Father, and of the Son, and of the Holy Ghost" (Matthew 28:19). Here He is associated with the Father and the Son in a way that of necessity points to His personality.

The second argument is based on the apostolic benediction in 2 Corinthians 13:14: "The grace of the Lord Jesus Christ, and the love of God, and the communion of the Holy Ghost . . ." Obviously the Holy Spirit is a person in line with the person of the Father and of the Son.

A most interesting way we can prove the personality of the Spirit is by showing that He is identified with us, with Christians, in a way that indicates that He is a person. In Acts 15:28 we read, "For it seemed good to the Holy Ghost, and to us, to lay upon you no greater burden than these necessary things." This was a decision arrived at by members of the early church, and as they were persons, so He must be a person. You cannot say, "It seemed good to a power and to us," because the power would be working in us. But here is someone outside us—"It seemed good to *him* and to *us*."

Personal qualities are ascribed to the Holy Spirit in the Scriptures. He is said, for example, to have knowledge. Paul argues, "For what man knoweth the things of a man, save the spirit of man which is in him? even so the things of God knoweth no man, but the Spirit of God" (1 Corinthians 2:11).

✦ A THOUGHT TO PONDER ✦

The Spirit is identified with us, with Christians, in a way that indicates that He is a person.

From *God the Holy Spirit*, pp. 10-11.

January 4

THE HOLY SPIRIT HAS A MIND

*And he that searcheth the hearts knoweth what
is the mind of the Spirit.*

ROMANS 8:27

The Holy Spirit clearly has a mind. In Romans 8:27 we read, "the mind of the Spirit"—this is in connection with prayer. He is also the one who loves, because we read that "the fruit of the Spirit is love" (Galatians 5:22); and it is His function to shed abroad the love of God in our hearts (Romans 5:5). And, likewise, we know He is capable of grief, because in Ephesians 4:30 we are warned not to "grieve" the Holy Spirit.

The ultimate doctrine about the Spirit, from the practical, experiential standpoint, is that my body is the temple of the Holy Spirit, so that whatever I do, wherever I go, the Holy Spirit is with me. I know nothing that so promotes sanctification and holiness as the realization of that. If only we realized, always, that in anything we do with our bodies, the Holy Spirit is involved! Remember also that Paul teaches that in the context of a warning against fornication. He writes, "Know ye not that your body is the temple of the Holy Ghost which is in you . . .?" (1 Corinthians 6:19). That is why fornication should be unthinkable in a Christian. God is in us, in the Holy Spirit: not an influence, not a power, but a *person* whom we can grieve.

I am going through these details not out of an academic interest, nor because I happen to have a theological type of mind. No, I am concerned about these things, as I am a man trying myself to live the Christian life, and as I am called of God to be a pastor of souls, and I feel the responsibility for the souls and conduct and behavior of others. Wherever you are, wherever you go, if you are a Christian the Holy Spirit is in you; and if you really want to enjoy the blessings of salvation, you do so by knowing that your body is His temple.

❧ A THOUGHT TO PONDER ❧
If you are a Christian, the Holy Spirit is in you.

THE SPIRIT PROHIBITED THEM

He shall testify of me.

JOHN 15:26

Actions are ascribed to the Spirit that can only be performed by a person. For instance, in 1 Corinthians 2:10 we are told that "the Spirit searcheth all things, yea, the deep things of God." He *searches*—that is the action of a person. We are also told clearly that He *speaks*. In Revelation 2:7 we read, "He that hath an ear, let him hear what the Spirit saith unto the churches." Then He also *makes intercession* for us. "We know not what we should pray for as we ought," says Paul in Romans 8:26, "but the Spirit itself maketh intercession for us with groanings which cannot be uttered."

He also *bears testimony*. Our Lord said, "He shall testify of me" (John 15:26). He bears testimony to the Lord. Only a person can do that. Then we are told, again by our Lord, "He will guide you into all truth" (John 16:13). Indeed, even in the Old Testament we are told that He teaches and instructs in the truth: "Thou gavest also thy good spirit to instruct them" (Nehemiah 9:20).

Another personal action of His is found in Acts 16:6-7 where we are told, "Now when they had gone throughout Phrygia and the regions of Galatia, and were forbidden of the Holy Ghost to preach the word in Asia, after they were come to Mysia, they assayed to go into Bithynia: but the Spirit suffered them not." Again, this is surely a very significant and relevant statement. All Paul's companions wanted to go and preach in Asia, but the Spirit prohibited them. Then they wanted to go into Bithynia, and again He would not allow them. That is a definite action by the Holy Sprit Himself, and it is proof positive that He is a person.

❧ A THOUGHT TO PONDER ❧

Actions are ascribed to the Spirit that can only be performed by a person.

From *God the Holy Spirit*, pp. 13-14.

THE COMFORTER

*It is expedient for you that I go away: for if I go not away, the
Comforter will not come unto you.*

JOHN 16:7

The very office to which the Holy Spirit was appointed is personal.
He is described as *the Comforter* ("another Comforter," says our
Lord in John 14:16), and a comforter is one who stands by our side
and helps us. The same word is sometimes translated *advocate*. So
our Lord was saying in effect, "As I have been with you during
these three years, as I have taught you and guided you, and as I
have sent you out on your missions, I will not leave you comfortless. I am going to send you another Comforter. You must not be
troubled; you are not going to be left as orphans." The Holy Spirit
is one who takes the place of our Lord. He is within us to lead us and
guide us, and that is why our Lord was even able to say, "It is expedient for you that I go away: for if I go not away, the Comforter
will not come unto you" (John 16:7). Obviously this is a personal
office.

Another big proof of the personality of the Holy Spirit is that,
according to the teaching of the Scriptures, the Holy Spirit is susceptible to personal treatment. In other words, we are told that we
can do certain things to the Spirit and that He reacts as only a person can react.

First, we are told that the Holy Spirit can be *lied to*. In the terrible case of Ananias and Sapphira in Acts 5, notice what Peter said:
"Ananias, why hath Satan filled thine heart to lie to the Holy Ghost,
and to keep back part of the price of the land?" (verse 3). Ananias
and Sapphira had declared that they had given everything, but Peter
charged them with having lied to the Holy Spirit. The Spirit is not
an influence therefore, not some vague power, but clearly a person.
Second, we are told that we can *blaspheme* against the Holy Spirit
(Matthew 12:31-32). Third, we see that He can be *insulted*
(Hebrews 10:29). Finally, He can be *grieved* (Ephesians 4:30).

❧ A THOUGHT TO PONDER ❧
The Holy Spirit is susceptible to personal treatment.

From *God the Holy Spirit*, pp. 14-15.

January 7

THE HOLY SPIRIT'S DEITY

Now there are diversities of gifts, but the same Spirit. . . .
And there are diversities of operations,
but it is the same God which worketh all in all.
1 CORINTHIANS 12:4, 6

We must demonstrate the Holy Spirit's deity. This is a vital part of the doctrine of the Trinity. It is only Christians who believe this doctrine; all other religions fail to do so, as do all errors and heresies. The Trinity is the key that unlocks all truth. So we must look at the evidence.

The Scripture itself specifically asserts the deity of the Spirit. I take you back to that terrible incident with Ananias and Sapphira. After asking, "Ananias, why hath Satan filled thine heart to lie to the Holy Ghost, and to keep back part of the price of the land?" Peter continued, "Thou hast not lied unto men, but unto God" (Acts 5:3-4). "The terrible thing that you have done," said Peter in effect, "is that you have not only been lying to men; you thought that you were just lying to us, the apostles, and to the other Christians, but no, you have been lying to *God.*" And just previously he had said that Ananias had lied to the Holy Spirit. So clearly that is a specific statement that the Holy Spirit is God.

But we also find that the Spirit's *name* is coupled with the name of God, and this not only establishes His personality but His Deity. This is seen in the baptismal formula, in the apostolic benediction, and also in 1 Corinthians 12, where Paul writes, "Now there are diversities of gifts, but the same Spirit. . . . And there are diversities of operations, but it is the same God which worketh all in all" (verses 4, 6). At one point we are told it is the Spirit who does this, and the next moment we are told that it is God—the same God who works all and in all, and He is the Spirit. Therefore the Spirit is God—His deity is proved.

✎ A THOUGHT TO PONDER ✎
Scripture specifically asserts the deity of the Spirit.

January 8

THE HOLY SPIRIT'S DIVINE DEEDS

The Spirit of God hath made me, and the breath of the Almighty hath given me life.

JOB 33:4

Certain things are done by the Spirit that we are told in the Scriptures can only be done by God. First of all, *creation*. In Genesis 1:2 we read, "The Spirit of God moved upon the face of the waters." There it is at the very beginning. Job says it also: "The Spirit of God hath made me, and the breath of the Almighty hath given me life." This is the creative work of the Holy Spirit, again a proof of His deity. And we must remember also that His is the special operation that we describe as *regeneration*. John 3:7 establishes that once and forever: "Ye must be born again." "Except a man be born of water *and of the Spirit* . . ." (John 3:5). This is the action of the Spirit; He gives the rebirth. Original creation and the new creation are both the special work of the Spirit. "It is the spirit that quickeneth," says our Lord again (John 6:63).

The work of *inspiration* is also the work of the Spirit. "No prophecy of the scripture is of any private interpretation," says Peter; ". . . holy men of God spake as they were moved"—carried along, driven; it does not matter which translation you use—"by the Holy Ghost" (2 Peter 1:20-21). All the Scriptures were written in that way: The Holy Spirit inspired and controlled the writers in an infallible manner. So we have our doctrine of the infallibility of the Scriptures, and it is proof positive to us that He is God. It is God alone who can give the truth and inspire men in their record of the truth.

The work of *resurrection* is also attributed to Him. Very often people are surprised by this. But it is to be found quite clearly in Romans 8:11: "But if the Spirit of him that raised up Jesus from the dead dwell in you, he that raised up Christ from the dead shall also quicken your mortal bodies by his Spirit that dwelleth in you." So we arrive at this—that the Holy Spirit is a person and a divine person.

◈ A THOUGHT TO PONDER ◈
The Holy Spirit is a person and a divine person.

From *God the Holy Spirit*, pp. 16-17.

SUBORDINATION

*He shall glorify me: for he shall receive of mine, and
shall show it unto you.*

JOHN 16:14

The Scriptures teach that the Spirit is subordinate to the Father and
to the Son. That is what is meant in John 16:13. Our Lord says,
"He shall not speak of himself," which means that He does not
speak from Himself—He is given what to speak. And indeed His
work, we are told, is to glorify Christ (John 16:14). The Spirit does
not glorify Himself; He glorifies the Son.

Is this not wonderful? Here is the subordination. Here is the division of the work. The Son says that He has come to glorify the
Father, and the Spirit's work is to glorify the Son. Each one reflects
the glory of the other. Thus we look into the mystery of this amazing doctrine of the blessed Trinity: "He shall glorify me: for he shall
receive of mine, and shall show it unto you" (John 16:14). This is,
to me, one of the most amazing and remarkable things about the biblical doctrine of the Holy Spirit. The Holy Spirit seems to hide
Himself and to conceal Himself. He is always, as it were, putting
the focus on the Son, and that is why I believe, and I believe profoundly, that the best test of all as to whether we have received the
Spirit is to ask ourselves, what do we think of, and what do we know
about, the Son? Is the Son real to us? That is the work of the Spirit.
He is glorified indirectly; He is always pointing us to the Son.

Yes, we must realize that He dwells within us, but His work in
dwelling within us is to glorify the Son, and to bring to us that
blessed knowledge of the Son and of His wondrous love to us. It is
He who strengthens us with might in the inner man (Ephesians 3:16-
19), that we may know this love of Christ.

✎ A THOUGHT TO PONDER ✎
The Spirit does not glorify Himself; He glorifies the Son.

THE HOLY SPIRIT AND THE CREATION OF THE WORLD

And the Spirit of God moved upon the face of the waters.
GENESIS 1:2

We are going to remind ourselves of what we are told in the Scriptures about the activity of the Holy Spirit before the Day of Pentecost.

First of all, we start at the very *creation of the world*. The second verse in the Bible says, "And the Spirit of God moved upon the face of the waters." He was operative in the creation of the world. God the Father has made everything through the Son by the Holy Spirit. The blessed Trinity is operative in the whole work, always, but the labor is divided up. And, of course, you will remember that the Holy Spirit is especially involved in connection with the creation of man.

The second is the work of the Holy Spirit in *sustaining or maintaining the creation*. Now there are many statements about this; I shall simply quote two. In Isaiah 40:7 we read, "The grass withereth, the flower fadeth: but the spirit of the LORD bloweth upon it." But still more strikingly, in Psalm 104 you will find a magnificent description of creation that is perhaps unsurpassed anywhere in the Bible. The psalmist makes the point that if the Lord withholds Himself or His power or His Spirit from creation, it all begins to droop and to wane, to perish and to die. If He puts His Spirit back again, it all revives. It is the Holy Spirit who sustains creation. Now you will find statements in the Scripture that say that the Son does that, and the answer is, of course, that the Son does it through the Holy Spirit. So the Holy Spirit has been active from the commencement in sustaining and maintaining the universe.

❧ A THOUGHT TO PONDER ❧
The Son sustains creation through the Holy Spirit.

From *God the Holy Spirit*, pp. 23-24.

THE HOLY SPIRIT AND COMMON GRACE

That was the true Light, which lighteth every man that cometh into the world.

JOHN 1:9

It is the Holy Spirit who is responsible for what is called *common grace*. Let me give you some definitions of what that means. Common grace is the term applied to those general blessings that God imparts to all men and women indiscriminately as He pleases—not only to His own people, but to all men and women, according to His own will. Or, again, common grace means those general operations of the Holy Spirit in which, without renewing the heart, He exercises a moral influence whereby sin is restrained, order is maintained in social life, and civil righteousness is promoted. That is the general definition. The Holy Spirit has been operative in this world from the very beginning, and He has had His influence and His effect upon men and women who are not saved and who have gone to perdition. While they were in this life and world they came under these general, non-saving operations of the Holy Spirit. That is what we mean by common grace.

Now, how does the Holy Spirit do this? Well, there are various answers to that question. You will remember that we are told in the prologue of John's Gospel about "the true Light, which lighteth every man" (John 1:9). It does not matter how you translate that verse. ". . . the true Light, which lighteth every man that cometh into the world," says the King James Version; "the Light that lighteth every man was coming into the world," says another. This light [that Christ puts in every person] is a kind of natural light, natural understanding. It is the light that is in the conscience, and there is that light of conscience in every person born into this world. Now that is one of the operations of the Holy Spirit in what is called common grace. It is a light that comes from Christ, because He is the Head of the human race, but it is the Holy Spirit who puts that light into everyone who is born.

～ A THOUGHT TO PONDER ～
Common grace is the term applied to those general blessings that God imparts to all men and women indiscriminately.

THE HOUSE OF CORNELIUS

And as I began to speak, the Holy Ghost fell on them,
as on us at the beginning.

ACTS 11:15

You can say that the Day of Pentecost was the day of public inauguration of the Church as the Body of Christ. There was something new there that had never been before. There is a sense in which you can speak of the Church in the Old Testament, yes, but it is not the same as the Church was subsequent to the Day of Pentecost.

Look at what happened in the house of Cornelius. Peter, of course, as a Jew would obviously have found it very difficult to believe that Gentiles could really come into this unity. That was why the vision was given to him as he was there on the top of the house. As he was praying he saw a great sheet coming down with clean and unclean animals and birds upon it, and he heard God's voice telling him to kill and eat. God said, "What God hath cleansed, that call not thou common" (Acts 10:15). But is there not a further suggestion that even that vision was not enough? Certainly it was enough to take Peter to the house of Cornelius and to preach as he did. But even while Peter was preaching, the Holy Spirit descended upon Cornelius and his household. And Peter and the Jews were amazed at this. They could not quite understand it, but they had to face the facts as they heard these other people speak with tongues and magnify God. "They of the circumcision which believed were astonished, as many as came with Peter, because that on the Gentiles also was poured out the gift of the Holy Ghost" (Acts 10:45).

The thing that Peter later emphasized was that while he was speaking, the Holy Spirit descended upon them: "And as I began to speak, the Holy Ghost fell on them, as on us at the beginning" (Acts 11:15). Now you see what was happening. God was declaring that the Church was to consist of Jews and Gentiles.

❧ A THOUGHT TO PONDER ❧

God was declaring that the Church was to consist of Jews and Gentiles.

From *God the Holy Spirit*, pp. 36-37.

THE SIGNIFICANCE OF PENTECOST

Would God that all the LORD's people were prophets, and that the LORD would put his spirit upon them!

NUMBERS 11:29

The great purpose of Pentecost is to give the final proof of the fact that Jesus of Nazareth is the Son of God and the Savior of the world. That is declared. The second thing is the great inauguration of the Church as His Body; and third, it is a proof of the fact that the various people who are added to the Church are members of the Body. Also, in the Old Testament we are told that the Holy Spirit was with men or that He came upon them. He worked upon them from without, as it were, and what David even said, you remember, was, "Take not thy holy spirit from me" (Psalm 51:11), as if the Holy Spirit was *with* him—that is the Old Testament terminology. The New Testament terminology is *in*, *within*; He works from within, and He abides. In the Old Testament He came upon men and left them. He comes, in the New Testament, because we are members of the Body of Christ and because the Spirit comes from Christ through the whole Body. Because we are members of the Body, the Spirit abides in us—perfectly; and that, it seems to me, is the essence of the teaching with regard to this matter.

On the Day of Pentecost the rushing mighty wind and the cloven tongues as of fire especially emphasized, not the filling with the Spirit, but the baptizing into the unity of the Body, the inauguration of the Church. That is why you have the special phenomena. The cloven tongues of fire were never repeated. The walls were shaken on another occasion, but this particular sound, this noise, the gathering together of the special phenomena places a uniqueness upon the event of the Day of Pentecost that has never been repeated. The filling with the Spirit is something that can be, and often is, repeated, but that is not the vital thing that happened at Pentecost. What is emphasized at Pentecost is that the Church became Christ's Body, and the Spirit was given to fill the Body.

❧ A THOUGHT TO PONDER ☙
Pentecost inaugurated the Church as Christ's Body.

From *God the Holy Spirit*, pp. 40-41.

THE WORD OF GOD AND THE SPIRIT

Being born again, not of corruptible seed, but of incorruptible,
by the word of God, which liveth and abideth for ever.

1 PETER 1:23

In order to do His work, *the Spirit uses the Word of God*. First, He reveals, through the Word, the great love of God to sinners in general: "God . . . for his great love wherewith he loved us . . ." (Ephesians 2:4) and so on.

Second, *He presents and offers salvation in Christ*; through His people, He states the facts about Christ. That is the business of preachers of the Gospel. It is to give the record of the life, the death, the resurrection, and the resurrection appearances of our Lord. What is preaching? It is proclaiming these facts about Christ. Not only that—it is an explanation of the fact, the meaning of the facts, how these facts constitute salvation and are the cause, the means, of salvation. So in the preaching of the Word in the power of the Holy Spirit, these facts and their interpretation are presented.

Then *the Holy Spirit calls us to repentance*. He calls everyone to repentance, all men and women everywhere, because of these facts, because of "that man whom he hath ordained," by whom the whole world is going to be judged in righteousness (Acts 17:31).

And finally *the Holy Spirit calls us to faith in Christ*. Take again those words of Paul in his farewell message to the church at Ephesus. What did Paul testify? What did he preach? It was "repentance toward God, and faith toward our Lord Jesus Christ" (Acts 20:21). He called men and women to faith in Christ in order that they might obtain forgiveness of sins and inherit eternal life. That was the way in which our Lord commissioned Paul on the road to Damascus. He said that He was going to send him to the people and to the Gentiles "to turn them from darkness to light, and from the power of Satan unto God, that they may receive forgiveness of sins, and inheritance among them which are sanctified by faith that is in me" (Acts 26:18).

✸ A THOUGHT TO PONDER ✸

The Spirit uses the Word of God.

From *God the Holy Spirit*, pp. 51-52.

January 15

REGENERATION

. . . that which is born of the Spirit is spirit.

JOHN 3:6

What is regeneration? It is the implanting of a principle of new spiritual life and a radical change in the governing disposition of the soul. The important thing to grasp is the whole idea of *disposition*. In addition to the faculties of our souls, there is something at the back of them that governs them all, and that is what we refer to as our disposition. Take two men. They have the same faculties, but one lives a good life, one lives a bad life. What makes the difference? The answer is that the good man has a good disposition, and this good disposition, this thing that is behind the faculties and governs them and uses them, urges him to use his faculties in the direction of goodness. The other man has an evil disposition; so he urges the same faculties in an entirely different direction. That is what one means by disposition.

When you come to think of it, and when you analyze yourself, your life and your whole conduct and behavior and that of other people, you will see at once that these dispositions are, of course, of tremendous importance. They are the condition, if you like, that determines what we do and what we are.

There is in every person a disposition that seems to determine the kind of person he or she is. It is this that directs the faculties and the abilities so that one person is artistic and the other scientific and so on. I am making this point to show that what happens in regeneration is that God so operates upon us in the Holy Spirit that this fundamental disposition of ours is changed. He puts a holy principle, a seed of new spiritual life, into this disposition that determines what I am and how I behave and how I use and employ my faculties.

✎ A THOUGHT TO PONDER ✎

Regeneration is a radical change in the governing disposition of the soul.

From *God the Holy Spirit*, p. 79.

A SEED OF LIFE

Except a man be born again, he cannot see the kingdom of God.
JOHN 3:3

The change in my disposition does not mean that I have a greater intellect now than I had before. No, I have exactly the same intellect, the same mind. But because the disposition governing it is changed, my mind is operating in a different realm and in a different way, and it seems to be a new mind. And it is exactly the same with the feelings. A man who used to hate the Gospel now loves it. A woman who hated the Lord Jesus Christ now loves Him. And likewise with the will: The will earlier resisted, it was obstinate and rebellious; but now it desires, it is anxious, it is concerned about the Gospel.

The next thing that we say is that it is a change that is instantaneous. Now do you see the importance of differentiating between generation and coming to birth? Generation, by definition, is always an instantaneous act. There is a moment, a flash, in which the germ of life enters, impregnates; that is one instantaneous action. In other words, there are no intermediate stages in regeneration. Life is either implanted or it is not; it cannot be partly implanted. It is not gradual. When I say that it is instantaneous, I am not referring to our consciousness of it, but to the thing itself, as it is done by God. The consciousness, of course, comes into the realm of time, whereas this act of germination is timeless, and that is why it is immediate.

So the next thing is that generation, the implanting of this seed of life and the change of the disposition, happens in the subconscious, or, if you prefer, in the unconscious. Our Lord explained that fully to Nicodemus (John 3). It is a secret, inscrutable operation that cannot be directly perceived by us; indeed, we cannot even fully understand it. The first thing we know about it is that it has happened, because we are conscious of something different, but that means that we do not understand it and that we really cannot arrive at its secret.

✎ A THOUGHT TO PONDER ✎

The will earlier resisted, it was obstinate and rebellious; but now it is concerned about the Gospel.

THE NEW BIRTH

No man is able to pluck them out of my Father's hand.

JOHN 10:29

If you are regenerate, you will remain regenerate. It seems to me that this is absolutely inevitable because regeneration is the work of God. Yet there are those who seem to think that people can be born again as the result of believing the truth, and then if they backslide or fall into sin or deny the truth, they lose their regeneration, but if they come back again and believe again, then they are regenerate again—as if one can be born again and die and be born again and die an endless number of times! How important doctrine is! How important it is that we should be clear as to what the Scripture teaches about these things! It tells us that regeneration is the work of God Himself in the depths of the soul and that He does it in such a way that it is permanent. "No man is able to pluck them out of my Father's hand" (John 10:29).

"I am persuaded," says Paul, and let us notice this, "I am persuaded"—he is certain—"that neither death, nor life, nor angels, nor principalities, nor powers, nor things present, nor things to come, nor height, nor depth, nor any other creature, shall be able to separate us from the love of God, which is in Christ Jesus our Lord" (Romans 8:38-39). And when Paul says that, he is expounding regeneration. It is not merely the relationship between us—it is because He has put this life in me that nothing can separate me from Him. And when we come to deal with the mystical union that follows directly from this, we see how still more inevitable this must be. This is a permanent work, and nothing can ever bring it to an end.

Regenerate people cannot go on sinning because they are born of God (1 John 3:9). They may backslide temporarily, but if they are born of God they will come back. It is as certain as that they have been born again. This is the way to test whether or not someone is born again.

✍ A THOUGHT TO PONDER ✍

Regeneration is the work of God Himself in the depths of the soul, and it is permanent.

From *God the Holy Spirit*, pp. 93-94.

IN CHRIST

For as in Adam all die, even so in Christ shall all be made alive.
1 CORINTHIANS 15:22

Paul draws a contrast between the union of the unbeliever with Adam and the union of the believer with Christ. This is the great argument in Romans 5, which is repeated in 1 Corinthians 15:22, 49. In Romans 5 the whole argument is that death passed on to all people because of Adam. Why? Because of their relationship to Adam; that is the whole doctrine of original sin. We are all condemned in Adam because of Adam's sin. He was our representative, he was our federal head; and not only that, we are bound to him, we were in the loins of Adam when he fell. In Adam all died. In Christ all shall be made alive again. That is it. The relationship of the believer to Christ is the same sort of union and relationship as that old relationship of the whole of Adam's posterity to Adam. We are all born in Adam, and we are related, we are joined in that way. Yes, but being born again, we are in the same sort of relationship to Christ.

Regeneration and union must never be separated. You cannot be born again without being in Christ; you are born again because you are in Christ. The moment you are in Him you are born again, and you cannot regard your regeneration as something separate and think that union is something you will eventually arrive at. Not at all! Regeneration and union must always be considered together and at the same time because the one depends upon the other and leads to the other; they are mutually self-supporting.

There is nothing that so strengthens my faith and fills me with a longing to be pure as He is pure and to live even as He did in this world as the realization of what I am and who I am because I am a Christian. I am a child of God, and I am in Christ.

❧ A THOUGHT TO PONDER ❧
Regeneration and union must never be separated.

From *God the Holy Spirit*, pp. 104-105.

A VITAL UNION

And of his fulness have all we received, and grace for grace.

JOHN 1:16

We are joined to Christ in a union with Him by means of the indwelling of the Holy Spirit in us. It is a vital union because our spiritual life is drawn directly from the Lord Jesus Christ. We are sustained by Him through the indwelling Holy Spirit. There is nothing more important in the Christian life than to realize that our union with Christ is a vital one. It is a living thing. It is not something mechanical or conceptual; it is not a thought or an idea; it is really a vital, spiritual union.

"And of his fulness have all we received, and grace for grace" (John 1:16). That says it all. That is our relationship to Him, says John; something of His fullness and of His life is passing into us, and we are receiving it.

The trouble with all of us is that we do not realize the truth of these things. But this is the truth given by the Lord Himself. It is His prayer for His people that they may know the meaning of this vital, spiritual relationship. And He does not hesitate to compare it with the relationship that subsists between the Father and Himself: As the Father is in Him, so He is in us, and we are in Him. But consider the statement of this truth that is made by the apostle Paul in Galatians 2:20: "I am crucified with Christ: nevertheless I live; yet not I, but Christ liveth in me." There is nothing greater than that, and what it does teach is that this is a life-giving relationship; it is a union of life. "Not I, but Christ liveth in me." And then Paul goes on to say, "And the life which I now live in the flesh I live by the faith of the Son of God, who loved me, and gave himself for me."

❧ A THOUGHT TO PONDER ❧

Our union with Christ is a vital, spiritual union.

From *God the Holy Spirit*, pp. 108-109.

OUR FELLOWSHIP IN HIS SUFFERINGS

That I may know . . . the fellowship of his sufferings.

PHILIPPIANS 3:10

I would now like to emphasize our fellowship in Christ's sufferings, and our fellowship even in His death. Paul says in Philippians 3:10, "That I may know him, and the power of his resurrection, and the fellowship of his sufferings, being made conformable unto his death." What great thoughts! We must work them out, think them out, and pray them out.

Paul put it another way in Colossians 1:24: "Who now rejoice in my sufferings for you, and fill up that which is behind of the afflictions of Christ in my flesh for his body's sake, which is the church." I do not pretend to understand that fully, but I do know that there is no higher statement of the doctrine of the union of the believer with His Lord. The apostle interprets his own sufferings in the flesh and in the body as, in a sense, filling up what remains of the sufferings and the afflictions of Christ Himself. Paul is bearing that in his own flesh. The result of the mystical union is that he enters into this mystical fellowship of the sufferings of Christ. There were people living in the Middle Ages of whom it is said that they so meditated upon and contemplated their Lord and all that He had done for them that some of them even developed in their physical hands the imprint of nails, the *stigmata*. It is not impossible. Such things do happen.

But all I am concerned to emphasize is that the more deeply we realize the truth about this union between us and our Lord, the more we shall know something of the fellowship of His sufferings. In this world He was "a man of sorrows, and acquainted with grief" (Isaiah 53:3). That was because of the sin of the world. And because He saw the enmity of the human heart against His Father, it hurt Him, it grieved Him, and He suffered. There is no more delicate test of our relationship to Him and our union with Him than the extent to which you and I know something of His suffering.

✎ A THOUGHT TO PONDER ✎

The result of the mystical union is mystical fellowship with the sufferings of Christ.

From *God the Holy Spirit*, pp. 115-116.

TEMPORARY CONVERSION

But he that received the seed into stony places,
the same is he that . . . is offended.
MATTHEW 13:20-21

Our Lord, because of the danger of a "temporary something" happening, was constantly dealing with this and seemed to be repelling people. Indeed, they charged Him with making discipleship impossible. Take that great sixth chapter of John where the people were running after Him and hanging onto His words because of the miracle of the feeding of the five thousand, and our Lord seemed to be trying deliberately to repel them.

Take also the parable in Matthew 13—the Parable of the Sower—and our Lord's own exposition of it. Notice particularly verses 20-21: "But he that received the seed into stony places, the same is he that heareth the word, and anon with joy receiveth it; yet hath he not root in himself, but dureth for a while: for when tribulation or persecution ariseth because of the word, by and by he is offended." But notice what our Lord says about this same man: he "anon with joy receiveth it [the Word]." That is what I mean by temporary conversion. He seems to have received the Word, he is full of joy, but he has no root in him, and that is why he ends up with nothing at all. Now that is our Lord's own teaching; there is the possibility of this very joyful "conversion," and yet there is nothing there in a vital, living sense, and it proves temporary.

Paul speaks in 1 Timothy 1:19-20 of "holding faith, and a good conscience; which some having put away concerning faith have made shipwreck." Now that is very serious teaching. He says the same thing in 2 Timothy 2. There is such a thing as temporary conversion, temporary believers, but they are not true believers. That is why it is so vital that we should know the biblical teaching as to what conversion really is.

❧ A THOUGHT TO PONDER ❧

There is the possibility of a joyful conversion proving to be temporary.

From *God the Holy Spirit*, pp. 119-120.

FAITH AND REASON

Unto you therefore which believe he is precious.

1 PETER 2:7

What is the relationship between faith and reason? The best answer I can give is that faith is not a matter of reason. Some people teach that it is. They say that if only men and women would use their minds, they would be bound to become Christians; they can reason themselves into Christianity. But that is thoroughly unscriptural. They cannot because the natural man's or woman's reason is also fallen. Not only that, there are supernatural and miraculous elements in faith to which reason cannot attain. So true faith is not entirely a matter of reason. Indeed, I would quote to you the statement of the great Blaise Pascal, perhaps the greatest mathematician that the world has ever known and who had an evangelical conversion. He said that the supreme achievement of reason is to teach us that there is an end to reason.

So what about faith and reason? Well, faith is not mere reason, but on the other hand, neither is it contrary to reason. It is not unreasonable; it is not irrational. That is the charge that is brought against us.

"Ah," people say, "but what you're teaching is a kind of irrationality. You say that faith isn't a matter of reason. Well then, is it opposed to reason?"

No, it is not. It is not reason; neither is it contrary to reason. What is it then? It is *supra-reason*. It means that our reason brings us to the point where we realize that reason is not enough, and at that point we have nothing to do but submit ourselves to revelation. And that is faith. Faith is accepting this revelation.

More and more I like to think of it like this: Faith means that I deliberately shut myself down to this Book, the Bible. I refuse to philosophize. I refuse to ask certain questions. People are always asking them. They want to understand the doctrine of the Trinity. You cannot. You will never understand it. It is too great. So you accept it; and you stop asking questions.

❧ A THOUGHT TO PONDER ☙

Reason brings us to the point where we realize that reason is not enough, and at that point we submit ourselves to revelation.

From *God the Holy Spirit*, pp. 147-148.

JUSTIFICATION BY FAITH

Therefore being justified by faith, we have peace with God.

ROMANS 5:1

Justification is opposed to condemnation, and nobody can bring an accusation because it is God who declares people just.

Justification is legal and forensic, and as you go on with the Scriptures you will find this in other places: "But ye are washed, but ye are sanctified, but ye are justified in the name of the Lord Jesus, and by the Spirit of our God" (1 Corinthians 6:11). And in Galatians 2:16 there is a statement that is parallel to those in Romans: "Knowing that a man is not justified by the works of the law, but by the faith of Jesus Christ, even we have believed in Jesus Christ, that we might be justified by the faith of Christ, and not by the works of the law: for by the works of the law shall no flesh be justified." Galatians is the great epistle that gave Martin Luther his liberty. His famous commentary on the epistle to the Galatians is a book that you should read, and the more you go on with it, the more you will enjoy it. Do not be put off by his polemic against the Roman Catholics. He had to do that because you must show what is wrong as well as what is right. People do not like that today, but Luther had to do it, and I think we must do it in our age and generation.

God makes a legal declaration that all the demands of the law upon us, as a condition of life, are fully satisfied with regard to all who believe on the Lord Jesus Christ. We are no longer in a state of condemnation: "Therefore being justified by faith, we have peace with God" (Romans 5:1). "There is therefore now no condemnation to them which are in Christ Jesus" (Romans 8:1). Why? Because God has declared it. He is the Lawgiver, and He says that Christ has satisfied the law. "For Christ is the end of the law for righteousness to every one that believeth" (Romans 10:4).

☙ A THOUGHT TO PONDER ☙

God is the Lawgiver, and He says that Christ has satisfied the law.

From *God the Holy Spirit*, pp. 171-172.

JUSTIFICATION AND SANCTIFICATION

But of him are ye in Christ Jesus, who of God is made unto us wisdom, and righteousness, and sanctification, and redemption.

1 CORINTHIANS 1:30

Let me show you the essential difference between justification and sanctification. Look at it like this: Justification is an act of God the Father; sanctification is essentially the work of God the Holy Spirit. There is this division of work in the blessed Persons of the Trinity. It is the Father who declares righteous and just. It is the Holy Spirit who sanctifies.

Second, justification takes place outside us, as in a tribunal; sanctification takes place within us, in our inner life. I stand in the court when I am justified, and the judge pronounces that I am free; it is a statement about me, outside me. But sanctification is something that is worked and takes place within.

Third, justification removes the guilt of sin; sanctification removes the pollution of sin and renews us in the image of God.

And therefore, last, by definition justification is a once-and-for-all act. It is never to be repeated because it cannot be repeated and never needs to be repeated. It is not a process but a declaration that we are pronounced just once and forever, by God. Sanctification, on the other hand, is a continuous process. We continue to grow in grace and in the knowledge of the Lord until we are perfect beyond the veil.

So there is nothing quite so erroneous and confusing and unscriptural as to mistake the essential difference between justification and sanctification. That is the whole trouble with Roman Catholic teaching and all Catholic piety. If you confuse sanctification with justification, you will be doubtful as to whether you are justified or not. If you bring in your state and condition and sin that you may commit, then you are querying your justification. But if you realize that justification is forensic, external, and declaratory, you know that you are justified whatever may be true about you.

✎ A THOUGHT TO PONDER ✐

Justification removes the guilt of sin; sanctification removes the pollution of sin.

From *God the Holy Spirit*, pp. 174-175.

THE PROOFS OF ADOPTION

For ye are all the children of God by faith in Christ Jesus.

GALATIANS 3:26

What are the proofs that any one of us can have that we have been adopted? Well, *you can find the scriptural proof.* "For ye are all the children of God by faith in Christ Jesus." Also in 1 Peter 1:3-6 you find it again: "Blessed be the God and Father of our Lord Jesus Christ, which according to his abundant mercy hath begotten us again unto a lively hope by the resurrection of Jesus Christ from the dead, to an inheritance incorruptible, and undefiled, and that fadeth not away, reserved in heaven for you, who are kept by the power of God through faith unto salvation ready to be revealed in the last time. Wherein ye greatly rejoice, though now for a season, if need be, ye are in heaviness through manifold temptations." We are the inheritance—that is, the children of God. This is for all of us who believe in Christ.

The second way of assurance is that *we are given "the Spirit of adoption,* whereby we cry, Abba, Father" (Romans 8:15); "we receive the adoption of sons" (Galatians 4:5). You can be assured of the fact that you have received adoption because you know that the Holy Spirit is dwelling within you. We have His testimony to our spirits that we are the children of God.

And then last of all I would offer the fact that *we are led by the Spirit.* This is Paul's argument: "For as many as are led by the Spirit of God, they are the sons of God" (Romans 8:14). Paul does not say, "As many as are actively acting as peacemakers or who are loving their enemies . . ." No! "As many as are led by the Spirit of God"; those who subject themselves to His leading and who rejoice in being led by Him—they are the sons of God.

❧ A THOUGHT TO PONDER ❧

You can be assured of the fact that you have received adoption because you know that the Holy Spirit is dwelling within you.

From *God the Holy Spirit*, p. 187.

THE RESULTS OF ADOPTION

I . . . will be your God, and ye shall be my people.
LEVITICUS 26:12

The first result of our adoption I shall mention is that if we have the spirit of adoption, *we have lost "the spirit of bondage again to fear"* (Romans 8:15). Positively, in the second place, *we have been given a spirit of liberty.* In other words, we are no longer afraid of the law and its condemnation; we are no longer afraid of death; we are enjoying something of the glorious liberty of the children of God. Third, *we receive this spirit of adoption through the indwelling Spirit.*

But then in addition there are these results: Because we have been adopted into God's family, *we are entitled to bear His name.* We can say that we are the children of God. We are members of the household of God. We belong to God's family. God's name is upon us. He has said, "I . . . will be your God, and ye shall be my people" (Leviticus 26:12). We are His people. Peter applies to Christians what God said to the nation of Israel of old: "But ye are a chosen generation, a royal priesthood, an holy nation, a peculiar people; that ye should show forth the praises of him who hath called you out of darkness into his marvellous light; which in time past were not a people, but are now the people of God: which had not obtained mercy, but now have obtained mercy" (1 Peter 2:9-10).

What else? Well, the fifth benefit is that *we enjoy the present protection and consolation that God alone can give, and the provision that He makes for His children.* "Even the very hairs of your head are all numbered" (Luke 12:7); nothing can happen to us apart from Him.

The next benefit, at first, is not so pleasurable—*fatherly chastisements.* That is the whole argument of the first half of Hebrews 12: "For whom the Lord loveth he chasteneth, and scourgeth every son whom he receiveth" (verse 6). He chastises His children, but not those who are not His children.

❧ A THOUGHT TO PONDER ❧

We are members of the household of God. We belong to God's family.

From *God the Holy Spirit*, pp. 187-188.

BECOMING HOLY

Be not conformed to this world.
ROMANS 12:2

The Scriptures place great emphasis on our part in sanctification, on what you and I have to do. What is the point of the mighty arguments of Paul and the apostles in their letters if sanctification is something that I am to receive? Why the exhortations?

Here is one exhortation from the apostle Peter: "Dearly beloved, I beseech you as strangers and pilgrims, abstain from fleshly lusts, which war against the soul" (1 Peter 2:11). Do you notice what he says? We do not receive our sanctification and are then delivered from these things. No; he tells us to abstain from them and to keep ourselves from them. And the tragedy is that so many people are spending their lives waiting to receive something, and in the meantime they are not abstaining from these fleshly lusts.

Take a statement from Paul: "Let him that stole steal no more" (Ephesians 4:28). That is what he is to do. He is not to wait to receive something; he is commanded to give up stealing. What can be more specific than that? And people who are guilty of foolish talking and jesting and other unseemly things are not to do them (Ephesians 5:4). "Be not conformed to this world" (Romans 12:2). You do not wait to receive something; if up to this moment you have been conforming to the world, you must stop.

People have often come to me about this and said, "You know, I've been trying so hard, but I can't get this experience." To which the reply is that the Scripture commands you to abstain: "Cleanse your hands, ye sinners; and purify your hearts, ye double minded" (James 4:8). And I repeat that these injunctions are quite pointless and a sheer waste of ink if sanctification is something that I can receive. If it is, we would surely be told, "You need not worry about this question of sin—you can receive your sanctification in one act, and all you do then is to maintain it and abide in it." But this is most certainly not the New Testament teaching.

❧ A THOUGHT TO PONDER ❧
The Scriptures place great emphasis on our part in sanctification.

Is Sanctification an Experience?

We all, with open face, beholding as in a glass the glory of
the Lord, are changed into the same image from glory to glory.
2 CORINTHIANS 3:18

Is sanctification an experience? There are large numbers of stories about people who have had marvelous experiences, of people, for example, who had a bad temper or something like that. I accept the experiences without any hesitation at all. Thank God, I am able to testify to some such experiences in my own life. So what of them? Well, here is my answer. First and foremost, there is no evidence at all in the New Testament that this kind of experience means sanctification. It may be a part of sanctification, it may greatly aid sanctification, but it is not sanctification in and of itself. We must not base our doctrine on experiences but on the teaching of the Word of God.

The teaching of the Scripture is that "We all, with open face, beholding as in a glass the glory of the Lord, are changed into the same image from glory to glory" (2 Corinthians 3:18). Sanctification is a growth, a development; it is a going forward. But it seems to me that the main trouble with this teaching about experience is that it confuses two things that are different, and the two things are these various experiences that we get in the Christian life and the grace of God in sanctification.

Sanctification is not an experience—it is a condition. It is my relationship to God: I am "changed into the same image [of Jesus Christ] from glory to glory" (2 Corinthians 3:18). Sanctification involves experiences and is helped by them, but in itself it is not an experience. Sanctification is that process of growth and development that starts the moment we are saved, the moment we are justified, the moment we are regenerated. The experiences are not the process of growth, but they do help and stimulate it.

❧ A Thought to Ponder ❧
We must not base our doctrine on experiences but on the teaching of the Word of God.

From *God the Holy Spirit*, pp. 216-218.

FILLED WITH THE SPIRIT

. . . in demonstration of the Spirit and of power.

1 CORINTHIANS 2:4

What does it mean to be *filled* with the Holy Spirit? Clearly there are two things at any rate that go with this term. It is something that happens that gives authority and power and the ability for service and witness. The apostles were given it at the very beginning, and the result was that they began to speak with other tongues, and Peter, filled with the Spirit, preached his sermon. Then again, after they had prayed, they were all filled with the Holy Spirit and spoke the Word of God with boldness. And when Paul was confronted by the opposition of that clever man, the magician Elymas, he was filled especially with the Spirit in order to pronounce a judgment, and the judgment fell upon the man. So it is clear that the filling with the Spirit happens for the sake of service; it gives us power and authority for service.

Let me emphasize this. This filling is an absolute necessity for true service. Even our Lord Himself did not enter upon His ministry until the Holy Spirit had descended upon Him. He even told the disciples, whom He had been training for three years, who had been with Him in the inner circle, who had seen His miracles and heard all His words, who had seen Him dead and buried and risen again, even these exceptional men with their exceptional opportunities He told to stay where they were, not to start upon any ministry, not to attempt to witness to Him, until they had received the power that the Holy Spirit would give them.

This is something, therefore, that is vital to our witness. It was the whole secret of the ministry of the apostle Paul. He did not preach with enticing words of human wisdom, but preached, he said, "in demonstration of the Spirit and of power" (1 Corinthians 2:4). He was filled with the Spirit for his task.

❧ A THOUGHT TO PONDER ☙

The filling with the Spirit happens for the sake of service.

From *God the Holy Spirit*, pp. 241-242.

THE IN-FILLING OF THE SPIRIT

*Be not drunk with wine, wherein is excess; but
be filled with the Spirit.*

EPHESIANS 5:18

The in-filling of the Spirit is essential to true Christian quality in
our life. That is why we are commanded to be filled with the Spirit.
It is a command to every single Christian: "Be not drunk with wine,
wherein is excess; but be filled with the Spirit." We are exhorted to
be filled with the Spirit. And this is commanded in order that our
graces may grow, in order that the fruit of the Spirit may develop in
us and may be evident to all. It is as we are filled with this life that
the fruit and the graces of this life will be manifest. Indeed, the filling of the Spirit is essential to a true act of worship. Did you notice
how Paul uses that commandment of his in that very connection? He
says, "Be not drunk with wine, wherein is excess; but be filled with
the Spirit"—and then goes on at once—"speaking to yourselves in
psalms and hymns and spiritual songs, singing and making melody
in your heart to the Lord; giving thanks always for all things unto
God and our Father in the name of our Lord Jesus Christ."

So the way to test whether we are filled with the Spirit is to ask,
Are we full of thankfulness? Are we full of the spirit of praise, of
thanksgiving, of worship and adoration?

What is a revival? It is God pouring out His Spirit. It is this
tremendous filling that happens to numbers of people at the same
time. You need not wait for a revival to get it; each of us is individ-
ually commanded to seek it and to have it and indeed to make sure
it is there. But at times of revival God, as it were, fills a number of
people together; they almost describe it as the Spirit *falling* upon
them. That is a revival, and that is the greatest need of the Church
today.

⌒ A THOUGHT TO PONDER ⌒

"Be filled with the Spirit" is a command to every single Christian.

From *God the Holy Spirit*, pp. 242-243.

THE GIFTS OF THE HOLY SPIRIT

*But all these worketh that one and the selfsame Spirit,
dividing to every man severally as he will.*

1 CORINTHIANS 12:11

There are some principles about the subject of spiritual gifts that stand out clearly in the biblical teaching. The first is that *spiritual gifts must be differentiated from natural gifts*. We all have natural gifts, but the spiritual gift that any one of us may possess is something separate from and entirely different from this. It is a gift that is given directly to us by the Holy Spirit. Some people have fallen into the error of thinking that a spiritual gift really means a person's natural gift taken hold of by the Holy Spirit and heightened so that it becomes a spiritual gift. But that is not what Scripture would have us believe. A spiritual gift is something new, something different.

The second principle is that *these gifts are bestowed upon us by the Holy Spirit in a sovereign manner*. This is emphasized very clearly in 1 Corinthians 12; notice verse 11, for instance: "But all these worketh that one and the selfsame Spirit, dividing to every man severally as he will." "As *he* will." It is He who decides and not us. He decides what particular gift to give to a particular person. Verse 7 enforces the same point: "But the manifestation of the Spirit is given to every man to profit withal." It is a gift, it is given, it is something that comes entirely from the Holy Spirit.

Third, *each Christian is given and therefore has some gift*: "But the manifestation of the Spirit is given *to every man* to profit withal." The clear implication there is that every single Christian is given some particular gift. So from this we deduce that every true member of the Body of Christ, every true Christian, who has been baptized into the Body of Christ by this one Spirit, has some particular spiritual gift.

The fourth principle taught in 1 Corinthians 12, obviously, is that *the gifts differ in value*; see verses 14-30.

❧ A THOUGHT TO PONDER ❧

Every single Christian is given some particular gift.

From *God the Holy Spirit*, pp. 265-266.

February

OUR GREAT
SALVATION

FROM

Saved in Eternity

THE RIGHT WAY AND THE WRONG WAY TO PRAY

Then they took away the stone. . . . And Jesus lifted up his eyes, and said, 'Father . . .'"

JOHN 11:41

Sometimes our whole idea of prayer is false. All too often we think of prayer only as guidance and requests. Now if you were to put that into practice in human relationships you would regard it as insulting. No, the thing the saint wants to know above everything else is that all is well between his soul and the Father. There is nothing the saint delights in more than to know God as his Father. He likes to maintain the contact and communion, to assure his heart before God and in the presence of God. The saint is in this difficult world; there are temptations from the outside, and the whole world is against him, and the saint is tired—sometimes he almost despairs. So he goes to God immediately, not to ask this or that but just to make certain that all is well there, that the contact is unbroken and perfect, that he can assure his heart and know that all is well.

That is what our Lord is doing in John 17, and that is the thing that stands out most frequently in that prayer. Our Lord is assuring His own human heart in the presence of His Father. He did this also when He was raising Lazarus from the dead; indeed He puts it in words for us: "Then they took away the stone. . . . And Jesus lifted up his eyes, and said, 'Father'"—He is praying—"'I thank thee that thou hast heard me'"—always He is assured in His heart—"'And I knew that thou hearest me always: but because of the people . . .'" (John 11:41-42). He just turns to God. He knows all is well, but He is assuring His heart in the presence of God.

Let me put it like this: The saints always prayed to God, and our Lord supremely did so, because they believed in God's power, because they believed in God's ability to help, and, above all, because they believed in God's willingness and readiness to help.

✎ A THOUGHT TO PONDER ✎

Our Lord is assuring His own human heart in the presence of His Father.

From *Saved in Eternity*, p. 32.

WHAT IS LEGITIMATE IN PRAYER?

O God, how long shall the adversary reproach?
PSALM 74:10

Pleas and arguments and requests are perfectly legitimate in prayer. Have you noticed how men of God prayed? They knew God was omniscient; so they not only made their requests known to Him but also pleaded with Him. And what I like above everything else is the way they argued with Him. Moses, for example, did so. On one occasion he came down from the Mount and found the people rebellious, and when he found God threatening to disown them and leave them to their own devices, Moses said to God, "You cannot do this."

Look too at the man in Psalm 74. "O God, how long shall the adversary reproach?" (Psalm 74:10). He says in effect, "Lord, why do You allow men to do these things?" I believe God as Father delights in listening to such pleas and reasonings and arguments. This flabby generation of Christians seems to have forgotten what our fathers used to delight in when they talked about "pleading the promises." They did not regard that as offensive. They had no sort of mock humility, but they felt they were entitled, according to this teaching, to go to God as the psalmist did and remind him of His own promises. They said, "Lord, I do not understand. I know it is my imperfection, but I am certain of these promises. Lord, help me to see how the promises are to be related to these perplexities."

So it is perfectly right to plead with God; our Lord pleaded with Him. In His great prayer in John 17 our Lord argued with God by bringing His requests. He reminded God of His own promises and of His own character. I believe God delights in this as Father, and as we do these things in this way our hearts will be reassured before Him, and often we shall be amazed and astonished at the answers that we receive.

◈ A THOUGHT TO PONDER ◈
Pleas and arguments and requests are perfectly legitimate in prayer.

February 3

THE POWER OF GOD

*And having spoiled principalities and powers, he made a show
of them openly, triumphing over them in it.*

COLOSSIANS 2:15

The plan of salvation displays to us, in a way that nothing else does, the power of God. The power of God was manifested in the Incarnation when He prepared a body for His Son and worked the miracle of the virgin birth—and what marvelous power! But not only that. I rather prefer to think of it like this: It is as we look at God in Christ and all that He did in Him and through this plan of salvation that we see His complete power to master everything that is opposed to Himself, everything that is opposed to the best interests of man, and everything that is opposed to the best interests of this world.

For the fact is that the whole problem has arisen in this way. One of the brightest of the angelic beings that were created by God rebelled against God and raised himself up against Him. That is the origin of Satan. He is a power, a person, an angel of great might. He is as great as this: He deluded a man and conquered him, thereby making himself the god of this world and "the prince of the power of the air" (Ephesians 2:2). The power of the devil is something that we seriously underestimate. He believed he had overturned all the work of salvation when the Son of God went to the cross.

But, says Paul in Colossians 2, it is there Satan made his greatest blunder, for by the cross God "spoiled principalities and powers, [and] he made a show of them openly, triumphing over them in it" (verse 15). Christ met Satan face to face in single combat and routed him; at the cross He fulfilled the promise given to man at the beginning, when Adam was told that the seed of the woman would bruise the serpent's head. This was the plan of salvation.

◈ A THOUGHT TO PONDER ◈
The plan of salvation displays to us the power of God.

From *Saved in Eternity*, pp. 50-51.

OUR SECURITY IN GOD

And I give unto them eternal life; and they shall never perish,
neither shall any man pluck them out of my hand.
JOHN 10:28

There is nothing uncertain about my acceptance with God, nor about my forgiveness, nor about my sonship. When I realize that I have been brought into God's plan, I know that nothing can frustrate this.

Now there are many people who talk about the Protestant Reformation and the influence it had upon the world. You find that certain statesmen do this. They say you cannot explain the history of England apart from the Protestant Reformation. Neither, they say, can you explain the United States of America apart from these things, because they all had their origin in that Reformation. But how little do these people really see what it all means and what it really represents, which is that these great truths are absolute and certain. Do you know why the Pilgrim Fathers made that attempt and succeeded in crossing the Atlantic? What was it that enabled men to do things like that and to do things that were even more hazardous? It was that they believed in what is called "the doctrine of the perseverance of the saints"; it was because they had seen themselves in the plan of God that cannot be broken and that cannot fail. It is as absolute as God Himself; He knows the end as well as the beginning. "Neither shall any man, " said Christ, "pluck them out of my hand." It is unthinkable.

If God has done all this for us in Christ, and especially in His death, we can be certain that He will carry on with the work until it is completed. That is Paul's argument: "He that spared not his own Son, but delivered him up for us all, how shall he not with him also freely give us all things?" (Romans 8:32). God, who is sufficiently concerned about me to send His Son to die on the cross of Calvary for me, is not going to let me down when any difficulty or temptation faces me.

✎ A THOUGHT TO PONDER ✎

God is not going to let me down when any difficulty or temptation faces me.

From *Saved in Eternity*, pp. 63-64.

OUR LORD'S GLORY ON EARTH

There is no beauty that we should desire him.
ISAIAH 53:2

Think about the glory of our Lord that we are told about when He was on earth: "There is no beauty that we should desire him . . . a man of sorrows, and acquainted with grief" (Isaiah 53:2-3). People would look at Him and say, "Who is this fellow?" "Is not this the carpenter, the son of Mary?" (Mark 6:3). He had laid aside the glory; He had not laid aside anything of His essential being or person or His essential deity. But neither had He held on to it. He had not clutched at the manifestation of His glory. He had laid that aside as one would a cloak and had come in the likeness of man.

Indeed, I must go further than this, because this is the wonder of it all. He decided that His glory should be veiled by flesh. Think of it like this: The glory is there still shining in all its power, but a veil of flesh has come over it so that mankind cannot see it.

Take an Old Testament illustration. In the wilderness Moses went onto the Mount and spoke with God, and when he came down his face was shining. The people saw the glory, and it was so bright that he had to put a veil over his face; the glory was still there, but it was hidden from them. Something like that happened to our Lord.

Yes, but He not only came as man, nor is it only true to say that His glory was veiled by flesh. It is not true to say simply that the eternal Son of God was made flesh. We are told that he was made "in the likeness of sinful flesh" (Romans 8:3). Indeed, He not only came into this world as a man—He took on Him "the form of a servant" (Philippians 2:7). It would have been a wonderful and astounding thing if this eternal King and Prince of glory had come on earth and lived in a palace as a human king with all the pomp and glory of an earthly kingship. But that is not what He did at all! He was born as a babe in very poor circumstances.

❧ A THOUGHT TO PONDER ☙
He had laid aside the glory.

From *Saved in Eternity*, pp. 72-73.

A GLIMPSE INTO ETERNITY

And now, O Father, glorify thou me with thine own self with the glory which I had with thee before the world was.

JOHN 17:5

The Lord is looking at what is before Him, and this is His prayer. Having completed all the work, having done everything that the Father had appointed Him to do, He asks, as it were, "Has not the time now arrived when I can come back to You, exactly where I was before? I have done the work. Father, 'glorify thou me with thine own self with the glory which I had with thee before the world was.'" But the astonishing thing for us to remember at this point is that He goes back as God-Man! In eternity He was God the Son, pure deity, and He shared the glory; but now He goes back as God-Man. And as God-Man, and our representative, the glory that He momentarily laid aside at the request of the Father is restored to Him, and thus as God-Man and Mediator He again shares this ineffable glory of the eternal God.

And so this prayer was answered. It began to be answered at the resurrection, the event that finally convinced even the disciples that He was the Son of God. They did not quite understand it before, but, as Paul puts it in writing to the Romans, our Lord was "declared to be the Son of God with power, according to the spirit of holiness, by the resurrection from the dead" (Romans 1:4). Who is this who has conquered death and the grave? He must be, He *is* the Son of God. Consider the appearances after the resurrection. You find the disciples in Jerusalem behind locked doors because they were afraid of the Jews, and suddenly He came in without the door being opened. "You see who I am," he says in effect. "I have flesh and bones, and I can eat." See the glorious person of this risen Lord.

✎ A THOUGHT TO PONDER ✐

In eternity He was God the Son, but now He goes back as God-Man.

From *Saved in Eternity*, pp. 77-78.

HISTORICAL EVENTS

. . . that he should give eternal life . . .
JOHN 17:2

If we base our position entirely upon experience, we will convince nobody. We are dealing with certain historical events and facts that we must never allow ourselves to forget. Indeed, I am prepared to go as far as to say that whatever I may feel at this moment, though I may feel that I am in a state of darkness and am utterly discouraged, my position is still safe, and I am secure because of these things that have been done in history outside of me and before I was ever born.

Thank God, I do not base my position on how I feel. Feelings are treacherous; they come and go, and what little control we have upon them! We have all had the following experience, have we not? We wake up one morning and find ourselves full of peace and joy and happiness. We have a marvelous day, we read our Bibles, we have freedom in prayer, and all is well. So we look forward to the next day being still more wonderful. But strangely enough, we find that when we wake up the next morning we are lifeless and dull.

If you are going to base your whole position upon experience and feelings, you are going to be a very unhappy person, and your Christian life is going to be very unstable. But the answer is this marvelous plan of salvation. I must, of course, know that I am related to it—that is essential. But what I am arguing for is that if you want to enjoy these blessings and if you want to live this Christian life truly, you do so by looking at these things, by resting upon them, and by saying, if you like, in the words of a hymn:

> *My hope is built on nothing less*
> *Than Jesus' blood and righteousness;*
> *I dare not trust my sweetest frame,*
> *But wholly lean on Jesus' name.*
> EDWARD MOTE

☙ A THOUGHT TO PONDER ❧
Thank God, I do not base my position on how I feel.

From *Saved in Eternity*, pp. 83-84.

THE PROMISE OF THE FATHER

. . . wait for the promise of the Father . . .

ACTS 1:4

The final manifestation of the glory of the Son was that which was given on the Day of Pentecost when the Holy Spirit was sent down upon the infant church gathered together at Jerusalem. That is the final proof of the fact that Jesus of Nazareth is the only begotten Son of God. The Scripture talks about "the promise of the Father." The Father had promised the children of Israel in the old dispensation that He would send His Spirit. He keeps on saying that He is going to make a new covenant with them, that the day is coming when He will take out their stony heart, give them a heart of flesh, and pour out His Spirit upon them. That is the thing to which they were looking forward, and in a sense the work of the Messiah, the Deliverer, the Savior, was to send this promise of the Father. And this is the very thing that happened on the Day of Pentecost when the Lord Jesus Christ sent the Holy Spirit.

Now in one place the Scripture tells us that the Lord Jesus Christ sent the Holy Spirit, and in another place it tells us that God the Father sent the Spirit after listening to the prayer of His Son. But it is the same thing, since the Spirit proceeds from the Father *and* from the Son. What I particularly want to emphasize is that "these words" of John 17:1 refer to the words that are recorded in chapters 14, 15, and 16 of John's Gospel, which all have to do with this promise of the coming of the Holy Spirit. Our Lord began to speak about this in chapter 14. He found that the disciples were crestfallen because He said that He was going to leave them. So He told them that He would give them another Comforter (14:16-17). Then He proceeded to teach them about the coming of the Holy Spirit.

✍ A THOUGHT TO PONDER ✍

The final manifestation of the glory of the Son was given on the Day of Pentecost.

From *Saved in Eternity*, pp. 84-85.

February 9

GLORY BE TO GOD

I have glorified thee on the earth: I have finished the work which thou gavest me to do.

JOHN 17:4

The coming of the Holy Spirit is part of this great and vital plan of salvation, and it is, of course, one of the most wonderful aspects of all. In the council in eternity, God the Father, God the Son, and God the Holy Spirit spoke together and planned the salvation of man. The Father stated the great scheme, and the Son accepted the decision that He should be the One to carry out the plan; and then it was equally decided that the Holy Spirit should complete what the Son had done for mankind.

This is what is sometimes called "the economy of the Trinity," the division of the work between the three Persons, and it is something that appears very clearly throughout the Scriptures. It appears, for example, in the very beginning, in Genesis, where we are shown how the creation itself was the work of the Trinity: "In the beginning God . . ." Then we are told that "the Spirit of God moved . . ." Everything was made through the Word, but in a sense the agency was still the Spirit.

The Father sends the Son, and the great business of the Son is to glorify the Father. He says, "I have glorified thee on the earth; I have finished the work which thou gavest me to do" (John 17:4). There is a sense in which the Lord Jesus Christ never glorified Himself. That is why He laid aside His glory, and why He was not born in a king's palace but in a stable. That, too, is why He took upon Himself the form of a servant; it was all to glorify the Father. All His life as a man was in a sense lived just in this way, in order that all the glory and power might be to God the Father.

✍ A THOUGHT TO PONDER ✍

Our Lord lived so that all the glory and power might be to God the Father.

From *Saved in Eternity*, pp. 85-86.

THE HOLY SPIRIT GLORIFIES THE SON

He shall glorify me.

JOHN 16:14

After the Lord Jesus Christ went back to heaven, He sent upon the church the Holy Spirit, and the business and work of the Holy Spirit is to glorify the Son. Now this is a marvelous statement. We do not see the Holy Spirit—He is invisible, and in a sense that is because His work is to glorify the Son. Indeed, we read about the Holy Spirit in John 16:14 the same thing that we read elsewhere about the Son. Our Lord says that the Holy Spirit does not speak of Himself, but "He shall glorify me: for he shall receive of mine, and shall show it unto you." We are told precisely the same thing about the Son in relation to the Father. Therefore, the great controlling thought we must hold in our minds is that the chief work of the Holy Spirit is to glorify the Lord Jesus Christ.

In a sense the final glorification of the Lord Jesus Christ was the coming of the Holy Spirit. We are told in John's Gospel that the Holy Spirit was not yet come because Jesus was not yet glorified. We see this in the great promise our Lord made one day in the Temple when He said, "If any man thirst, let him come unto me, and drink. He that believeth on me, as the scripture hath said, out of his belly shall flow rivers of living water" (John 7:37-38). And John expounds on that: "But this spake he of the Spirit, which they that believe on him should receive: for the Holy Ghost was not yet given; because that Jesus was not yet glorified." So the Holy Spirit could not be given until Christ had finished the work the Father had given Him to do, until He had died and risen again, until He had ascended and taken His seat at the right hand of God. God then said, in effect, "I give You the promise; You send it upon the people."

◈ A THOUGHT TO PONDER ◈
The chief work of the Holy Spirit is to glorify the Lord Jesus Christ.

From *Saved in Eternity*, pp. 86-87.

THE HOLY SPIRIT REVEALS THE PERSON OF CHRIST

No man can say that Jesus is the Lord, but by the Holy Ghost.
1 CORINTHIANS 12:3

How does the Holy Spirit glorify Christ? It seems to me that the best way to look at this is to divide it into three main headings. First of all, He reveals the Lord Jesus Christ and His person. Paul in his letter to the Corinthians talks about the Lord of glory. Paul writes: "But we speak the wisdom of God in a mystery . . . which none of the princes of this world knew: for had they known it, they would not have crucified the Lord of glory" (1 Corinthians 2:7-8). But we, he says, have received the Spirit, and "the Spirit searcheth all things, yea, the deep things of God" (verse 10).

Do you see what that means? When the Lord Jesus was here as man, the Pharisees and the doctors of the law did not recognize Him; it was they who incited the people to cry out, "Away with Him, crucify Him." The Greeks did not know Him either, nor did the great philosophers; they all rejected Him. They said it was nonsense and impossible that a carpenter like that should be the Son of God. And the reason they did not know Him was they had not received the Holy Spirit. Paul says in 1 Corinthians 12:3, "No man can say that Jesus is the Lord, but by the Holy Ghost."

Have you not often been perplexed by the fact that many able men in this modern world of ours do not believe in the deity of Jesus Christ? They say that He was only a man. They praise Him and say He is the greatest man or teacher the world has ever known, but they do not see in Him the Son of God. We should never be happy about that. To recognize the Lord Jesus Christ is not a matter of intellect, but the greatest brain can never come to see it and believe it. It is a *spiritual* truth and something that is spiritually discerned. The Holy Spirit alone can reveal the person of Christ, but He *can* do it, and He can do it to anybody and to everybody.

✎ A THOUGHT TO PONDER ✍
The Holy Spirit alone can reveal the person of Christ.

From *Saved in Eternity*, pp. 88-89.

THE HOLY SPIRIT REVEALS THE WORK OF CHRIST

Now we have received, not the spirit of the world, but the Spirit which is of God; that we might know the things that are freely given to us of God.

1 CORINTHIANS 2:12

The Holy Spirit not only reveals the *person*—He also reveals the *work* of the Lord Jesus Christ. The preaching of Christ, says Paul, is a stumbling block to the Jews and foolishness to the Greeks (1 Corinthians 1:23). These so-called wise men frequently stumble at the cross especially. You see, the preaching of the first disciples was not only that Jesus of Nazareth is the Son of God, but that He came into the world in order to deal with the problem of sin. They taught that the meaning of His death upon the cross was not merely that He was arrested by the Romans at the instigation of the Pharisees and put to death by crucifixion. No; they taught also that God had made Him to be sin for us—it was a great transaction between the Father and the Son. To the philosophers this was nonsense. They did not understand because they did not receive the Holy Spirit. But "we," says Paul again to the Corinthians, "have received, not the spirit of the world, but the Spirit which is of God; that we might know the things that are freely given to us of God" (1 Corinthians 2:12).

I want to ask a simple question here: Have you understood this matter of the atonement? Are you clear about the work of Christ? Do you see and know that the Lord Jesus Christ has taken your sins upon Himself and has died for them on the tree? If you are in difficulty, it is because you have not been enlightened by the Holy Spirit. The only way you can come to know this is not to try to understand it intellectually, but to ask God to enlighten you by the Spirit and to enable you to see and receive this truth as the Spirit unfolds the work of Christ.

❧ A THOUGHT TO PONDER ☙
Ask God to enlighten you by the Spirit.

From *Saved in Eternity*, pp. 89-90.

THE HOLY SPIRIT REVEALS THE TEACHING OF CHRIST

*When he, the Spirit of truth, is come, he will
guide you into all truth.*

JOHN 16:13

The Holy Spirit not only reveals the *person* and the *work* of Christ—
He also reveals the *teaching* of Christ. Our Lord said to the disciples before He left them, "I have yet many things to say unto you, but ye cannot bear them now. Howbeit when he, the Spirit of truth, is come, he will guide you into all truth" (John 16:12-13). That is, "He will remind you of the things I have said and that you cannot grasp now, and He will make them plain to you."

So if you are in trouble about the understanding of the Gospel, ask God to give you His Spirit in all His fullness, and you will begin to understand. The fatal thing in these matters is to bring your natural intellect to bear upon them: "The natural man receiveth not the things of the Spirit of God . . . neither can he know them, because they are spiritually discerned" (1 Corinthians 2:14).

Read 1 Corinthians 2, and understand that these things are in a different realm, they belong to a different order, and the only way to understand the teaching of the New Testament about Christ's personal work and teaching is to have the eyes of your understanding enlightened by the Holy Spirit. Therefore, if you are in trouble, do not waste your time trying to read books of philosophy about these matters; do not try to grasp them with the natural intellect, for that is impossible. We are dealing with miracles. We are in the realm of the supernatural and the spiritual, and the only hope for us is that the Holy Spirit will come with that unction, with His eye salve, to anoint our eyes so that they will be opened to the blessed truth.

❧ A THOUGHT TO PONDER ❧

We are in the realm of the supernatural and the spiritual, and the only hope for us is the Holy Spirit.

From *Saved in Eternity*, pp. 90-91.

THE HOLY SPIRIT APPLIES CHRIST'S WORD

When he is come, he will reprove the world of sin.

JOHN 16:8

The Holy Spirit not only *reveals Christ*—He also *applies His Word*, which convicts us of sin. I have met people who said to me, "I do not understand this teaching about sin. I do not feel I am a sinner." Well, if you do not feel you are a sinner, it is simply because you do not know yourself, and you do not know yourself because the Holy Spirit has not convicted you. Some of the best people who have ever trodden this earth have been those who have been most conscious of their sinfulness. I cannot imagine a worse state for anybody to be in than for him or her to say he or she does not feel he or she is a sinner. The Holy Spirit convicts and convinces of sin, and if He has not done it for you, if you value your own soul, ask Him to do it. Christ came to die for sinners, not for the righteous, and the first work of the Spirit is to convict of sin, of righteousness, and of judgment. We come to Christ for salvation after the Spirit has convinced us of sin, because the Lord Jesus Christ is the answer to our need.

The Holy Spirit then gives us assurance of our acceptance and our forgiveness. He is a seal given to us to show that we belong to God. He testifies with our spirits that we are the children of God. No Christian has a right to be uncertain about his or her salvation; the Holy Spirit has been given in order that we might be certain, for "the Spirit itself beareth witness with our spirit, that we are the children of God" (Romans 8:16). If any Christian who is reading this is uncertain or is lacking in assurance and in happiness, let me urge this upon you—ask for the gift of the Spirit in His fullness, ask for this blessed assurance, tell God you long for it, do not give yourself rest or peace, and in a sense do not give God rest or peace until you have it.

❧ A THOUGHT TO PONDER ❧

No Christian has a right to be uncertain about his or her salvation.

From *Saved in Eternity*, pp. 91-92.

THE HOLY SPIRIT AT WORK IN US

*For it is God which worketh in you both to will and
to do of his good pleasure.*

PHILIPPIANS 2:13

Our Lord said in John 15 that we are bound to Him as are the branches to the vine; His life is in us, and it is a part of this blessed work of the Spirit. Then He goes on to work in us, sanctifying and perfecting us. "Work out your own salvation," says Paul in Philippians 2:12-13, "with fear and trembling. For it is God which worketh in you both to will and to do of his good pleasure." He even helps us in our prayers: "We know not what we should pray for as we ought: but the Spirit itself maketh intercession for us with groanings which cannot be uttered" (Romans 8:26). He then goes on to produce the fruit of the Spirit in us: "love, joy, peace, longsuffering, gentleness, goodness, faith, meekness, temperance" (Galatians 5:22-23).

The work of the Spirit is to make the Lord Jesus Christ real to us. So do not waste your time trying to picture the Lord Jesus Christ. Do not go and look at portraits of Him that are wholly imaginary. There is a sense, I believe, in which nobody should ever try to paint Him—it is wrong. I do not like these paintings of Christ; they are the efforts of the natural mind. If you want a photograph of the Lord Jesus Christ, the Holy Spirit will give it to you in the inner man. Christ said Himself, in John 14:21, "He that hath my commandments, and keepeth them, he it is that loveth me: and he that loveth me shall be loved of my Father, and I will love him, and will manifest myself to him." That is the work of the Spirit—to make Christ living, to make us certain He is there, so that when we speak to Him, and He to us, the Spirit makes Him real, and He is formed in us.

✎ A THOUGHT TO PONDER ✐

The work of the Spirit is to make the Lord Jesus Christ real to us.

THE HOLY SPIRIT GIVES US HIS POWER

My speech and my preaching was not with enticing words of man's wisdom, but in demonstration of the Spirit and of power.

1 CORINTHIANS 2:4

The Holy Spirit gives us His power, and, thank God, He not only gave it to the first apostles, He has also given it to quite unknown people throughout the centuries. He has enabled some simple people to speak just the right word at the right moment. John Bunyan tells us in his autobiography, *Grace Abounding*, that one of the greatest blessings and helps he ever had was one afternoon listening to three uneducated women who were doing some knitting together in the sunshine, outside a house, talking about the Lord Jesus Christ. He got more from them than from anybody else. And you find that is what happens. God gives this power to the simplest, humblest Christian to testify to the Lord Jesus Christ, sharing what He has done and the difference He has made to human life. This is how the Holy Spirit glorifies the Son. When He works in us, what He does is to make us glorify the Lord Jesus Christ. The man in whom the Spirit dwells does not talk about himself; whether he is a preacher or whatever he may be, you do not come away talking about him.

You and I have the inestimable privilege of being men and women who in this life and in our daily work and vocation can be glorifying the Lord Jesus Christ. Oh, God grant that we all may be filled with this Spirit, the Holy Spirit, of God, that we may "know him, and the power of his resurrection, and the fellowship of his sufferings, being made conformable unto his death" (Philippians 3:10); that we may know what He has done for us; that we may know we are the children of God and joint heirs with Christ; that we may have glimpses of the glory that awaits us and that we may find our lives transformed and filled with His power, so that we may say with Paul, "I live; yet not I, but Christ liveth in me" (Galatians 2:20).

❧ A THOUGHT TO PONDER ❧

You and I have the inestimable privilege of being men and women who in our daily work can glorify the Lord Jesus Christ.

GOD FORGIVES SIN

God is light, and in him is no darkness at all.
1 JOHN 1:5

God, being God, cannot simply forgive sin. Now the common idea about God, the one that we have instinctively, is that when we admit we have sinned, all that is necessary is that we should come to God, say we are very sorry, and God will forgive us. But according to the Bible that is impossible, and I do not hesitate to use that word. As a preacher of the Christian Gospel, I am compelled to say this, and I say it with reverence: God, because He is God, cannot just forgive sin like that.

If you want me to prove what I am saying, this is how I do it. If God could have forgiven sin just by saying, "I forgive," He would have done so, and Christ would never have been sent into this world. The work that was given to Him to do, this work, this assignment, this task, was given to the Lord Jesus Christ because, I say again, without it God cannot forgive sin. He must not only justify the ungodly—He must remain just. The way of salvation must be consistent with the character of God. He cannot deny Himself; He cannot change Himself; He is unchangeable. "God is light, and in him is no darkness at all" (1 John 1:5). He is "the Father of lights, with whom is no variableness, neither shadow of turning" (James 1:17). He is eternally the same, and He is absolutely righteous and holy and just. He cannot remain that and simply forgive sin.

It is wrong to say, "God is love, and because He is love, He will forgive me." My friend, He cannot, because He *is* God! The work of Christ was essential because of the character of God, and it was essential because of man being in sin; something had to be done to render man fit for God.

❧ A THOUGHT TO PONDER ❧
God, being God, cannot simply forgive sin.

WHAT WE COULD NOT DO FOR OURSELVES

I have finished the work which thou gavest me to do.
JOHN 17:4

The work of salvation was something that Christ Himself had to do, and He could therefore speak of it as being done. "I have finished the work which thou gavest me to do." Now I want to put that in the form of a negative like this: The Lord Jesus Christ did not come into this world to tell us what *we* have to do; He came Himself to do something for us that we could never do for ourselves. These negatives are all so essential, because there are people who believe in the deity of the Lord Jesus Christ, but if you ask them what He came into this world to do, their answer will be that He came to tell us what we must do ourselves. Or they talk about good works and say that if we do this or that, we will make ourselves Christian and make ourselves right with God. No! Our Lord says here, "*I have finished the work which thou gavest *me* to do.*"

The truth that we have to take hold of is that which is emphasized here, and the best way to understand it is to consider what it was He did, and, too, what He was doing beforehand. He came to do certain things Himself, and we are saved by what Christ has done for us, and not by what He tells us to do. The work of salvation is His work and His doing, and He came specifically to do it; and here, in these words, He looks ahead, as it were, to His death on the cross, as well as back to what He has already done. Under the shadow of the cross, he reviews the whole work, and He is able to say, "I have finished the work which thou gavest me to do." "I have completed it." So a very good way of testing whether we have a right or wrong way of looking at salvation is to ask ourselves whether we see Christian salvation as something that is exclusively and entirely the work of the Lord Jesus Christ.

❧ A THOUGHT TO PONDER ❧

Christ came to do something for us that we could never do for ourselves.

From *Saved in Eternity*, pp. 100-101.

THE WORK HAS BEEN DONE

It is finished.

JOHN 19:30

We need to be delivered from the power of the devil, we need death and the grave to be conquered—and our Lord Jesus Christ has done it all. And beyond all that, we need a new nature, because we need not only forgiveness of sins, but to be made fit to have communion and fellowship with God. We need to have a nature that can stand before God, for "God is light, and in him is no darkness at all" (1 John 1:5). And Christ has come and given Himself, His own nature, the eternal life of which he speaks in John 17:1-5. So here, looking at it all, He can say, "I have finished the work which thou gavest me to do" (verse 4).

He has done everything that is necessary for man to be reconciled to God. Have you realized, my friends, that this work is finished? Have you realized that it is finished as far as you are concerned? You are asked whether you are a Christian, and you reply that you are hoping to be, but that you need to do this, that, and the other. No! Christ says, "I have finished the work which thou gavest me to do." The work has been done, and what proves whether we are truly Christians or not is whether we know and realize that the work has been done and that we then rest, and rest only, upon the finished work of our blessed Lord and Savior Jesus Christ. If we see it all in Him and the work done and completed in Him, it means we are Christians.

The way for you to know God and to be reconciled to Him is wide-open in the Lord Jesus Christ and His perfect work on your behalf. If you have never entered in before, enter in now, rest upon the finished work of the Lord Jesus Christ, and begin to rejoice, immediately, in your great salvation.

⮜ A THOUGHT TO PONDER ⮞

The way for you to know God, and to be reconciled to Him, is wide-open in the Lord Jesus Christ.

From *Saved in Eternity*, pp. 105-106.

THE GARDEN OF GETHSEMANE

This is your hour, and the power of darkness.

LUKE 22:53

What does our Lord mean exactly when He says in the Garden of Gethsemane, "This is your hour, and the power of darkness"? It seems to me that the only possible explanation must be that this hour would never have come to pass were it not for the power of darkness. What makes this hour and all that it involves necessary and essential? It is again the problem of sin and of evil, the problem of Satan and of hell. It is the kind of hour that the devil has staged and brought into being, for in one sense he has manipulated it, though in a much higher sense he has not. I think this is the way to look at it—it is the work of the devil that makes the hour essential from God's standpoint; it is because of what Satan has produced by sin and evil that God has to do this in order to overcome it.

So it is, in a sense, the hour of evil men, and it is there that we really see the essence of evil and of sin. The devil has produced such a situation that this hour alone can deal with it.

So this hour can be described as "your hour" and the hour of the glorification of the Son at the same time, and that is why He prays that His Father may glorify Him. It is in going through this hour, which has been produced by Satan and hell, that our Lord really is glorified. It is there we know for certain that He is the Son of God. No one had ever before had to meet Satan and conquer him; no one had been able to destroy the power that Satan had over death. The author to the Epistle to the Hebrews puts it like this: "That through death he might destroy him that had the power of death" (2:14). And thus He sets the children free, and Christ has done this through His glorification. Christ's death and resurrection are proof that He is the Son of God.

⚓ A THOUGHT TO PONDER ⚓

Christ's death and resurrection are proof that He is the Son of God.

February 21

THE RESULTS OF THE HOUR

*Now is the judgment of this world: now shall the prince
of this world be cast out.*

JOHN 12:31

The results of the hour are put very plainly by Jesus in John 12:31. What an hour this is! Do you not begin to see that it is the most momentous hour of all time? We talk about the pivotal points of history, but they are all nothing when you look at this. "Now is the judgment of this world"—the whole world, in the sense that it is the hour in which the world was really revealed for what it is. It was there that sin was revealed. There, shown plainly and clearly once and forever, is the whole state of mankind apart from God.

The cross does not only reveal sin for what it is—at one and the same time it pronounces doom on the whole world and everything that belongs to that realm. The cross of Jesus Christ makes this great proclamation. Unless I believe in Him, unless I believe that His death at that hour is the only thing that reconciles me to God, I remain under the wrath of God. If I do not see that the wrath of God against my sin has been borne there by the Son of God, then the alternative is that I must experience the wrath of God. That is the essence of the Christian Gospel. I either believe that my sins have been punished in the body of the Son of God, or else they will be punished in me. It is the judgment of the world.

The world apart from Him is under the wrath of God, it is doomed, it is damned, and He alone can save it in that way. There was no other way, for God would never have allowed His Son to endure all that if there had been another way. It is the only way; so it is the judgment of the world.

☙ A THOUGHT TO PONDER ❧

This hour is the most momentous hour of all time.

February 22

JESUS PEOPLE

And this is life eternal, that they might know thee the only true
God, and Jesus Christ, whom thou hast sent.

JOHN 17:3

The end of salvation is that we should have eternal life. What is a Christian? What is Christianity? The definition given by the New Testament is that a Christian is a person who possesses eternal life. Perhaps the best way of emphasizing that is to consider how it is that we hold such a low view of Christianity and the Christian life. What is the average person's conception of a Christian and what makes one a Christian?

Some people seem to think of it in terms of country. They still speak about Christian countries and non-Christian countries, as if the whole country could be Christian. Others think in terms of church membership. Others think in terms of living a good life, following Christ and His teaching, trying to apply it personally, and getting other people to do the same.

But according to the New Testament, all that does not even begin to make one a Christian, and the world is very often quick to detect the hollowness of the claims in such people who call themselves Christians. I was reading of a distinction that I think was common among many Chinese people in past years. They called all the ordinary foreigners Christians, but others they called "Jesus people." What they meant was that they regarded everybody who went to China from the West as Christians, because they came from so-called Christian countries, and most of them claimed that they were Christians. But the Chinese saw that they were often drunkards and immoral and so on, and they felt that if that was Christianity, they did not want it. Then they found that there were other people who came from the same countries and who also called themselves Christians. But these lived a pure, holy, and kind life. They seemed to help people and were altogether different, and the Chinese began to call them "Jesus people," because they seemed to be like the Lord Jesus Christ Himself.

✒ A THOUGHT TO PONDER ✒
The end of salvation is that we should have eternal life.

From *Saved in Eternity*, pp. 125-126.

HIGHEST POWER

As thou hast given him power over all flesh, that he should give
eternal life to as many as thou hast given him.

JOHN 17:2

There is only one person who can give us the gift of eternal life, and that is the One who is praying: "As thou hast given him power over all flesh, that he should give eternal life to as many as thou hast given him." Christ alone can give us this eternal life.

There is the terrible danger of mysticism here, or at any rate of the mysticism that does not make Christ central. There are many people in the world who are anxious to possess this life of God. You will find them writing about it, and one of the most remarkable examples of this has been Aldous Huxley, who used to be a complete skeptic, but who came to believe that nothing can save the world but mysticism, and who became a Buddhist for that reason. Such men believe that there is this eternal life of God to be had, that what we need is that life of God in ourselves, and that our trouble is that we have not got it. But these people think that they can get this life of God in themselves without mentioning the Lord Jesus Christ at all. You get it, they say, by contemplation of the Absolute, by increasingly sinking into the eternal and being lost in him, because as you do so, you are receiving life from him.

But, my friends, it is Christ and He alone who can give eternal life. He claims it here, and Scripture says it everywhere: "As thou hast given him power over all flesh, that he should give eternal life . . ." There is no one else who can give eternal life to man except the Lord Jesus Christ. If it were possible in any other way, why did He ever come to earth? Why the death on the cross? There is no other way; the whole plan of salvation centers on Him.

❧ A THOUGHT TO PONDER ☙
Christ alone can give us this eternal life.

From *Saved in Eternity*, pp. 132-133.

KNOWING GOD

I am the way, the truth, and the life: no man cometh unto the Father, but by me.

JOHN 14:6

We must realize as we approach God that His ultimate, gracious purpose with regard to man has been revealed to us, and it is a purpose of love and mercy and of kindness and compassion. This is something that is only known fully and finally in and through the Lord Jesus Christ. That is why this statement must be put like this: "And this is life eternal, that they might know thee the only true God, and Jesus Christ, whom thou hast sent" (John 17:3). This truth is an absolute necessity. That is why our Lord said, "I am the way, the truth, and the life: no man cometh unto the Father, but by me" (John 14:6). He is the way to God. He is the truth about God, and apart from the life He gives, we will never share or know the life of God. So there is no knowledge of God apart from Him; through Him comes this ultimate true and saving knowledge, the saving relationship.

Notice what John 17:3 tells us about our Lord Jesus Christ: "That they might know thee the only true God, *and* Jesus Christ." The name *Jesus* reminds us of the truth of the Incarnation: This eternal Son of God was made man—the man Jesus. But the man Jesus is One who is God and who is co-equal with Him and whom, therefore, you think of in terms of being God and being with God— "and Jesus."

But He is also Jesus *Christ*, and "Christ" means "Messiah," the One who has been anointed to do this special work of bringing men and women to God and of giving God's life to humankind. You see how all this mighty doctrine is put here as it were in a nutshell for us—"and Jesus Christ." It is all there—the ultimate object is to know this "only true God"; yes, and the way to know Him is to know Jesus Christ.

∽ A THOUGHT TO PONDER ∾

Christ is the way to God; He is the truth about God.

From *Saved in Eternity*, pp. 143-144.

ETERNAL LIFE

. . . that he should give eternal life . . .
JOHN 17:2

Let us try to understand exactly what is true of this life. Let me give you some of the New Testament definitions of it. We are told that as a result of having this life we become sons of God or children of God: "For ye are all the children of God," says the apostle Paul in Galatians 3:26. Another phrase, used by John in his first epistle, is that we are "born of God" (1 John 5:1); and in John 3:8 we read that we are "born of the Spirit."

The apostle Peter describes it by saying that we become "partakers of the divine nature" (2 Peter 1:4)—an astounding statement. In another place he tells us that we are "begotten . . . again" (1 Peter 1:3)—we are regenerated.

Now all those terms, and others too, are used in the New Testament in order to give us some conception and understanding of the quality and nature of eternal life. And it was in order to give us this marvelous life that the Lord Jesus Christ came into the world. That is why He went to the cross, that is why He was buried and rose again—so that you and I might become sons of God, children of God, born of God, partakers of the divine nature, that we might be regenerated and made anew and receive a new life. But I must hasten to add, it is very important that we should not misconstrue any of these great, exalted terms.

Not one of them means that you and I become divine. We do not cease to be human. We are not turned into gods. We must never put such a meaning to those great terms. It does not mean that the divine essence, as it were, is infused into us. We are still human, though we are partakers of the divine nature.

✎ A THOUGHT TO PONDER ✐

Christ went to the cross that we might become children of God and receive a new life.

From *Saved in Eternity*, pp. 150-151.

A NEW PRINCIPLE

*For after that in the wisdom of God the world by wisdom
knew not God, it pleased God by the foolishness of preaching
to save them that believe.*

1 CORINTHIANS 1:21

We are meant to use all our God-given natural faculties. That is
why when God wants a great teacher of the Christian Gospel, he
chooses a man like the apostle Paul. Yes, but Paul was no more a
Christian than the most ignorant person in the church at Corinth.
It is the *principle* that matters. We must not merely consider this in
terms of understanding and ability; it is something much more wonderful and glorious than that. And that is why Paul was able to say
in 1 Corinthians 1:21, "For after that in the wisdom of God the
world by wisdom knew not God, it pleased God by the foolishness
of preaching to save them that believe."

God, he says, takes the ignorant, and by means of them He confounds the wise, and He takes the weak and confounds the mighty—
because of this new principle that He introduces.

What, then, is the effect of the introduction of this principle?
This life eternal about which we are speaking is something that
affects the entire person. But it is especially interesting to observe
the way in which it affects a man's understanding and apprehen-
sion of spiritual things. And the way to look at that is to contrast
the natural, unregenerate man, who is not a Christian, with the
man who is a Christian. According to Scripture, the natural man is
spiritually dead. May I be so bold as to put it like this: If there is
anybody to whom these things about which I am speaking are really
utterly meaningless, then, as I understand Scripture, it means that
such a person is spiritually dead and has not received eternal life
because, as Paul puts it, "The natural man receiveth not the things of
the Spirit of God: for they are foolishness unto him" (1 Corinthians
2:14). They are meaningless to him.

✍ A THOUGHT TO PONDER ✍

God takes the ignorant, and by means of them He confounds the
wise—because of this new principle that He introduces.

From *Saved in Eternity*, pp. 153-154.

THE WILL OF GOD

Nevertheless not my will, but thine, be done.

LUKE 22:42

The person who has eternal life loves to do the will of God. This is the logical sequence. The man who loves is the man who is anxious to please the object of his love. There is no better test of love than that, and unless you desire to please someone whom you claim to love, then I assure you, you do not love that person. Love always wants to be pleasing and to give itself, and anyone who loves God wants to do the will of God.

If you look at Christ, you see that the whole of His life, His one object, was to do the will of His Father. He did not care what it was; even in the Garden of Gethsemane when He faced the one thing He did not want, even there He said, "Nevertheless not my will, but thine, be done." He says, "I do not want to drink this cup, but if it is doing Thy will, I will do even that." That is love at its maximum and its best, and it is true of all who have His life. The chief end of the true Christian is the glory of God;, therefore he spends his time seeking to know the will of God and doing it.

He strives to do it, and he loves to do it. He is controlled by this one idea. Having learned what God has done for him and what God is to him, having realized something of this love of God, he says, "Love so amazing, so divine, demands my soul, my life, my all." Any man, therefore, who has eternal life has this as the supreme object and desire of his life—to do the will of God.

The ultimate manifestation of the possession of eternal life is that it produces certain results in our lives. Fortunately for us they have all been set out in a very brief compass in Galatians 5:22-23, where the apostle Paul speaks of the fruit of the Spirit. These verses are rightly called "the shortest biography of Christ that has ever been written."

◈ A THOUGHT TO PONDER ◈

The true Christian spends his time seeking to know the will of God and doing it.

From *Saved in Eternity*, pp. 168-169.

HINDRANCES REMOVED

I have glorified thee on the earth: I have finished the work
which thou gavest me to do.

JOHN 17:4

One basis of security and assurance about eternal life, according to our Lord, is that every hindrance and obstacle to our receiving this gift of eternal life has been removed by the blessed work of the Lord Himself. "I have glorified thee on earth: I have finished the work which thou gavest me to do."

Many things had to be done before I could receive the gift of eternal life. As a natural man I wondered how I could get it. Eternal life really means that we are sharers of the life of God and are in communion with Him. Is it not obvious, therefore, that a great many things have to happen before we can come into that condition? But it has all been done. There is nothing that has been left undone. Christ has dealt with the problem of my guilt by removing it. He has reconciled me to God; the law of God has been satisfied. "Who shall lay any thing to the charge of God's elect?" (Romans 8:33). He Himself has done it, for "It is Christ that died, yea rather, that is risen again, who is even at the right hand of God" (verse 34).

Christian people, this is the position we are meant to occupy. Here is a quotation from an Augustus Toplady hymn:

> *The terrors of law and of God*
> *With me can have nothing to do.*
> *My Savior's obedience and blood,*
> *Hide all my transgressions from view.*

That is not boasting, for I am not relying upon myself, but upon Him: "My Savior's obedience and blood, / hide all my transgressions from view."

❧ A THOUGHT TO PONDER ☙

Every obstacle to our receiving eternal life has been removed by the blessed work of the Lord Himself.

From *Saved in Eternity*, pp. 180-181.

CAN YOU LOSE THE GIFT?

Neither death, nor life, nor angels, nor principalities, nor powers,
nor things present, nor things to come, nor height, nor depth,
nor any other creature, shall be able to separate us from the love
of God, which is in Christ Jesus our Lord.

ROMANS 8:38-39

I find it quite extraordinary that anybody calling himself a Christian can believe that he can receive the gift of the life of God and then, because of sin, lose it and then accept it again and then lose it once more. You cannot go on being born and dying! No. If you receive the life of God, then God Himself gives you this gift through His Son, and the very quality, the nature, and the character of the life means that it is imperishable. Our Lord had already said in John's Gospel, "Neither shall any man pluck them out of my hand" (John 19:28); it is impossible. Or again, the apostle Paul says, "Neither death, nor life, nor angels, nor principalities, nor powers, nor things present, nor things to come, nor height, nor depth, nor any other creature, shall be able to separate us from the love of God, which is in Christ Jesus our Lord" (Romans 8:38-39).

Furthermore, this is especially true because He Himself has given us this life. So we are in this new relationship, we belong to the family of God, we are separated out of the world, we are separated unto God, we are a part of His plan and purpose, and we belong to Him. That is why Paul can say with such confidence that "the sufferings of this present time are not worthy to be compared with the glory which shall be revealed in us" (Romans 8:18).

We are saved by hope, hope that is sure and certain, because it is based upon the character, indeed upon the life, of God Himself. Therefore, if we know that we have eternal life, that should encourage us and strengthen us. It should enable us to know that because God has given us that gift, it is indeed, as God Himself has said, an *eternal* life.

❧ A THOUGHT TO PONDER ❧

We are saved by hope that is based upon the life of God Himself.

From *Saved in Eternity*, pp. 182-183.

March

JESUS' PRAYER FOR US

FROM

Safe in the World

AND

Sanctified Through the Truth

OUR SAVIOR PRAYS FOR US

*I pray for them: I pray not for the world, but for them which
thou hast given me; for they are thine.*

JOHN 17:9

Our Lord prays for His followers here. Some would put it as strongly as to say that He pleads for them; He does not merely make requests—He produces arguments and makes statements. This is a point that we must surely observe, for it is of great value to us. It reminds us that God's omniscience is no reason for our not telling Him things that He already knows.

You must have often found yourself facing a particular difficulty or situation. You feel that because God knows everything, there is no point in telling Him anything about it. God knows our need, He knows all about us before we get on our knees to pray; so why then do we need to tell Him anything? What seems to be the obvious conclusion to that thought is that there is no need to pray at all: If God knows all about us, why not let things take their course and all will be well.

Now the answer to that is what we find in John 17. Our Lord knew, in a way we can never know, about God's omniscience, His perfect and complete knowledge, and yet He told His Father certain things about those disciples, things that God knew already. He prayed about them and repeated them, and, of course, that is characteristic of Bible prayers everywhere—not only the prayers of our Lord but also those of the apostles and of the saints of the Old Testament. This is something that is wonderful the moment you begin to contemplate it. God after all desires us to think of Him as our Father. It is a kind of anthropomorphism; God is stooping to our weakness.

So when we come into the presence of God with our requests and our petitions, let us never fear to bring the details, for nothing is too small for God's loving care and attention.

✎ A THOUGHT TO PONDER ✎

God's omniscience is no reason for our not telling Him things that He already knows.

WHY OUR LORD PRAYS FOR THESE PEOPLE

I pray for them.

JOHN 17:9

Why does our Lord pray for these people at all? He is facing His own death, the greatest and most terrible moment in His life is at hand, and yet He pauses to pray for them. Why does He do it? The answer is all here. He does it first and foremost *because of His great concern for the glory of God*. While He is on earth, the glory of God is, in a sense, in His hands. He has come to glorify His Father, and that is the one thing He wants to do above everything else. And now as He is going to leave these people, over and above His own concern about dying is His concern about the glory of God; it is the one thing that matters.

Second, He prays for them *because of who and what they are*. They are the people to whom He has manifested the name of God, the people who have been given to Him, the people to whom He has given the Word, people who believe certain things. That is the definition of a Christian, and they, and they alone, are the people for whom He prayed.

Then He prays for them *because of their task*, because of their calling. He is going away, and He is leaving them in the world to do something; they have work to do, exactly as He had been given work to do. You see the logic of it all? God sent Him, He sends them, and He prays for them especially in the light of their calling and their task—the work of evangelizing. There are other people who are going to believe on Him through their word, and so they must be enabled to do this work.

He also prays for them *because of their circumstances*, the circumstances in which they were placed in the world. He says that they are going to have trouble in the world (verse 14).

❧ A THOUGHT TO PONDER ❧

Over and above Christ's own concern about dying is His concern about the glory of God.

From *Safe in the World*, pp. 11-12.

March 3

WHAT OUR LORD PRAYS FOR

I pray not that thou shouldest take them out of the world,
but that thou shouldest keep them from the evil.

JOHN 17:15

The primary object of Christ's prayer is not so much that His followers may be one with one another as that *they may be kept in true unity with Him,* with God the Father, and therefore with each other. That is the nature of communion. Obviously this has to be worked out in greater detail, and never perhaps was this more necessary than today.

The next thing He prays for them is that *they may be kept from the evil one*—the devil, the god of this world, the prince of the power of the air—and the evil that is in the world as the result of his activities and efforts. Our Lord does not pray that they may be taken out of the world. We sometimes wish we could pray that; the idea of monasticism is somewhere down in the depths of all of us. We want to retire out of the world and arrive in some magic circle where nothing can disturb us. There is a longing in the suffering, persecuted Christian to get out of the world. But our Lord does not pray that they may be taken out of the world in any sense, nor that they may be taken out of it by death, but rather that in it they may be kept from the evil.

Your business and mine as Christian people is to be in the midst of this world and its affairs and still remain true and loyal to God and be kept from the evil. "Pure religion and undefiled before God and the Father is this," says James, not to retire out of every vocation in life, but rather "to visit the fatherless and widows in their affliction, and to keep himself unspotted from the world" (James 1:27). The task of the Christian is to be in the midst of this world and its affairs in order that he or she may do this work of evangelism.

✎ A THOUGHT TO PONDER ✎
Our Lord does not pray that they may be taken out of the world but rather that in it they may be kept from the evil.

WHAT WE SEE ABOUT
OUR LORD HIMSELF

For I have given unto them the words which thou gavest me;
and they have received them, and have known surely that I came
out from thee, and they have believed that thou didst send me.

JOHN 17:8

Notice what we see here about the Lord Himself. Here He is praying for His followers—not only for those immediately of His own time, but for all those who are going to believe in Him throughout the centuries, and therefore for us. Let us look at Him as He thus prays; let us look at certain things that stand out very clearly about His person.

Notice His claims. He says, for instance, "They . . . have known surely that I came out from thee." Here is One who appears to be just a man. He is to be taken by cruel people in apparent helplessness and weakness and is to be crucified on a cross. Yet He speaks of Himself as One who has come from God. Here is another great assertion of His unique deity: He is proclaiming that He is the eternal Son of God come from heaven to earth to dwell among men. He repeats it by saying, "Thou didst send me." He is not One who has just been born like everybody else—He has been sent by God into this world.

Then in verse 10 He does not hesitate to say, "I am glorified in them"—a tremendous assertion that He is not only man, He is the Son of God, verily God Himself, and that as He is the glory of the Father, so the disciples are to be His glory. He has glorified the Father, and He is glorified in them by what they are going to be and what they are going to do. You notice our calling, you notice that we, as Christians, have the privilege of being men and women in Him—that through us the Lord Jesus Christ Himself is glorified.

⮞ A THOUGHT TO PONDER ⮜

He is praying for all those who are going to believe in Him throughout the centuries, and therefore for us.

From *Safe in the World*, pp. 15-16.

OUR LORD'S CARE FOR HIS FOLLOWERS

I have manifested thy name unto the men which thou gavest me out of the world: thine they were, and thou gavest them me; and they have kept thy word.

JOHN 17:6

Observe our Lord's care for His followers. He reminds His Father that He kept them while He was in the world. How easy it is to read the Gospels without seeing that all the while He is watching them and keeping them and shielding them against the enemy. But now He is going out of the world, and in John 17 He is praying to His Father to keep them. He pleads with Him to look after them and commits them to His care. They are His Father's, but they have been given to Him, and He gives them back: "keep them from the evil" (John 17:15). If we but realized the concern of our Savior for us as we are tried and tempted and beset by sin and Satan, it would revolutionize our whole attitude toward everything.

We should also note His loving attitude toward His followers. Some astounding things are said here. Indeed we would almost be right to query them when we read what He says of these disciples: "I have manifested thy name unto the men which thou gavest me out of the world." Then notice: "thine they were, and thou gavest them me; and they have kept thy word" (John 17:6). How can He say that? As we read the Gospels and look at these disciples, we see them quarreling with one another, we see their jealousy of one another and their desire for preeminence over one another, and finally we read how at the end they all forsook Him and fled. Yet He said about them, "they have kept thy word." He did not criticize them; He prayed for them. I thank God for this above everything else.

✎ A THOUGHT TO PONDER ✐
He did not criticize them; He prayed for them.

THE CHARACTER OF THE CHRISTIAN

They are not of the world, even as I am not of the world.

JOHN 17:16

We must consider what our Lord has to say about the Christian. Here is the character of the Christian. The first thing I notice is a negative. He says in John 17:6, "I have manifested thy name unto the men which thou gavest me *out of the world*." Now that is the first thing He says about the Christian. He is not of this world. In verses 6-19 Jesus repeats that four times. In addition to verse 6, He says in verse 9, "I pray for them: I pray not for the world, but for them which thou hast given me"; again in verse 14, "I have given them thy word; and the world hath hated them, because they are not of the world, even as I am not of the world"; and then in verse 16, "They are not of the world, even as I am not of the world." Our Lord goes on repeating that phrase because He wants to impress it upon us. The first thing that is true about the Christian is that he does not belong to this world.

In the light of this, it is vital that we should ask ourselves the question, am I of the world or am I not? That is the fundamental distinction that runs through the Bible from beginning to end. There are only two groups of people in the world today—those who are of the world and those who belong to Christ. In the last analysis there is no other division or distinction that has the slightest importance or relevance. That is why most of us are defeated by life in this world—we recognize other distinctions that are quite unimportant. But when we all come to die, does it make the slightest difference which political party we belong to? Does it matter whether we are rich or poor, learned or otherwise? There is only one fundamental distinction, and that is whether we belong to the world or to Christ.

❧ A THOUGHT TO PONDER ❧
The Christian does not belong to this world.

GOD'S PEOPLE

And all mine are thine, and thine are mine; and
I am glorified in them.

JOHN 17:10

Why are Christian people not of the world? It is because they are God's people. "I have manifested thy name"—to whom?—"unto the men which thou gavest me out of the world: thine they were, and thou gavest them me" (John 17:6). That is the answer. That is the first and indeed the ultimate explanation, the one that includes all the others.

The importance of this doctrine can be seen at a glance in John 17. Whenever our Lord repeats a thing, we can be quite sure that He regards it as absolutely vital. We are familiar with the fact that whenever He introduces a statement by saying, "Verily, verily" we ought to pay unusual attention to it. So if He repeats a statement frequently in a short space, we can be equally certain that it is something that we should lay hold of very firmly.

Now you notice how He repeats this thought in John 17:6-19. We have noted it in verse 6, but we have it again in verse 9: "I pray for them: I pray not for the world, but for them which thou hast given me; for they are thine." In verse 10 He says, "And all mine are thine, and thine are mine; and I am glorified in them," and then again in verse 11, "And now I am no more in the world, but these are in the world, and I come to thee. Holy Father, keep through thine own name those whom thou hast given me, that they may be one, as we are." Finally, in verse 12 He says, "While I was with them in the world, I kept them in thy name: those that thou gavest me I have kept, and none of them is lost, but the son of perdition; that the scripture might be fulfilled." Nothing, then, ought to establish in our minds the all-importance of this doctrine and teaching more than that.

❧ A THOUGHT TO PONDER ❧

Why are Christian people not of the world? It is because they are God's people.

From *Safe in the World*, pp. 33-34.

GOD'S SPECIAL PEOPLE

Ye are a chosen generation, a royal priesthood, an holy nation,
a peculiar people.
1 PETER 2:9

The doctrine that Christians are God's special people is given in a very remarkable way in John 17, but it is taught everywhere throughout the New Testament. It is found, for instance, in that mighty first chapter of the Epistle to the Ephesians, but especially in Paul's prayer for the church at Ephesus. He prays that the eyes of their understanding may be enlightened. He wants them to grasp this truth with their minds and with their understanding because it is so vital. He prays that they may know what is the hope of their calling and then, second, what are "the riches of the glory of his inheritance"—God's inheritance—"in the saints." I want you to know, he says, and to see yourselves as God's inheritance. I want you to grasp this idea of God's special people. It is his prayer, above everything else, that these people might know this.

Consider, too, what he wrote to Timothy. Timothy was very troubled and worried about certain things that were happening in some of the churches for which he was responsible, and Paul in effect said, "Timothy, you need not be troubled, 'The Lord knoweth them that are his.'" God knows His own people, and that means that He not only knows them, but He looks after them, He keeps His eye upon them. Then in Hebrews 2:13 these words are applied to the Lord: "Behold I and the children which God hath given me." That is how the Lord Jesus Christ refers to Christians and to the members of His church. Peter also writes on the same theme in his epistle: "Ye are a chosen generation, a royal priesthood, an holy nation, a peculiar people" (1 Peter 2:9), which means a people for God's special interest and possession.

God has chosen and marked out and separated a people for Himself.

✒ A THOUGHT TO PONDER ✒
Christians are a people for God's special interest and possession.

From *Safe in the World*, pp. 34-36.

GOD'S PARTICULAR POSSESSION

*That ye may know what is the hope of his calling, and
what the riches of the glory of his inheritance in the saints.*
EPHESIANS 1:18

God desires us as His own particular possession and portion, and ultimately as those who are to share His glory. Look again at Paul's prayer for the Ephesian church in Ephesians 1. It is that they may know what is "the hope of his calling, and what the riches of the glory of his inheritance in the saints" (verse 18). To talk about God's "inheritance in the saints," the God who made everything and to whom all things belong and by whom all things are, to talk in this way is the most amazing and daring piece of anthropomorphism that Paul ever produced, and yet he has put it like that in order to give believers an understanding of it. What he means is that these are the people in whom God delights and whom God is going to enjoy.

Let me give an illustration in order to make this point clear. Take a child who has many toys, all of which he likes. Yes, but there is one particular favorite, the toy that is always with him. The child is fond of them all, but that one is something special. And it is the same with us. We all have certain possessions that we prefer to others; there is always something especially dear and of interest to us. That is the idea—that the great Lord of the universe has a special object of interest and affection—His own people, those whom He has taken and, as Paul puts it in writing to the Galatians, separated out of this evil world and put into a special category and compartment. That is the whole message of the Bible—God preparing for Himself a people who are going to be His joy throughout eternity.

◈ A THOUGHT TO PONDER ◈

These are the people in whom God delights and whom God is going to enjoy.

From *Safe in the World*, pp. 37-38.

LOVED BY THE FATHER AND THE SON

I have manifested thy name unto the men which thou gavest me out of the world.

JOHN 17:6

Consider the place we occupy in the interest and love of the Father and the Son. I confess that I am almost overwhelmed when I think of this. I so often spend my time, as I am sure many of you do, wondering why it is that I do not experience more of the love of God; why God does not, as it were, love me more and do things for me. What a terrible thing that is! The trouble is that I do not realize His love for me—that is my difficulty. People often say, "I feel my love for God is so small." Quite right, I say the same thing myself:

> *Lord, it is my chief complaint,*
> *That my love is weak and faint.*
>
> WILLIAM COWPER

That is true, but the best cure is not to try to do things within yourself and work up some love from the depths of your being. The way to love God is to begin to know God's love to you, and this doctrine is the high road to that love. Before time, before the creation of the world, He set His eye upon you, He set His affection upon you; you were marked, you were already put among His people. And all that has been done, all the person and the work of Christ, all this manifestation of His ineffable love, was done because of God's love to you. Therefore, realize His interest in you. The God who has loved you to the extent of sending His only begotten Son to endure and to suffer all that for you loves you with a love that you will never understand, a love that passes knowledge. If we but knew God's love to us, it would revolutionize our lives.

☙ A THOUGHT TO PONDER ❧

The way to love God is to begin to know God's love to you.

From *Safe in the World*, pp. 41-42.

THE NAME OF GOD

I have manifested thy name . . .
JOHN 17:6

In Scripture the name always stands for the character; it represents what a person really is. Let me remind you of some of the names that are used for God in the Scriptures. God is given the name Jehovah-nissi, the Lord Our Banner, in Exodus 17:15. That is the name He revealed to the children of Israel after a great victory, a victory won not by their own strength, nor by their own military prowess, but because God enabled them to obtain the victory—the Lord Our Banner. You and I have enemies to meet in this world—sin and temptation. The world is full of these subtle enemies, and behind them all is the devil himself with all his power. Do you know what it is to be attacked by him? Do you know, for example, what it is to have blasphemous thoughts insinuated into your minds? The saints of God have had to experience that. The devil hurls fiery darts, says Paul, and who are we to meet such a foe? We are small and weak and helpless, but thank God, we know One whose name is Jehovah-nissi, the Lord Our Banner, who can help us smite every foe and rout and conquer every enemy.

But let me give you another: Jehovah-shalom—The Lord Is Peace. That was the name by which God revealed Himself to Gideon. Gideon was fearful and unhappy, but God told him that He was Jehovah-shalom (Judges 6:24), and this is one of the most precious promises. It does not matter what kind of turmoil you are in or how heart-sore you may be. If you are beside yourself and cannot understand why things are happening to you, go to Him. He has promised to give you peace. Remember that noble statement in Hebrews 13:20, ". . . the God of peace, that brought again from the dead our Lord Jesus." Jehovah-shalom, The Lord Is Peace—He makes peace with His people.

❧ A THOUGHT TO PONDER ❧

We know One whose name is Jehovah-nissi, the Lord Our Banner.

From *Safe in the World*, pp. 46, 51-52.

GOD'S NAME MANIFESTED

*I have manifested thy name unto the men which thou gavest me
out of the world.*

JOHN 17:6

Notice that our Lord says here that He has "manifested" the name
of God unto men whom God had given Him out of the world. He
does not say merely that He told them about it. He goes beyond that.
He says, "I have manifested . . ."—there has been a revelation, there
has been an expounding of the name. That which was concealing it
has been taken away, and there has been an unveiling or an unfolding—that is the meaning of the word "manifested." Our Lord has
made the name appear, and He has put it obviously before them.
This is a very rich and comprehensive term, and our Lord undoubtedly uses it deliberately so that these men who are listening to Him
as He prays to God might realize the variegated and manifold character of this manifestation of the name of God that He has given.

So how does the Lord Jesus Christ manifest the name of God,
and especially how does He do so in a way that is superior to the Old
Testament revelation? The author of the letter to the Hebrews argues
for the preeminence of Christ. The Old Testament was a true revelation, but it was only in part and in pieces; now, in Christ, it has
come in all its fullness and glory.

Here, then, our Lord says that because He is the Son of God,
He has manifested the name of God in a way that nothing and no
one else could ever have done. He puts it like this: "They have
received them [the words God gave Him], and have known surely
that I came out from thee." "These," He says in essence, "are Your
people; these are true Christians because they know that I have come
out from You." That is just another way of saying that these people
knew that He was, in a unique and absolute sense, the Son of God.

☙ A THOUGHT TO PONDER ☙

These people knew that He was, in a unique and absolute sense,
the Son of God.

From *Safe in the World*, pp. 59-60.

JOY

And now come I to thee; and these things I speak in the world,
that they might have my joy fulfilled in themselves.

JOHN 17:13

How in practice do we have this joy? The first thing is to avoid concentrating on our own feelings. Many Christian people spend the whole of their lives looking at their own feelings and always taking their own spiritual pulse, their own spiritual temperature. Of course, they never find it satisfactory, and because of that they are miserable and unhappy, moaning and groaning.

The secret of joy is the practice of meditation—that is the way to have this joy of the Lord. We must meditate upon Him, upon what He is, what He has done, His love to us, and God's care for us who are His people.

And obviously—this almost goes without saying—we must avoid everything that tends to break our fellowship with God. The moment that is broken, we become miserable. We cannot help it; whether we want it to or not, our conscience will see to that. It will accuse us and condemn anything that breaks our fellowship with God and His Son. The joy of the world always drives out the other joy, as does any dependence on the world; so we must avoid sin in every shape and form. Let us stop looking to the world, even at its best, for true joy and for true happiness. But above all, we must look at "these things" (John 17:13) that He speaks of, these truths that He unfolded. Let us meditate upon them, contemplate them, dwell upon them, revel in them, and I will guarantee that as we do so, either in our own personal meditation or in reading books about them, we will find ourselves experiencing a joy we have never known before. It is inevitable; it follows as the night the day.

✒ A THOUGHT TO PONDER ✒

Let us stop looking to the world. We must meditate upon Him, upon what He is, what He has done.

From *Safe in the World*, pp. 116-118.

JUDAS ISCARIOT

*. . . none of them is lost, but the son of perdition; that the
scripture might be fulfilled.*

JOHN 17:12

If there is one thing in the Scriptures that proves more conclusively
than anything else the absolute necessity of the rebirth, it is the case
of Judas Iscariot. What differentiates the Christian from the non-
Christian is not that the Christian lives a better life than he did before,
nor that he knows more of the Scriptures and all these other good
things. Judas knew all that, and he probably lived a good outward
moral life during the three years he was among the disciples. What
makes a man a Christian is that he is born again; he has received the
divine nature; he has indeed become indwelt by the Spirit of the living God. It is this that gives understanding and everything that Judas
did not have. It was because Judas was never renewed and given the
new life that he remained "the son of perdition."

And here I want to utter a solemn, terrible word. The end of
the non-Christian, even though he may be highly religious, is perdition, which means perishing. Though Judas was in the company of
the apostles all along, he really belonged to the world, and the fate
of the world is to perish. Whatever its appearance may be, it end is
destruction, with no hope whatsoever; because it has not truly
believed in the name of the only begotten Son of God, it perishes.

This is an unpleasant subject, and yet we have to face it, because
in the very center of this most wonderful prayer our Lord had to
mention it as a solemn warning. He was not praying for Judas—He
was praying for those who were God's people, those who belong to
God.

My dear friends, are we *certain* that we belong to God? Do not
rely upon anything but the certain knowledge that you have received
life from God.

❧ A THOUGHT TO PONDER ❧
The end of the non-Christian, even though he may be highly religious, is perdition, which means perishing.

From *Safe in the World*, pp. 129-130.

THE DEMAS WAY

Demas hath forsaken me, having loved this present world.

2 TIMOTHY 4:10

The world is opposed to Christians, and it shows its opposition by means of hatred. "Yea," says Paul to Timothy, "and all that will live godly in Christ Jesus shall suffer persecution" (2 Timothy 3:12). But the world has another way of showing its opposition. That is what I would call the Demas way: "Demas hath forsaken me, having loved this present world." The world does not care very much how it attacks Christ's followers. If by throwing them into prison it can wrest them from Christ, it will do so; but if that does not work, it will try some other method. "Demas hath forsaken me"—the love of ease, love of the things of the world, its wealth, its position, its so-called pomp and show, the lust of the flesh, the lust of the eye, and the pride of life. How many good men have been ruined by that! Prosperity can be very dangerous to the soul, and the world is prepared to use that. If direct opposition will not work, it will pamper us, it will dangle these things before us and thus try to wean us from Christ. So it is not surprising that He asked the Father to keep us in His name.

Another way in which the world does the same thing is by what may be described as the Barnabas method. We are told in Acts 15 that a dispute had taken place between Barnabas and Paul. Barnabas wanted to take his relative John Mark on their second missionary journey, but Paul said that he would not have him. Paul felt that John Mark had let them down and deserted them when they had taken him on their previous journey and that he was not therefore the man to accompany them. Here we have worldly relationships, such as family relationships, interfering in God's work. It is the tendency not to judge things in a spiritual way.

✍ A THOUGHT TO PONDER ✍

The world does not care very much how it attacks Christ's followers.

TRIALS

I pray not that thou shouldest take them out of the world,
but that thou shouldest keep them from the evil.

JOHN 17:15

God's way is not to take us out of the difficulties and trials, not to avoid them. His way is to enable us and to strengthen us, so that we can go through them with heads erect and undefeated, more than conquerors in them and over them. And that is a wonderful thing.

We must never grumble at our lot, nor ask doubting questions. We must rather believe that there is always a purpose in these trials, if we can but see it; we must believe that God has laid this thing upon us and that He has left us in this situation in order that we may show forth His glory. The disciples were left in the world to do that, and you and I can be certain that whatever we may be passing through at this moment is a part of God's plan and purpose for us to show forth His glory.

The world may not recognize you; it may ignore and dismiss you, and others may get all they want from the world. Do not worry about it. The saints have experienced the same thing, and Christ knew something similar: "Woe unto you, when all men shall speak well of you!" (Luke 6:26). All is well—you are fulfilling the glory of God even as you go through a trial. Paul came to see that about his thorn in the flesh. "All right, God," he says in effect, "I asked You three times to remove it, but You are leaving it. I see now that Your glory is going to be shown through me. Very well, I will glory in this infirmity. I will stop asking You to take it away. It is really when I am weak that Your power is made manifest in me and through me." So we must never grumble. We must gladly accept what He allows and remember that we are fulfilling the glory of God.

✎ A THOUGHT TO PONDER ✐

We must never grumble at our lot, nor ask doubting questions.

From *Safe in the World*, pp. 155-156.

"Sanctify Them"

Sanctify them through thy truth: thy word is truth.
JOHN 17:17

What does our Lord mean when He prays, "Sanctify them through thy truth" or "in thy truth"? We need to be very careful at this point in our definition of the term *sanctify*, because we must interpret it bearing in mind that the same word is used in John 17:19: "And for their sakes I sanctify myself, that they also might be sanctified through the truth." In verse 19 our Lord uses exactly the same word about Himself as He uses with regard to His followers here. So we must start by arriving at a true definition of what is meant by "sanctify."

Now it is generally agreed that there are two main senses in which this word is used throughout the Bible. The first sense of "sanctify"—and we must always put this one first because it is the one most emphasized in Scripture—is *to set apart for God and for God's service*. So you will find that this term *sanctify* is not only used of men—it is used even of a mountain, the holy mount on which the law was given to Moses. Mount Sinai was sanctified, it was set apart for a special function and purpose, in order that God might use it to give His revelation of the law. The word is used, too, of buildings and of vessels, instruments and utensils, and various things that were used in the Tabernacle and the Temple. Anything that is devoted to or set aside for God and for His service is sanctified. So there is a double aspect to this primary meaning of the word. It means, first, a separation from everything that contaminates and perverts, and the second, positive aspect is that something or someone is devoted wholly to God and to His use.

❧ A THOUGHT TO PONDER ❧
To sanctify is to set apart for God and for God's service.

From *Sanctified Through the Truth*, pp. 8-9.

THE PRIMARY MEANING OF "SANCTIFY"

But ye are washed, but ye are sanctified, but ye are justified in the name of the Lord Jesus, and by the Spirit of our God.
1 CORINTHIANS 6:11

You will find that the primary meaning of the word *sanctify* is often applied to Christian people. Read, for instance, 1 Corinthians 6:11, where Paul tells the Corinthians that there was a time when some of them were guilty of terrible sin—drinking, adultery, etc. "But," he says, "ye are washed, but ye are sanctified, but ye are justified in the name of the Lord Jesus, and by the Spirit of our God." You notice he says they are "sanctified" before he says they are "justified." Now with our superficial and glib ideas about sanctification, we always say, "Justification first and sanctification afterward." But Paul puts sanctification first, which means that *they have been set apart by God and taken out of the world.* That is the primary meaning of sanctification, and in that sense it comes before justification.

Or take 1 Peter 1:2: ". . . elect according to the foreknowledge of God the Father, through sanctification of the Spirit, unto obedience and sprinkling of the blood of Jesus Christ." Sanctification comes before believing and sprinkling with the blood and justification. So in its primary meaning this word is a description of our position. It means that as Christians we are separated from the world. Our Lord has already said that in John 17:16: "They are not of the world." Now He says, "Sanctify them through thy truth" (John 17:17). "They have been set apart," He says in effect; "set them still more apart." It means separation from the world. In 1 Peter 2:9 this is applied to the Christian church: "Ye are . . . a peculiar people," a special possession for the Lord. The same is true of all Christian people. We are a holy people, set apart for God and for His service and for His purpose. That is the primary meaning.

✎ A THOUGHT TO PONDER ✎
Notice that Paul says they are sanctified before he says they are justified.

From *Sanctified Through the Truth*, pp. 9-10.

THE SECONDARY MEANING OF "SANCTIFY"

Ye shall be holy: for I the LORD your God am holy.
LEVITICUS 19:2

There is a secondary meaning to the word *sanctify*, and this is equally clear from the Scriptures. This is that we are not only *regarded* as holy—we are *made holy*. And obviously we are made holy because that is how we are regarded. God sets us apart as His peculiar or special people, and because of this we must be a holy people: "Ye shall be holy: for I the LORD your God am holy," says God. So we are to *be* holy because we *are* holy, and that is the great New Testament appeal for sanctification.

So this second meaning is that *God does a work within us—a work of purifying, cleansing, and purging*; and this work is designed to fit us for the title that has been put upon us. We have been adopted, taken out of the world, and set apart, and we are now being conformed increasingly to the image, the pattern, of the Lord Jesus Christ, so that we may in truth be the people of God, in reality as well as in name.

So this is obviously progressive work. The first meaning involves something that is done once and for all, and it is because we are set apart that we are justified. God has looked upon His people from all eternity and has set them apart. He sanctified them before the foundation of the world, and because of that they are justified, and also because of that they are sanctified in this second sense.

So the question is, which of these two meanings is to be attached to the word in John 17:17: "Sanctify them through thy truth"? It seems to me that there is only one adequate answer to that: Obviously both meanings are involved. Our calling demands that we must be a holy people since we cannot represent a holy God unless we ourselves are holy.

⟜ A THOUGHT TO PONDER ⟝
We are to *be* holy because we *are* holy.

THE DESIRE TO SIN

I pray not that thou shouldest take them out of the world,
but that thou shouldest keep them from the evil.

JOHN 17:15

The church and the Christian and the Gospel are not so much concerned about removing the occasions for sin as removing from man the desire to sin. "I pray not that thou shouldest take them out of the world, but that thou shouldest keep them from the evil. . . . Sanctify them" (John 17:15, 17). Our Lord is saying in effect, "I am not so concerned that You should take the occasion for sin away, but that You should take out of the man the desire to take advantage of the occasion." Do you see the difference? The Gospel of Jesus Christ does not so much take the Christian out of the world as take the world out of the Christian. That is the point. "Sanctify them": Whatever the world is like around and about them, if the world is not in them, the world outside them will not be able to affect them. That is the glory of the Gospel; it makes a man free in the midst of the devil's work in this world.

Or let me put it like this: The Gospel is not so much concerned about changing the conditions as about changing the man. Oh, the tragedy of the folly and the foolishness that has been spoken about this! People say, "But surely you must clear up the slums before these people can become Christians?" My friends, one of the most glorious things I have ever seen is a man who has become a Christian in the slums and then, though remaining in the same place, has transformed his home and house there. You need not change the man's conditions before you change the man. Thank God, the Gospel can change the man in spite of the conditions.

∞ A THOUGHT TO PONDER ∞

The Gospel of Jesus Christ does not so much take the Christian out of the world as take the world out of the Christian.

From *Sanctified Through the Truth*, pp. 17-18.

EVANGELISM AND SANCTIFICATION

*As thou hast sent me into the world, even so have I also
sent them into the world.*

JOHN 17:18

Our Lord's disciples are to be sent to evangelize the world. How are they to do it? What is the first thing to consider? You notice what our Lord puts first: It is sanctification: "Sanctify them, for the work needs to be done in them before it can ever be done in the world."

There is nothing that appalls me so much as the almost incredible way in which Christian people seem to ignore entirely the teaching of the Scriptures with regard to methods of evangelism. In the Scriptures from beginning to end, the emphasis is on the messenger, not his external methods—on his character and his being and on his relationship to God.

Take the case of Gideon. A mighty enemy army was facing the children of Israel, and at first Gideon collected an army of thirty-two thousand people. Then God began to reduce them until in the end there were only three hundred. God in effect said to Gideon, "I am not going to do this through the great army of thirty-two thousand, but in My way." So He reduced the thirty-two thousand to three hundred, and then He sent them out, not with great armaments, but with pitchers with lamps inside them, along with trumpets to blow. And with that ridiculous equipment they conquered the army of the enemy. That is God's way. God has always done His greatest works through remnants. If there is one doctrine that runs through the Scriptures more prominently than any other, it is the doctrine of the remnant. How often God has done everything with just one man. Do you remember the story in 1 Samuel 14 of Jonathan and his armor-bearer? They did not spend their time arguing about the condition of the enemy. One man, with his armor-bearer, trusting in the living God, could conquer an entire army!

✎ A THOUGHT TO PONDER ✍

God has always done His greatest works through remnants.

CHRIST'S SANCTIFICATION OF HIMSELF

I sanctify myself.

JOHN 17:19

We must engage our attention about the meaning of Christ's sanctification of Himself. Clearly He cannot mean that He will do anything to increase His own holiness. That is impossible. He was perfect from the beginning, without blemish, without sin and without fault. So when He says He is going to sanctify Himself, He cannot mean He is going to make Himself more holy than He was before. What it means, obviously, is that He is using the term in the primary sense of sanctification—namely, dedication, consecration, a setting apart for the special work of God and for God's purpose in Him and through Him. It means an entire offering of oneself to God for His glory and for His purpose.

Then, in order to grasp the full meaning of this statement, the next word we must look at is "myself." "I sanctify myself," our Lord says. And by that He clearly means Himself as He is in His total personality, everything that He is, as God and man, all His powers, all His knowledge, all His perfection, all His ability, everything. There is no word more inclusive than this word "myself." It means my total self, all that I am in and of myself, all my relationships, all my privileges, all my abilities, and all my possessions. I sanctify myself in the full totality of my being and my personality. So what our Lord is really saying at this point is that all He is and has, He is now giving entirely and utterly to God "for their sakes" (John 17:19a)—they being the Christians then in existence—and for our sakes too, those who are going to come into existence—all those people He has been talking so much about in this prayer, the people who had been given to Him by God, and for whom He has come into the world.

✺ A THOUGHT TO PONDER ✺

Jesus' sanctification means an entire offering of Himself to God for God's glory and for His purpose.

From *Sanctified Through the Truth*, pp. 34-35.

"FOR THEIR SAKES"

*And for their sakes I sanctify myself, that they also might be
sanctified through the truth.*

JOHN 17:19

This wonderful statement tells us what led Christ to do all He did for us. It is all here! "For their sakes I sanctify myself." If only we could see this. This is the thing that leads to sanctification. "For their sakes," He says, He is going to do all this. Who are these people for whom He does it? Enemies of God and therefore enemies of Christ, self-willed creatures, people who listen to Satan rather than to God, people who deliberately believe the lies against God, people who have set themselves up and put their own wills and desires against the will of God, people who delight in evil, who are full of malice, envy, lust, and passion—you and I as we were in sin and in evil, as the result of the Fall.

"For *their* sakes." We must recognize, guilty sinners as we are, that it is for us that He has done all this. "I sanctify myself," says the eternal Son of God, the holy and pure One, the blameless and spotless One, the One whose supreme joy was to do the will of His Father. Can you imagine a greater contrast than that between "they" and "I"? And yet He says, "I sanctify myself," which not only means the totality of His personality, but also that He did it voluntarily and willingly. There was nothing in us to recommend this; there was no motive that could arise from anything in us. Man in sin is so damned and hopeless that he does not want to be saved or even asks to be. No request ever went out from man to God for salvation; it has come entirely from God. "Here am I," says our Lord. "Send Me."

❧ A THOUGHT TO PONDER ❧

Man in sin is so damned and hopeless that he does not want to be saved or even asks to be.

From *Sanctified Through the Truth*, pp. 42-43.

GOD'S WORK THROUGH THE TRUTH

Sanctify them through thy truth: thy word is truth.

JOHN 17:17

Some teach that all we have to do, having told God that we want to be delivered, is to believe He has done it, and then we shall eventually find that it has happened. Now that teaching is also put like this: You must say to a man who is constantly defeated by a particular sin, "I think your only hope is to take it to Christ, and Christ will take it from you." But what does Scripture say in Ephesians 4:28 to the man who finds himself constantly guilty of stealing, to a man who sees something he likes and takes it? What am I to tell such a man? Am I to say, "Take that sin to Christ and ask Him to deliver you"? No. What the apostle Paul tells him is this: "Let him that stole steal no more." Just that. Stop doing it. And if it is fornication or adultery or lustful thoughts, again, stop doing it, says Paul. He does not say, "Go and pray to Christ to deliver you." No. You must stop doing that, he says, as becomes the children of God.

My friends, we have become unscriptural. If you want further evidence, lest somebody thinks it is only the teaching of Paul, let me come to the teaching of the apostle Peter, which is exactly the same—it is the whole teaching of Scripture, which we seem to have forgotten. We read in 1 Peter 1:14-15, "As obedient children, not fashioning yourselves to the former lusts in your ignorance: But as he which hath called you is holy, so be ye holy in all manner of conversation." It is something that *you* have to do. You must turn your back on these things because you are a child of God. Peter does not say, "Surrender it to Christ and ask Him to deliver you from it." What he says is, "Realize who you are and stop doing it."

✒ A THOUGHT TO PONDER ✒

You must turn your back on these things because you are a child of God.

From *Sanctified Through the Truth*, pp. 54-55.

SANCTIFICATION—A CONTINUOUS PROCESS

Sanctify them through thy truth: thy word is truth.
JOHN 17:17

We must not think of sanctification as something that happens suddenly. People seem to think (and here they are logical though they are wrong) that if it is a gift and to be received, then obviously it must be something that happens suddenly; when you receive a gift, it happens suddenly. But surely this is incompatible with the New Testament teaching on this matter. It is, rather, characteristic of the cults, of a man-made idea of sanctification.

We always like to do things suddenly and to have anything we want at once. So you find that those false teachings always offer a kind of short cut, and that is their appeal to the carnal mind, because we are always so impatient, always in such a desperate hurry. But this very verse that we are now considering makes it quite impossible for sanctification to be something that happens suddenly. "Sanctify them," says our Lord, "through thy truth."

Our Lord has already said the same thing in John 8:31-32. He said to certain men who appeared to believe, "If ye continue in my word, then are ye my disciples indeed; and ye shall know the truth, and the truth shall make you free." It is always the truth, therefore, that does it, and that is something that is progressive. We do not grasp the whole of the truth at once; we go through stages, from babies to full, matured age, from being a child to being an old man, as it were, in terms of faith. We see the same thing again in Philippians 2:12: "Work out your own salvation with fear and trembling"—it is something you keep doing. "Not as in my presence only," says Paul, "but now much more in my absence." The exhortation in all these writings is to be steadfast, to progress, and to go on with the work.

✒ A THOUGHT TO PONDER ✒

John 17:17 makes it quite impossible for sanctification to be something that happens suddenly.

PARTICULAR SINS

. . . the eyes of your understanding being enlightened;
that ye may know what is the hope of his calling.
EPHESIANS 1:18

The New Testament method of dealing with particular sins is never to concentrate upon the particular sin as such, but to bring it into the light and the context of the whole Christian position. I cannot emphasize that principle too strongly. Speaking out of pastoral experience, I have found in practice that this particular principle is probably the most important of all. May I give you one illustration? I remember a lady once, some twenty years ago, coming to tell me of a crippling problem in her spiritual life. She told me that she had a terrible horror and dread of thunderstorms. Apparently she had once been in a bad thunderstorm, and it had looked as if she might be killed. Ever since then the fear of thunder and lightning had gripped her, and it had come to such a pass that if she was going to a place of worship and happened to see a large cloud, she would begin to say to herself, "A thunderstorm is coming!" So there would be a terrible conflict within her, and it usually ended in her turning back and going home. It seemed to her that the one problem of her life was this fear and dread of thunderstorms. She told me she had struggled with this problem and had done her best to get rid of it.

Now it seemed to me that the one thing to say to that woman was this—and it came as a shock to her, "Stop praying about this particular fear, for while you are praying, you are reminding yourself of it. You must stop thinking about yourself in terms of fear. Never think about thunderstorms; turn your back upon that altogether. You must think of yourself as a disciple of the Lord Jesus Christ and as one who belongs to Him. You must concentrate upon positive Christianity, not upon a negative fear."

✍ A THOUGHT TO PONDER ✍

Bring a particular sin into the light and into the context of the whole Christian position.

From *Sanctified Through the Truth*, pp. 77-78.

THE ESSENCE OF SANCTIFICATION

. . . that ye should show forth the praises of him who hath
called you out of darkness into his marvellous light.

1 PETER 2:9

The essence of sanctification is that I love the God in whom I believe and who has been revealed to me with the whole of my being. Indeed I do not hesitate to assert that if I think of sanctification in any lesser terms than that, I am being unscriptural. This is scriptural holiness. This is the holiness, the sanctification, that is produced and promoted by the truth of God, because it is the truth concerning God. Then it follows from that—I think directly—that a man who thus loves God with all his heart and soul and mind and strength does so because he is called upon to do so and is commanded to do so. To such a man the main thing in life is to glorify God and to show forth His praises.

This is the argument of the apostle Peter when he reminds the people to whom he is writing that at one time, before they became Christians, they were not a people. "Which in time past," he says in 1 Peter 2:10, "were not a people but are now the people of God." You who are called out of darkness into light are a "peculiar people" (verse 9). Why? What is the object of it all? "That ye should show forth the praises of him who hath called you out of darkness into his marvellous light" (1 Peter 2:9). "Praises" there means "excellencies" or "virtues"; it means the glorious, marvelous attributes of God. And so sanctification is that condition in which we praise God just by being what we are. Of course, it includes not doing certain things, but it is not only that. It is much more. By being what we are in all the totality of our personalities and in the whole of our lives, we reveal and manifest the virtues and the excellencies of God.

☙ A THOUGHT TO PONDER ❧

Sanctification is that condition in which we praise God just by being what we are.

From *Sanctified Through the Truth*, pp. 91.

NEW CREATURES

Therefore we are buried with him by baptism into death:
that like as Christ was raised up from the dead by the glory of
the Father, even so we also should walk in newness of life.

ROMANS 6:4

There is no point in our saying that we believe that Christ has died for us and that we believe our sins are forgiven unless we can also say that for us old things are passed away and all things are become new, that our outlook toward the world and its method of living is entirely changed. It is not that we are sinless, nor that we are perfect, but that we have finished with that way of life. We have seen it for what it is, and we are new creatures for whom everything has become new.

But I can imagine somebody saying, "Don't you think that this is rather a dangerous doctrine? Don't you think it is dangerous to tell people that they are dead to sin, dead to the law, dead to Satan, and that God regards them as if they had never sinned at all? Won't the effect of that make such people say, 'All right, in view of that, it does not matter what I do'?" But Paul says that what happens is the exact opposite, and that must be so because to be saved and to be truly Christian means that we are in Christ, and if we are in Christ, we are dead to sin, dead to Satan, dead to the world, dead to our old selves. We are like our Lord.

Let me put that positively. We have not only died with Christ— we have also risen with Him: "Therefore we are buried with him by baptism into death: that like as Christ was raised up from the dead by the glory of the Father, even so we also should walk in newness of life" (Romans 6:4). We live in "newness of life." We have been raised with Christ.

❧ A THOUGHT TO PONDER ❧

If we are in Christ, we are dead to sin, dead to Satan, dead to the world, dead to our old selves.

From *Sanctified Through the Truth*, pp. 120-121.

CHRIST IN US

Know ye not that your body is the temple of the Holy Ghost which is in you?
1 CORINTHIANS 6:19

The New Testament tells me that Christ is in me, and I am meant to live a life of constant fellowship and communion with Him. Sin is to look away from Him, to be interested in anything that the world can give rather than in Him. Oh, if it is something foul it is ten times worse; but the best that the world can give me is an insult to Him if I put it before Him.

There are endless statements of this. Paul puts it in terms of the Holy Spirit: "Know ye not that your body is the temple of the Holy Ghost which is in you?" (1 Corinthians 6:19). The argument is about fornication and adultery. Paul does not merely give a moral lecture on immorality; he says in effect, "What is wrong about that is that you are joining your body, which is a temple of the Holy Spirit, to another, and you have no right to do it. The way to overcome that sin is not to pray so much that you may be delivered from it; it is to realize that your body is the temple of the Holy Spirit and that you have no right to use it in that way." Another way he puts it is this, and it is very tender: "Grieve not the Holy Spirit of God" (Ephesians 4:30). He is tender, He is sensitive, He is holy; do not grieve Him.

If you and I would only think of our lives like that, it would very soon begin to promote our sanctification. May I commend to you a simple morning rule: When you wake up, the first thing you should do (and I need to do the same) is to say to yourself, "I am a child of God. Christ is in me. That old self is gone: I died with Christ. 'I live; yet not I, but Christ liveth in me.' Everything I do today must be in the light of this knowledge."

❧ A THOUGHT TO PONDER ❧

The Holy Spirit is tender, He is sensitive, He is holy; do not grieve Him.

From *Sanctified Through the Truth*, pp. 135-136.

SANCTIFICATION IN THE LIGHT OF THE RESURRECTION

. . . who was delivered for our offences, and was raised again for our justification.

ROMANS 4:25

It is only in the light of the resurrection that I finally have an assurance of my sins forgiven. It is only in the light of the resurrection that I ultimately know that I stand in the presence of God absolved from guilt and shame and every condemnation. I can now say with Paul, "There is therefore now no condemnation to them which are in Christ Jesus" (Romans 8:1) because I look at the fact of the resurrection. It is there that I know it.

You notice how Paul argues in 1 Corinthians 15:17 when he says, "If Christ be not raised, your faith is vain; ye are yet in your sins." If it is not a fact that Christ literally rose from the grave, then you are still guilty before God. Your punishment has not been borne, your sins have not been dealt with, you are yet in your sins. It matters that much: Without the resurrection you have no standing at all; you are still uncertain as to whether you are forgiven and whether you are a child of God. And when one day you come to your deathbed you will not know, you will be uncertain as to where you are going and what is going to happen to you. "Who was delivered for our offences, and was raised again for our justification" (Romans 4:25). It is in the resurrection that I stand before God free and absolved and without fear and know that I am indeed a child of God. So you see the importance of holding on to this doctrine and why we must insist upon the details of doctrine, and not be content with some vague general belief in the Lord Jesus Christ.

If you are concerned about your life in this world and the fight against the world, the first thing to do, says the apostle Paul, is to take an overall look at the great doctrine of the resurrection of our Lord.

✎ A THOUGHT TO PONDER ✎

Without Christ's resurrection you have no standing at all.

From *Sanctified Through the Truth*, pp. 144-145.

A STIMULUS TO SANCTIFICATION

Awake to righteousness, and sin not.

1 CORINTHIANS 15:34

The trouble, says Paul, is that "some have not the knowledge of God: I speak this to your shame" (1 Corinthians 15:34). The real trouble with a man who is living a life of sin and who is not sanctified is that he lacks the knowledge of doctrine. That is his trouble: He does not know these things. And if you and I are not more determined than ever to "awake to righteousness" and to forsake sin, then the only explanation is that we do not believe the doctrine of the resurrection. And if we do not, we are yet in our sins and are destined for hell, and may God have mercy on us.

But then to crown it all, in the last verse of 1 Corinthians 15 Paul uses the word "Therefore." That is the argument, you see the logic—you cannot get away from it. It is not just beautiful language. You have heard people reveling in a beautiful service and saying, "How marvelous, how beautiful, how perfect—the balance, the cadence, and the lilt of the words!"

But that is not what the apostle wants you to feel. He wants you to say, "Therefore"—"Therefore, my beloved brethren, be ye stedfast, unmoveable." Let them say what they like about you—stand on your doctrine like a man, unmovable, "always abounding in the work of the Lord," in your personal life and living, in your life in the church and in the whole of your life, "forasmuch as ye know that your labour is not in vain in the Lord." The doctrine of the resurrection—what a stimulus to our sanctification!

Let nothing come between us and this mighty truth. This is life. This is everything.

> *Love so amazing, so divine*
> *Demands my soul, my life, my all.*
> ISAAC WATTS

☙ A THOUGHT TO PONDER ☙

The doctrine of the resurrection—what a stimulus to our sanctification!

From *Sanctified Through the Truth*, pp. 152-153.

April

THE CROSS OF CHRIST

FROM

The Cross

SOWING AND REAPING

Be not deceived; God is not mocked: for whatsoever a man soweth, that shall he also reap. For he that soweth to his flesh shall of the flesh reap corruption; but he that soweth to the Spirit shall of the Spirit reap life everlasting.

GALATIANS 6:7-8

Life is a matter of sowing and reaping, and what a man sows, that shall he also reap. There are certain moral laws in operation in this world that are absolute. All of us are responsible beings, and we shall all die and stand before God in judgment and give account of the deeds done in the body. And our eternal destiny will depend upon what we have done in this life and in this world. Life therefore is a tremendous matter. It is the most serious thing conceivable, because what we get in this life and what we will get through all eternity depends upon whether we sow to the flesh or whether we sow to the Spirit.

Very well then, the most important thing to discover in this world is, how does one sow to the Spirit? How am I so to live that I shall reap the blessing of joy and happiness and peace in this world and in the world to come forever and forever? The great apostle Paul answers the question. He puts it in this glorious and tremendous statement: "God forbid that I should glory . . ." The thing is unthinkable, he says, that I should glory in anything ". . . save in the cross of our Lord Jesus Christ, by whom the world is crucified unto me, and I unto the world" (Galatians 6:14). This is the thing that he preached. And this by the grace of God is the thing that I am privileged to preach to you. The preaching of the cross, the preaching of the death of the Lord Jesus Christ on the cross, is the very heart and center of the Christian Gospel and the Christian message.

✎ A THOUGHT TO PONDER ✐

What we will get through all eternity depends upon whether we sow to the flesh or whether we sow to the Spirit.

From *The Cross*, pp. 17-18.

PREACHING ABOUT THE CROSS OF CHRIST

But God forbid that I should glory, save in the cross of our Lord Jesus Christ.

GALATIANS 6:14

The preaching of the cross of Christ was the very center and heart of the message of the apostles, and there is nothing I know of that is more important than that every one of us should realize that this is still the heart and the center of the Christian message. In order to emphasize that, let me put it negatively first. What is the message of the Christian Gospel and of the Christian church? Now at the risk of being misunderstood I will put it like this: It is not primarily the *teaching* of our Lord. I say that, of course, because there are so many today who think that this is Christianity. They say, "What we need is Jesus' teaching. He is the greatest religious genius of all times. He is above all philosophers. Let us have a look at His teaching, at the Sermon on the Mount and so on. That is what we want. What the world needs today," they say, "is a dose of the Sermon on the Mount—a dose of His ethical teaching. We must preach this to people and teach them how to live."

But according to the apostle Paul, this is not their first need. And I will go further. If you only preach the teaching of the Lord Jesus Christ, not only do you not solve the problem of mankind, but in a sense you aggravate it. You are preaching nothing but utter condemnation, because nobody can ever carry it out.

So they did not preach His teaching. Paul does not say, "God forbid that I should glory, save in the Sermon on the Mount" or "God forbid that I should glory save in the ethical teaching of Jesus." He does not say that. It was not the teaching of Christ, nor the example of Christ either. What they preached was His death on the cross and the meaning of that event.

❧ A THOUGHT TO PONDER ❧

The preaching of the cross of Christ was the very center and heart of the message of the apostles.

From *The Cross*, pp. 18-21.

THE PURPOSE OF THE CROSS

The LORD hath laid on him the iniquity of us all.

ISAIAH 53:6

In the Old Testament the Israelites transferred their guilt to a lamb, and then the lamb was killed, and his blood was offered. Why did Jesus Christ, the Son of God, come? John the Baptist, who went around before Him, gave the answer. John the Baptist had only one sermon, and he kept repeating it, and this was it: "Behold," he says in essence, "I am not He. I am unworthy to undo the laces of His shoes. Behold, behold, behold, 'the lamb of God, which taketh away the sin of the world.'" All the others were types and shadows, indications and adumbrations. The Lamb of God has come. God has provided His own sacrifice; it is His own Son—the Lamb of God. This is what happened on Calvary's tree. God took your sins and mine, and He put them on the head of His own Son, and then He smote Him, He punished Him, He struck Him, He killed Him. The wages of sin is death.

So what was happening on the cross was that God Himself was laying your sins and mine upon His own dearly beloved Son, and Christ paid the penalty of our guilt and our transgressions. "For he hath made him to be sin for us, who knew no sin; that we might be made the righteousness of God in him" (2 Corinthians 5:21). "The LORD hath laid on him the iniquity of us all" (Isaiah 53:6). That is what the Father did. What did the Son do? He was passive as a lamb. He did not grumble; He did not complain. He took it all upon Himself. He allowed it to happen. He surrendered Himself deliberately and freely. As the apostle Paul puts it: "Who gave himself for [on behalf of] our sins, that he might deliver us from this present evil world, according to the will of God and our Father" (Galatians 1:4).

∾ A THOUGHT TO PONDER ∾

On the cross God Himself was laying your sins and mine upon His own dearly beloved Son.

From *The Cross*, pp. 33-34.

THE OFFENSE OF THE CROSS

But we preach Christ crucified, unto the Jews a stumblingblock,
and unto the Greeks foolishness.

1 CORINTHIANS 1:23

The test of whether someone is teaching the cross rightly or wrongly is whether it is an offense to the natural man or not. If my preaching of this cross is not an offense to the natural man, I am misrepresenting it. If it is something that makes him say "how beautiful," "how wonderful," "what a tragedy," "what a shame," I have not been preaching the cross truly. The preaching of the cross is an offense to the natural man. So it becomes the test of any man's preaching.

Or let me put it in terms of the congregation. If this element of offense in the cross has never appeared to you, or if you have never felt it, then I say that you likewise have never known the truth about the cross of Christ. If you have never reacted against it and felt that it is an offense for you, I say you have never known it. It is *always* an offense to the natural man. Invariably, there is no exception. So if you have never felt it, you have never seen it because you are a natural man. Nobody is born a Christian into this world. We have to be born again to become Christians, and as long as we are natural men and women, the cross is an offense.

So if we have never known this element of offense, either we have not seen it or we have had some misrepresentation of it. The cross is an offense to the mind of the natural man. It cuts across all his preconceived notions and ideas. It was a stumbling block to the Jews for this reason. They were expecting a Messiah to destroy the Roman conquerors. So when they found the One who claimed to be the Messiah dying in apparent weakness upon the cross, they were deeply wounded and offended.

❧ A THOUGHT TO PONDER ❧
As long as we are natural men and women, the cross is an offense.

From *The Cross*, pp. 45-46.

GLORYING IN THE CROSS

*God forbid that I should glory, save in the cross of our
Lord Jesus Christ.*
GALATIANS 6:14

The Christian is one who glories in the cross. "God forbid that I should glory, save in the cross of our Lord Jesus Christ." Let us look at this. Paul does not merely say that he admires it, that the cross is simply beautiful and marvelous. No; he does not stand there just admiring it or merely praising it. I want to go further—he does not just believe it. He does not merely accept its message intellectually. I am going to test you, my friends. The Christian is a man who does not only believe in the cross—he glories in it!

What do you mean by that? says someone. Well, I mean the same as the writer of the hymn when he says:

> *In the Cross of Christ I glory,*
> *Towering o'er the wrecks of time;*
> *All the light of sacred story*
> *Gathers round its head sublime.*
> J. BOWRING

He rejoices in it. The word that the apostle actually uses here is a very strong one. He says "God forbid that I should *boast*." He makes his boast of it. He says these Jews are the people who want to have you circumcised in order that they may boast about their converts. They want to boast in your flesh. They are out for their own success and their own name. "Oh," says the apostle, "I boast in nothing, and God forbid that I should, save in the cross of Christ."

❧ A THOUGHT TO PONDER ❧
The Christian is a man who does not only believe in the cross—he glories in it!

From *The Cross*, pp. 53-54.

April 6

THE CROSS AND CHRIST'S LOVE

. . . the Son of God, who loved me, and gave himself for me.
GALATIANS 2:20

Looking at our Lord on the cross, what I see above everything else is the love that made Him do it all. "Love so amazing, so divine." What does it mean? Let the apostle himself answer the question. This is how he puts it: "For when we were yet without strength, in due time Christ died for the ungodly. For scarcely for a righteous man will one die: yet peradventure for a good man some would even dare to die. But God commendeth his love toward us, in that, while we were yet sinners, Christ died for us. Much more then, being now justified by his blood, we shall be saved from wrath through him. For if, when we were enemies, we were reconciled to God by the death of his Son, much more, being reconciled, we shall be saved by his life" (Romans 5:6-10).

It comes to this, my dear friends: He is dying there because of His love for you, His love for me, His love for those who are sinners, those who are rebels, those who are enemies. He died for people who hated Him. As He was dying there, Saul of Tarsus was hating Him, but He was dying for Saul of Tarsus. As Paul (to give his subsequent name) puts it later: ". . . the Son of God, who loved me, and gave himself for me" (Galatians 2:20). He did not wait until Paul was converted before He loved him. He loved him even when Saul of Tarsus was blaspheming His holy name, ridiculing His claim that He was the Son of God and the Lord of Glory, ridiculing the idea that He came to teach us and to die for us and to save us, pouring his blasphemous scorn upon Him. While Paul was doing that, Christ was dying for Paul. And He was doing the same for you and for me.

✑ A THOUGHT TO PONDER ✑
He died for people who hated Him.

WHY DID THE CROSS HAPPEN?

. . . brought as a lamb to the slaughter, and as a sheep . . .
ISAIAH 53:7

Why is the Son of God there on the cross? The first thing the Scriptures say is that it is not merely the action of men. Oh, but, you say, it is men who are hammering in those nails. I agree, but that would be the remark of a very superficial observer. What made the men do it? Is there nothing behind them? You see, the whole trouble in the world today is that we are all looking at everything superficially. We choose some activity, then we set up a royal commission to look into it, and we have a little superficial reporting. It makes no difference, nothing is any different, because we are superficial in our diagnosis—we are not able to see the depths of things beneath the surface. It is the same here.

Why do I say that it was not merely the action of men? Why am I saying that it was not merely an accident? My answer is, of course, that it was something that had been prophesied. Take the passage in Isaiah 53, an exact prophecy of what happened on the cross. Again, read the 22nd Psalm. That is another perfect prophecy of the death of our Lord upon the cross. It is prophesied many times in the Old Testament. Indeed, you will see it if you go back to books like Leviticus and other books of the law that people say they find utterly boring and beyond their understanding. If you only know how to read them, you will find that they are all pointing to the cross. Or go back to Exodus and the story of the exodus of the children of Israel from the captivity of Egypt. Why did they have to kill that lamb, the paschal lamb as we call it, at night and put its blood on the doorposts and the lintels? It is a prophecy of this. Everything in the Passover story points to this event.

❧ A THOUGHT TO PONDER ☙
Everything in the Passover story points to the cross.

THE CROSS AND THE GRACE OF GOD

By grace are ye saved through faith; and that not of yourselves:
it is the gift of God.
EPHESIANS 2:8

If you want to know God, if you want to know the everlasting and eternal God, this is the way, the only way: Look at the cross. Gaze on, meditate on, survey the wondrous cross. And then you will see something of Christ.

The first thing you will see is the *grace* of God. Grace is a great word in the Bible, the grace of God. It is most simply defined in these words—it is favor shown to people who do not deserve any favor at all. And the message of the Gospel is that any one of us is saved and put right for eternity solely and entirely by the grace of God, not by ourselves. "By grace are ye saved through faith; and that not of yourselves: it is the gift of God" (Ephesians 2:8). My friend, is it not about time we all admitted it? Do what you like, you will never save yourself. You will never save yourself from the world, the flesh, or the devil; you will never save yourself from your own misery. Still less will you save yourself from the law of God and judgment and hell. You cannot do it. Men have tried it throughout the centuries. They have all admitted failure.

> *Not the labors of my hands*
> *Can fulfill thy law's demands;*
> *Could my zeal no respite know,*
> *Could my tears for ever flow,*
> *All for sin could not atone;*
> *Thou must save, and thou alone.*
> A. M. TOPLADY

ᏍᎧ A THOUGHT TO PONDER ᏍᎧ
Do what you like, you will never save yourself.

From *The Cross*, pp. 74-75.

THE CROSS AND THE LOVE OF GOD

God commendeth his love toward us, in that, while we were yet sinners, Christ died for us.

ROMANS 5:8

The most wonderful thing of all about the cross is that it reveals the love of God to us. It is not surprising that Paul should say to the Romans, "God commendeth his love toward us, in that, while we were yet sinners, Christ died for us." How do we see the love of God in the cross? Ah, says the modern man, I see it in this way, that though man rejected and murdered the Son of God, God in His love still says, "All right, I still forgive you. Though you have done that to My Son, I still forgive you." Yes, that is part of it, but it is the smallest part of it. That is not the real love of God. God was not a passive spectator of the death of His Son. That is how the moderns put it—that God in heaven looked down upon it all, saw men killing His own Son, and said, "All right, I will still forgive you." But it was not we who brought God's Son to the cross. It was God. It was the predeterminate counsel and foreknowledge of God.

If you really want to know what the love of God means, read what Paul wrote to the Romans: "For what the law could not do, in that it was weak through the flesh, God sending his own Son in the likeness of sinful flesh, and for sin, condemned sin in the flesh" (Romans 8:3). God condemned sin in the flesh of His own Son. This is the love of God. Read again Isaiah 53, that wonderful prophecy of what happened on Calvary's hill. You notice how he goes on repeating it: "Surely he hath borne our griefs, and carried our sorrows . . . it pleased the LORD to bruise him; he hath put him to grief" (verses 4, 10). These are the terms. And they are nothing but a plain, factual description of what happened on the cross.

✎ A THOUGHT TO PONDER ✎

It was not we who brought God's Son to the cross. It was God.

GAINING THE WORLD

*For what shall it profit a man, if he shall gain the whole world,
and lose his own soul?*

MARK 8:36

What if you are the most handsome man or woman the world has
ever known and are always dressed in a most gorgeous manner,
and what if you have the greatest palace to live in and have the greatest collection of motor cars and everything else? What if you have the
whole world—but lose your own soul? That is what Christ says
about the world, and He says it supremely upon the cross. "Or
what shall a man give in exchange for his soul?" (Mark 8:37).

Why did He die? He died for the souls of men—not for our
material welfare, not to reform this world, but to save our souls.
"The Son of man is come to seek and to save that which was lost"
(Luke 19:10). And it is the *soul* that is lost. The world knows nothing about the soul, but it is in you and in all of us—this imperishable thing in us that goes on beyond death and the end. Christ
exposed the lie of this world for what it really is.

He spoke a parable about Dives and Lazarus. The rich man sat
in his palace, dressed gorgeously, in wonderful robes, eating with
all his companions until he had his fill, while the poor beggar sat at
the gate with the dogs licking his sores. The Lord says in effect,
"Do not judge superficially—that is not the end of the story." He
gives us a picture of Lazarus in Abraham's bosom and Dives in the
torment of hell. You can see the difference between the mind and
outlook of the world and the mind and outlook of the Father and the
Son of God. He exposes the world for what it is.

✎ A THOUGHT TO PONDER ✐

You can see the difference between the outlook of the world and
the outlook of the Father.

From *The Cross*, pp. 100-101.

THE CROSS AND JUDGMENT

He will judge the world in righteousness.
ACTS 17:31

Christ on the cross says, "Now is the judgment of this world" (John 12:31). He prophesies what is going to happen. He is to be the judge. "He [God] will judge the world in righteousness," says the apostle Paul to the Athenians, "by that man whom he hath ordained; whereof he hath given assurance unto all men, in that he hath raised him from the dead." And Revelation 20:12-13 tells us that the books will be opened, and every man will have to stand before Him. Those who died at sea, those who died on land, those who were blown to nothing in the air—all will come back before Him in the final judgment.

And the simple message of the whole of the Bible is that the world, everything that is opposed to God and trusts in man and in his own power, is all going to be judged and condemned to everlasting misery and destruction. Now you see why Paul glories in the cross. It is the cross alone that saves any one of us from the destruction that is coming to the world. The whole world lies guilty before God, "for the wrath of God is revealed from heaven against all ungodliness and unrighteousness of men, who hold the truth in unrighteousness" (Romans 1:18). The whole world is going to be judged and is going to be destroyed. We are all born in the world and of it. And unless we can be separated from that world, we will share its fate. God forbid that I should glory, save in the cross of the Lord Jesus Christ, by which the world is crucified unto me, and I am separated from it. How? Let me make it clear. On that cross, the Lord Jesus Christ took upon Himself the punishment that is coming to all who belong to the world. That is why He died; He was receiving the punishment of the sins of men.

ᐸᕽ A THOUGHT TO PONDER ᕽᐳ

It is the cross alone that saves any one of us from the destruction that is coming to the world.

From *The Cross*, pp. 102-103.

April 12

THE CROSS AND THE WORLD

. . . greater is he that is in you, than he that is in the world.
1 JOHN 4:4

What is a Christian? Paul tells the Colossians that a Christian is a person who has been translated from the kingdom of darkness into the kingdom of God's dear Son. I no longer belong to the world—I belong to the kingdom of Christ, the kingdom of light, the kingdom of glory, the kingdom of God. Here I am, and the world has nothing to do with me. I am not of it. I am in this other kingdom. Oh, I am still existing in this world, but I no longer belong to it. I have been translated. And my citizenship is now in heaven, from whence also we look for the Savior, and we know that we shall ever go on and be with the Lord. He, by dying on the cross, separates me from the world, puts me into His own kingdom, introduces me to God, and makes me a child of God and an heir of eternal bliss.

He delivers me from the world. He died so that "whosoever believeth in him should not perish, but have everlasting life." He does more—He gives me a power that is greater than the world. Listen to John: ". . . greater is he that is in you, than he that is in the world," and "this is the victory that overcometh the world, even our faith," our faith in Him (1 John 4:4; 5:4).

And thank God, He gives us occasional glimpses of that other world, that real world, that pure, holy world that is yet going to be. This old world can never be improved and reformed. He will set up a new world: "new heavens and a new earth, wherein dwelleth righteousness" (2 Peter 3:13). A renovated cosmos, a perfected universe, with glory everywhere. The glory of the Lord shall cover everything as the waters cover the seas.

⇜ A THOUGHT TO PONDER ⇝
I am still existing in this world, but I no longer belong to it.

THE CROSS AND RECONCILIATION

2 CORINTHIANS 5:19

On the cross our Lord was reconciling us unto God. "God was in Christ, reconciling the world unto himself, not imputing their trespasses unto them." Christ had to pay this penalty. The law had to have its way, and He has borne the punishment. And because of that, if we believe in Him we are free from the punishment and free of the condemnation. We are reconciled to God, and the power of God takes over and delivers us from the devil and his cohorts and transfers us into the kingdom of God. That is why the apostle puts it like this in Colossians 1:13: "who hath delivered us from the power of darkness, and hath translated us into the kingdom of his dear Son." That is how it happens. That is what was happening upon the cross. The devil thought he was defeating Christ, but Christ was reconciling us to God, defeating the devil and delivering us out of his clutches. He does it by paying the penalty and putting us right with God. The power of God comes into us, and we are born again, receiving new natures and becoming new people. The Holy Spirit is put within us, and Christ's presence is ever at hand to help us.

That is why John was able to say, "and the whole world lieth in wickedness," but "that wicked one toucheth him not" (1 John 5:18-19). The enemy not only touches the world—he embraces it, and the world cannot get out of his clutches. But Christ takes us out of his clutches and puts us into His own kingdom, and the devil cannot touch us. He can frighten us perhaps, he can shout at us, but he cannot touch us. He thought he was finishing Christ. He was really bringing about his own defeat. Christ has conquered him.

✒ A THOUGHT TO PONDER ✒

Christ takes us out of the devil's clutches and puts us into His own kingdom, and the devil cannot touch us.

From *The Cross*, pp. 126-127.

April 14

THE CROSS AND OURSELVES

The Son of man is come to seek and to save that which was lost.

LUKE 19:10

The first thing the cross does is to show us to ourselves. Of course, we always defend ourselves, do we not? It isn't my fault, we say, it is his. If only he understood. Or take husbands and wives, when they separate from one another. You listen to the story of the husband: "This woman is impossible!" Then you listen to the woman: "This man of mine—I could not live with him. He is an impossible man!" It is always somebody else, is it not? We are never wrong—we are very wonderful. If only we could be understood. It is always somebody else, always that other person.

Do you know what the Gospel does, what the cross does? It shows you to yourself. And nothing else in the whole world does that but the cross. There is nothing that will ever humble a man or a nation but the cross of Christ. The cross tells us the simple, plain truth about ourselves.

Think of it like this. Why did the Son of God ever come into this world? Why did He leave the courts of glory? Why was He born as a little babe? Why did He take unto Him human nature? There is only one answer. He came because man could not save himself. He said that. "The Son of man," he says, "is come to seek and to save that which was lost" (Luke 19:10). And when I look at the cross and see Him dying there, what He tells me is this: You have nothing whereof to boast. The cross tells me that I am a complete failure, and that I am such a failure that He had to come from heaven not merely to teach and preach in this world, but to die on that cross. Nothing else could save us.

✎ A THOUGHT TO PONDER ✐

And when I look at the cross and see Him dying there, what He tells me is this: You have nothing whereof to boast.

April 15

THE CROSS HUMBLES US

But what things were gain to me, those I counted loss for Christ.
PHILIPPIANS 3:7

It is the cross of Christ that brings us all down to the same place. "All have sinned, and come short of the glory of God." The differences between nations and groups within them and individuals are nothing when you look at the cross of Christ. We are all miserable, helpless, hopeless sinners.

There is nothing in which we can boast. As the apostle puts it in Philippians 3:7-9, "But what things were gain to me, those I counted loss for Christ. Yea doubtless, and I count all things but loss for the excellency of the knowledge of Christ Jesus my Lord: for whom," he says, "I have suffered the loss of all things, and do count them but dung, that I may win Christ, and be found in him, not having mine own righteousness, which is of the law, but that which is through the faith of Christ, the righteousness which is of God by faith."

Once you really see this message of the cross, you see yourself groveling on the dust and the floor, a miserable failure, a hopeless sinner. You can do nothing, and neither can your neighbor; you are together in your complete helplessness and hopelessness. But thank God it does not leave you there. You both look up together into face of the one and only Savior, the Savior of the world, "the Lamb of God, which taketh away the sin of the world." He is not only the Savior of the western world. He is also the Savior of the Iron Curtain. He can save Communists as well as He can save capitalists.

✒ A THOUGHT TO PONDER ✑
We are all miserable, helpless, hopeless sinners.

From *The Cross*, pp. 147-148.

THE CROSS SPEAKS TO US

. . . the blood of sprinkling, that speaketh better things
than that of Abel.

HEBREWS 12:24

Has the cross of Christ ever spoken to you? Have you heard its message? The cross of Christ preaches. The cross of Christ speaks. The blood of the cross speaks. It has something to say. Have you heard it? The writer to the Hebrews thanks God that this blood speaks something better than the blood of Abel spoke. You remember the story of Cain and Abel, the first two sons of Adam and Eve, and the story of how Cain slew his brother Abel and shed his blood. He murdered him. And the blood of Abel, spilled there upon the ground, spoke as it cried out for vengeance, punishment, and retribution. The blood of Abel spoke. And God tells us through the writer to the Hebrews that is not the blood that you and I have come to. We have come to a blood of sprinkling that "speaketh better things than that of Abel." This is why all these men in the New Testament rejoice in it. This is why the saints of the ages rejoiced in it. The blood speaks, and it speaks the best things that the world has ever heard.

Let me call your attention to some of the things that the cross of Christ, the blood of the cross, speaks and says to men and women today. In other words, let us listen to the cross speaking in the form of exposition. There is nothing that so expounds the truth of God to us as the cross of Christ. The Bible expounds the same truth. The cross of Christ lays it open before us and makes it speak to us. Have you ever regarded it as a sermon and sat and listened to it, and have you heard what it has to say to you? What an exposition of truth there is in that cross on Calvary's hill!

◆ A THOUGHT TO PONDER ◆

There is nothing that so expounds the truth of God to us as the cross of Christ.

THE CROSS AND THE SOUL OF MAN

Or what shall a man give in exchange for his soul?

MARK 8:37

The cross expounds the truth that the soul of man is something that is very precious. You remember our Lord's own teaching about this. He said: "For what shall it profit a man, if he shall gain the whole world, and lose his own soul? Or what shall a man give in exchange for his soul?" (Mark 8:36-37). The cross talks about the soul of man; our Lord is on the cross because of the preciousness of a man's immortal soul. So at once you see that the cross tells me something about myself and the nature of this manhood that God has given me. It tells me also about the whole purpose of life in this world. This is my soul; this is the thing that matters. Now my body is important, and I must not despise it. Many other things are important, too, in this world. It is no part of the preaching of the Gospel to depreciate legitimate things or to ridicule them. But I would say that it is the business of the Gospel to say that it is the soul of man that matters, that part of us that goes on even when we die—something imperishable, something that goes on into eternity. The cross puts tremendous emphasis upon that. He came there not in order that our bodies might be healed, not in order that we might be better fed or clothed or have more information and knowledge; no, He came to save the soul. "The Son of man is come to seek and to save that which was lost" (Luke 19:10), and what was lost is man's soul.

Here is this tremendous statement, therefore, coming from the cross to us. Have you heard it—have you realized that the most important thing about you is this soul of yours?

✆ A THOUGHT TO PONDER ✆

Have you realized that the most important thing about you is this soul of yours?

From *The Cross*, pp. 156-157.

THE CROSS IS PROCLAMATION

. . . to be a propitiation through faith in his blood, to declare his righteousness for the remission of sins . . .

ROMANS 3:25

The cross, thank God, is not only exposition. The cross is also proclamation, a mighty declaration. I like the word that the apostle uses there in Romans 3, and especially the way in which he repeats it. He likes it himself obviously. "Whom God hath set forth," he says "to be a *propitiation* through faith in his blood, to declare his righteousness for the remission of sins . . . to declare, I say . . ." (Romans 3:25-26). Have you got it, have you heard it, were you listening? says the apostle. Wake up, you sleepy listeners. ". . . to declare, I say . . ." Have you heard the declaration? Have you heard the mighty proclamation? What does this blood declare to me?

Let me sum it up in another word that this same apostle used in 2 Corinthians 5:19, 21. This is the declaration: "God was in Christ, *reconciling* the world unto himself, not imputing their trespasses unto them. . . . For he hath made him to be sin for us, who knew no sin, that we might be made the righteousness of God in him." What does all this mean? Let me put it in modern terms. The cross tells me that this is the declaration. This, it says, is God's way of dealing with the problem of man's sin. It has already said that there is a problem. It is a terrible one; it is the greatest problem of all time and of the whole cosmos. There is nothing greater than this. There is the exposition of the problem. Then comes the mighty declaration. This, it says, is God's answer.

Now our Lord had been saying that in His teaching, but they could not understand it. They were blinded, even His own disciples. They were thinking as Jews, in terms of a kingdom on earth. Man will always materialize the great and glorious blessings of God's kingdom.

❧ A THOUGHT TO PONDER ☙

The cross, thank God, is not only exposition. The cross is also proclamation, a mighty declaration.

THE CROSS IS A MIGHTY DECLARATION

*Whom God hath set forth to be a propitiation through faith
in his blood, to declare his righteousness for the remission of sins
that are past, through the forbearance of God.*

ROMANS 3:25

The cross is a mighty declaration. And what it says is this: The Son is a propitiation. In other words, God on the cross was punishing sin. He said that he would, and He has done it.

God has always said that sin is to be punished, that His holy wrath is upon it, and that He cannot deal with sin in any other terms. And He has done exactly what He promised. On the cross He is doing it publicly. There He is, once and for all, at the central point of history, pouring out His wrath upon the sins of man in the body of His own Son. He is striking Him; He is smiting Him; He is condemning Him to death. Christ dies, and His blood speaks. It is God's punishment of sin and evil. It is a mighty declaration that God has done what He has always said He would do—namely, that He would punish sin, and the wages of sin is death. And there you see it happening upon the cross. It is an announcement, a proclamation, that this is God's way of dealing with the problem of sin.

I hasten to say this. It is obviously the only way to deal with sin, and the cross says that.

> *There was no other good enough*
> *To pay the price of sin;*
> *He only could unlock the gate*
> *Of heaven and let us in.*

MRS. C. F. ALEXANDER

It is not surprising that the Gospel of the cross and the blood of Christ has produced some of the greatest poetry the world has ever known.

✎ A THOUGHT TO PONDER ✐

The cross is an announcement, a proclamation, that this is God's way of dealing with the problem of sin.

From *The Cross* pp. 163-164.

THE CROSS IS AN INVITATION

Look unto me, and be ye saved, all the ends of the earth.

ISAIAH 45:22

The cross is an invitation. "... the blood of sprinkling, that speaketh better things than that of Abel" (Hebrews 12:24). Abel's blood has no invitation in it. Abel's blood cries out for retribution, for punishment; there is no invitation there to anybody, except to the wrath of a holy God. But in this other blood "that speaketh better things than that of Abel," there is a word of invitation. And from your standpoint and mine, looking at it very practically, there is nothing more wonderful about the cross than this. We know that the cross is a historical event. It is a setting forth in public of this great act of God. But thank God it does not stop there. It is an appeal; it is an invitation; it asks us to listen as we value our own immortal souls.

You know the Old Testament prophets had seen something of this. But they had not seen it very clearly. They were not meant to, and they could not see so far off. They saw something of the sufferings of Christ and the glory that was to follow, but they had not seen this. One of them, at the height of his prophetic inspiration, put what he saw into the mouth of the Messiah that was to come when he said, "Look unto me, and be ye saved, all the ends of the earth" (Isaiah 45:22). "Look unto me." It is an invitation. That is not only proclamation—that is an invitation. "Look unto me"!

I like the way the apostle Paul puts it in Ephesians 2. It is so wonderful. He says, "For he is our peace, who hath made both one, and hath broken down the middle wall of partition between us; having abolished in his flesh the enmity, even the law of commandments contained in ordinances ... that he might reconcile both unto God in one body by the cross" (verses 14-16).

✎ A THOUGHT TO PONDER ✎

The cross is an appeal; it is an invitation; it asks us to listen as we value our own immortal souls.

WHO DOES THE CROSS INVITE?

*Come unto me, all ye that labour and are heavy laden,
and I will give you rest.*

MATTHEW 11:28

To whom does the invitation of this cross come? It comes to failures, the people who know they have gone wrong, the people who are filled with a sense of shame, the people who are weary and tired and forlorn in the struggle. "Come unto me, all ye that labour and are heavy laden, and I will give you rest." You know He is talking about people who are laboring to live a good and clean and straight life. That is what He means by laboring and being heavy-laden—by the law of God, the commandments, moral ideals. You have tried and sweated and fasted. You are laboring, like Martin Luther before he saw the truth, like John Wesley before he saw it. Like all these people before they saw it, you are laboring, trying to live the good life, but failing; we are miserable failures, weary and forlorn.

The hymns of the church have always expressed this.

> *I heard the voice of Jesus say,*
> *"Behold, I freely give*
> *The living water, thirsty one;*
> *Stoop down, and drink, and live."*
>
> *I came to Jesus as I was,*
> *Weary, and worn, and sad . . .*
> H. BONAR

That is how they have come. The invitation is to such—the weary and worn.

☙ A THOUGHT TO PONDER ☙

The invitation of the cross comes to failures.

THE CROSS AND JUSTIFICATION

*Therefore being justified by faith, we have peace with God
through our Lord Jesus Christ.*

ROMANS 5:1

The cross is the door that leads to all blessings. Without it there is nothing. Without the cross and all it means, we have no blessings from God at all. But the cross opens the possibility to all of the endless blessings of the glorious God.

What are they? The apostle Paul never got tired of saying these things. Read what he says in Romans. He puts it like this: "Therefore being justified by faith, we have peace with God through our Lord Jesus Christ." "Justified by faith" means that the moment you believe in what happened on the cross and see that is God's way of reconciling you unto Himself, you are immediately regarded as just, your sins are all forgiven and blotted out, and you are clothed in the righteousness of Christ.

"Therefore," says Paul, "being justified by faith, we have peace with God." That is the first thing that comes out of this belief. There is no more important word in the letter of Paul than the word *therefore*. Note it. He always brings in this word "therefore" at a point of this kind. He has been laying down the doctrine, and especially the doctrine of the cross, and then he says, "therefore"—in the light of that, because of that, this is what follows.

And here is the first thing that follows. "Being justified by faith, we have peace with God." Do you realize what that means? Do you realize that is the most important and most wonderful thing that can ever happen to you, that you are given peace and made at peace with God? All our troubles in this life as human beings are due to the fact that we are in the wrong relationship to God. It is as simple as that.

✑ A THOUGHT TO PONDER ✑

Being justified by faith means that the moment you believe in what happened on the cross, you are immediately regarded as just.

From *The Cross*, pp. 178-179.

THE CROSS AND PEACE

. . . peace with God . . .
ROMANS 5:1

Before man can ever know peace, and in particular peace with God, the two sides must be dealt with. Man is at enmity with God, and God's wrath is upon man. Something has to happen on God's side, and the message of the cross is that this has happened. When our Lord died upon the cross, He was fulfilling every demand of God's holy law. The righteousness and the justice and the holiness of God were fully satisfied. God poured out His wrath upon sin in the body of His own Son. Christ's soul was made an offering for sin, and all the demands of God on His holiness were satisfied there. And, thank God, it works on our side also. We have a feeling that God is against us. We think of God as some great ogre or monster waiting to pounce upon us and to punish us; we feel that He hates us and that He is against us and spoiling our lives. We do not want to be bothered by Him and want to go our own way.

Then the moment comes when we look at that cross and see that God sent His only begotten, dearly loved Son into this world in order that He might go to the cross. It was God who sent Him to it. "God was in Christ, reconciling the world unto himself . . ." It was God who "laid on him the iniquity of us all." It was God who smote Him and struck Him and gave Him the punishment that we deserved. As you look at the cross, I say again, our whole attitude toward God, and our whole opinion of God, changes completely. There we see that God is love and full of mercy and of compassion, that God loves us with an everlasting love. So you see that by the cross, God's wrath is satisfied and appeased, and our folly and our rebellion are taken away, and God and man are brought together, and our peace is made with God.

⮞ A THOUGHT TO PONDER ⮜
By the cross God and man are brought together.

From *The Cross*, pp. 182-183.

A NEW CREATURE

*For sin shall not have dominion over you: for ye are not
under the law, but under grace.*

ROMANS 6:14

A Christian can have an entirely new birth, a new start, a new
nature, a new life. He dies with Christ; he rises with Christ. He is in
Christ. And so he becomes a new man.

Now, this is, of course, the very thing that had happened to the
apostle Paul. In his old life he was a self-satisfied, proud Pharisee, a
religious and highly moral man—a very good man and a very nation-
alistic Jew, despising everybody else and proud of himself. That is
what he was, and yet he was miserable and wretched and unhappy
and disturbed. But once he realized the meaning of the death of the
Lord Jesus Christ on the cross, he made an absolutely new start. Saul
of Tarsus died, and the apostle Paul began to live. He says, "If any
man be in Christ, he is a new creature: old things are passed away;
behold, all things are become new" (2 Corinthians 5:17).

He is a man in a new universe. He is delivered from that old
Adamic state and nature, and he is in Christ, alive unto God. It is
the cross that does that. There is nothing that will get rid of the old
man that we all are by nature except Christ's death on the cross.
But if you believe in Him and in the purpose of that death and what
that death accomplished, you are truly dead to your old Adamic
nature. You know that your old man was crucified with Christ and
that he is gone forever. And as a result of this, our whole position and
status is entirely changed. The apostle expressed that in this great
statement: "For sin shall not have dominion over you: for ye are
not under the law, but under grace" (Romans 6:14).

❧ A THOUGHT TO PONDER ☙

There is nothing that will get rid of the old man that we all are by
nature except Christ's death on the cross.

From *The Cross*, pp. 186-187.

A NEW NATURE

Therefore if any man be in Christ, he is a new creature.
2 CORINTHIANS 5:17

The cross of the Lord Jesus Christ makes an entire change. You are "not under the law," Paul says, "but under grace" (Romans 6:14). You who have believed in the Lord Jesus Christ and His death upon the cross have been taken from that position; you are in an entirely new position. You are under grace, and grace is unmerited favor. It is kindness shown to people who deserve nothing but punishment. Grace means that God, because He is God, looks upon us with favor when we do not deserve anything at all. That is what "under grace" means. It means that God is no longer just a lawgiver to you—He is your Father. He is your Father who loves you with an everlasting love. He is your Father who looks upon you and desires to bless you. He is the one who says, "You are My child—I am your Father. I will give you My own nature. I will count the very hairs of your head. I will number them all. Nothing shall happen to you apart from Me." That is what it means to be under grace.

Do you see the difference? It is the difference between being in a relationship of law and a relationship of love. You are in an entirely new position, and the cross puts you there. You are under grace, and you do not tremble before God with a craven fear. You know that though you are unworthy, He is your Father, and you say, "My Father, who art in heaven, hallowed be thy name, thy kingdom come." And you know that He looks upon you with a smile. You know that He is patient, that He is long-suffering. You know that He is determined to bring you back to the perfection in which He originally made you, and that all the forces of His love and grace and compassion are working in your favor.

❧ A THOUGHT TO PONDER ❧

It is the difference between being in a relationship of law and a relationship of love.

From *The Cross*, pp. 189-190.

April 26

THE CROSS AND PRAYER

God heareth not sinners.
JOHN 9:31

The cross opens the door of heaven to me, and I can begin to pray. And we have all known, have we not, what it is to turn to God in prayer? Some of us remember during the last war [World War II], and during the 1914-18 war (World War I), reading of the terrible experiences of men torpedoed at sea. There they might be, in their little dinghies, for days on end. The food had ended, so had the water, and they were just drifting, and it seemed that everything had finished, and there was nobody in sight to save them. They were frantic and did not know what to do. Then somebody would say, "What about prayer?" None of them had prayed for years or had ever thought about God, but in their trouble they remembered Him.

We have all known what it is to turn to God in prayer, but the vital question is this: Can we pray? Have we any right to pray? What is prayer? Prayer means entering into the presence of God. It means addressing that almighty, holy God who is in heaven while we are on earth, the God we have ignored and spurned and reviled and rejected. How can we go into His presence? The answer is that we cannot go into His presence as we are.

"God heareth not sinners" (John 9:31). There is only one way whereby a man can pray with any confidence and assurance, and it is in believing in the cross of our Lord Jesus Christ. Listen to the apostle: "Therefore being justified by faith, we have peace with God through our Lord Jesus Christ: by whom also we have access by faith into this grace wherein we stand. . . ." He is fond of saying this—we find it everywhere. "For through him," says Paul to the Ephesians—by Christ—"we both have access by one Spirit unto the Father" (2:18).

❧ A THOUGHT TO PONDER ❧

There is only one way whereby a man can pray with any confidence and assurance, and it is in believing in the cross of our Lord Jesus Christ.

From *The Cross*, pp. 191-192.

THE CROSS OPENS THE GATE OF HEAVEN

*Having therefore, brethren, boldness to enter into the holiest
by the blood of Jesus . . .*

HEBREWS 10:19

Prayer means speaking to God who is in heaven, who is all-powerful to bless. How can you do that? There is only one way.

Read again as the author to the epistle to the Hebrews puts it in his own incomparable manner: "Seeing then that we have a great high priest, that is passed into the heavens, Jesus the Son of God, let us hold fast our profession. For we have not an high priest which cannot be touched with the feeling of our infirmities; but was in all points tempted like as we are, yet without sin. Let us therefore come boldly unto the throne of grace, that we may obtain mercy, and find grace to help in time of need" (Hebrews 4:14-16).

That is the problem. What do I do when I need help? What do I do when I am failing, when I am in an agony, in a crisis? I want grace to help in time of need. How can I get it? What right have I to speak to God? And there is only one answer. My only right to speak to God is that Christ has borne my punishment and has reconciled me to God and has made me at peace with God. Or, as it is put in Hebrews 10:19-22, "Having therefore, brethren, boldness to enter into the holiest by the blood of Jesus, by a new and living way, which he hath consecrated for us, through the veil, that is to say, his flesh; and having an high priest over the house of God; let us draw near with a true heart in full assurance of faith, having our hearts sprinkled from an evil conscience, and our bodies washed with pure water." He opens the gate of heaven and enables me to pray.

✎ A THOUGHT TO PONDER ✍

Prayer means speaking to God who is in heaven, who is all-powerful to bless.

From *The Cross*, pp. 192-193.

THE CENTRALITY OF THE CROSS

For the love of Christ constraineth us; because we thus judge,
that if one died for all, then were all dead.

2 CORINTHIANS 5:14

Everything proceeds from the cross. A Christian is a man who glories in the cross. If the cross is not central to you, you are not a Christian. You may say that you admire Jesus and His teaching, but that does not make you a Christian.

The apostle tells us that the cross governs his view of himself and that he has a new view of himself as a result of the cross. This is one of the most glorious aspects of the doctrine of the cross. It gives a man an entirely different view of himself.

Now, how does that happen? If you read 2 Corinthians 5, you will find that he there expands this aspect in a particularly clear manner. He has two great things to say: "Wherefore," he says in verse 16, "henceforth know we no man after the flesh: yea, though we have known Christ after the flesh, yet now henceforth know we him no more." That is one. But here is another in verses 14-15: "For the love of Christ constraineth us; because we thus judge, that if one died for all, then were all dead: and that he died for all, that they which live should not henceforth live unto themselves, but unto him which died for them, and rose again."

What he is saying in that chapter is all summarized in verse 17 when he puts this astonishing statement before us: "Therefore if any man be in Christ, he is a new creature: old things are passed away; behold, all things are become new." And among the "all things" that have become new is man's view of himself. This is one of the most glorious deliverances a man can ever know, to be free and delivered from himself.

❧ A THOUGHT TO PONDER ❧

If the cross is not central to you, you are not a Christian.

From *The Cross*, pp. 199-200.

A RANSOM

For ye are bought with a price.
1 CORINTHIANS 6:20

What Paul has learned from the cross is that the Lord Jesus Christ had died for him there in order to deliver him. Now, many terms are used to explain this, and one of them is the term of paying a ransom, paying a price. Man has become the slave to the devil and of sin and of evil, and he has to be bought. The apostle says that he discovered that what was happening on the cross was that the Lord Jesus Christ was purchasing him. So he writes to the Corinthians about morality and behavior, and he puts it like this: "What? know ye not that your body is the temple of the Holy Ghost which is in you, which ye have of God, and ye are not your own? For ye are bought with a price: therefore glorify God in your body, and in your spirit, which are God's" (1 Corinthians 6:19-20).

Now then, here the new view comes in. He was the slave of the devil, the slave of the world, the slave of sin and of evil. He could not get free, try as he would. But he has been bought. He has been delivered; he has been set free. He has been translated from the kingdom of darkness into the kingdom of God's Son. He has been redeemed. And now he has a new view of himself. He is not his own; he does not belong to himself anymore. He formerly lived to himself, but no longer; he has been bought with a price. He has a new life; he is in a new world. You know, this so grips and thrills this man that he cannot stop saying it. Listen to him saying it in Galatians 2:20: "I am crucified with Christ: nevertheless I live; yet not I, but Christ liveth in me: and the life which I now live in the flesh I live by the faith of the Son of God, who loved me, and gave himself for me."

❧ A THOUGHT TO PONDER ❧

What Paul has learned from the cross is that the Lord Jesus Christ had died for him there in order to deliver him.

THE CROSS TEACHES HOW TO SUFFER

Christ also suffered for us, leaving us an example,
that ye should follow his steps.

1 PETER 2:21

Christ teaches us how to live, and He also teaches us how to suffer. Because we live in a world of suffering and we need to be taught how to suffer, He teaches us how to suffer. The cross teaches us how to suffer—not only how to live morally and ethically, but how to suffer. "The slings and arrows of outrageous fortune" come to us all: people misunderstanding us, injustices done to us, the failure of trusted friends, people in whom we reposed every confidence letting us down, disappointments, loneliness, physical pain. How do you stand up to these things? These are the things that come to all of us. How do we meet them—how do we live? Read what the apostle Peter says about this: "Christ also suffered for us, leaving us an example, that ye should follow his steps: who did no sin, neither was guile found in his mouth: who, when he was reviled, reviled not again; when he suffered, he threatened not; but committed himself to him that judgeth righteously: who his own self bear our sins in his own body on the tree" (1 Peter 2:21-24).

There is the only way—the cross. Christ experienced misunderstanding, injustice, the treachery of friends, loneliness, even his disciples forsaking Him and fleeing from Him. In the dark night, they all forsook Him. And so no experience can ever fall to your lot but that he has gone through it. The treachery, the misunderstanding, the abuse, the injustice, the loneliness, the agony, the sweat.

In every pang that rends the heart,
The Man of Sorrows had a part.

M. BRUCE

Yes, in the light of the fact that He has been made in the likeness of sinful flesh and "was in all points tempted like as we are, yet without sin," He is able to succor us.

❧ A THOUGHT TO PONDER ☙

No experience can ever fall to your lot but that Christ has gone through it.

From *The Cross*, pp. 213-215.

May

THE GOSPEL OF
JESUS CHRIST

FROM

The Heart of the Gospel

AND

Truth Unchanged, Truth Unchanging

NO OTHER PERSON

There is none other name under heaven given among men,
whereby we must be saved.

ACTS 4:12

The New Testament says that the most important question that we must face is that of Jesus Christ; for, it tells us, our life in this world here and now, the whole meaning of death, and indeed our life throughout eternity depends entirely and solely upon our answer to this question: "Art thou he that should come, or do we look for another?" The New Testament does not hesitate to say that. Listen to the apostle Peter saying it unequivocally in one of his first recorded sermons: "There is none other name under heaven given among men, whereby we must be saved" (Acts 4:12)—this name of the Lord Jesus Christ.

Now that is a dogmatic assertion, I agree, but there is no more dogmatic book in the world than the New Testament. It never comes and says, "You have read many other books and been interested in their theories—now read me and see what you make of me. Perhaps you will find me more interesting than the others." No; rather, it makes a definite pronouncement. Here, it tells us, is the only way for men and women to know God and to be reconciled to Him. Here is the only way whereby they can be delivered from the thralldom and the serfdom of life in this world and from its sin and its evil. Here is the only way whereby they can be delivered forever from the fear of death and the grave. And here, says the New Testament, is the one and only way in which men and women can avoid spending eternity in a state of misery and wretchedness and torment. That is its statement, nothing less. "He that believeth on the Son hath everlasting life: and he that believeth not the Son shall not see life; but the wrath of God abideth on him" (John 3:36). It is one or the other; everything is dependent upon this person.

⟡ A THOUGHT TO PONDER ⟡

There is no more dogmatic book in the world than the New Testament.

May 2

UNDERSTANDING MIRACLES

Great is the mystery of godliness.
1 TIMOTHY 3:16

If what the Bible says about Jesus Christ is right and true, then of necessity it is something that transcends human intellect and reason. "Quite right," you say. "I cannot understand miracles." Of course you cannot; no one can understand a miracle. It would cease to be a miracle if you could. "I cannot grasp the supernatural." Most certainly you cannot. There never has been a man who could understand the doctrine of the Incarnation. I think of the Incarnation, and I take my stand on the side of the apostle Paul who said, "Great is the mystery of godliness." My mind is too small to understand it; my intellect cannot span the infinities and the immensities and the eternities. My little pygmy reason and logic are not big enough to see or to take in such a conception as the self-emptying and the humiliation of the Son of God.

I do not claim to understand it; who could understand an idea such as the Virgin Birth? It is beyond understanding; it is beyond reason. Who can understand the doctrine of the two natures of Christ, unmixed, remaining separate, unmingled and yet both there, still only one person? We cannot understand the doctrine of the Trinity—the Father, Son, and Holy Spirit, and we should never try to do so.

The claim of the Gospel is that it is in a realm that is beyond human reason and understanding. It is a revelation, a statement that comes to us, an announcement; it is the gift of God. That is why instead of reasoning around and around in circles and trying to span and grasp the infinite and the everlasting, I say, go to Him!

✍ A THOUGHT TO PONDER ✍

If what the Bible says about Jesus Christ is right and true, then of necessity it is something that transcends human intellect and reason.

ACCEPTING AND SUBMITTING

The common people heard him gladly.

MARK 12:37

If it were a matter of understanding and abstract reasoning, then this Gospel of the New Testament and salvation would just be for a handful of people in this world. You would have to be an expert philosopher; you would have to go to colleges and universities to be trained in philosophy. So there would be no gospel for the common, ordinary man. But thank God, here is a Gospel that tells us that "the common people heard him gladly."

Philosophers cannot preach to the poor; the poor could not follow them, and all the Greek philosophers have nothing to say to such people. But the Gospel is preached to the poor. Here, then, is a proof of the whole thing. It is not understanding that is essential—it is accepting and submitting; it is giving yourself to Jesus Christ.

So we see that the message of the Gospel is that if you are in trouble and in difficulty about Him, don't stop with arguing and going around in circles. I say this with feeling because I have known myself what that means. I did it for years, arguing and reasoning, and you come back exactly to where you began. I do not hesitate to say that if you persist in trying to understand the essence of this Gospel, you will die in the same position as you are now—you will never understand. Do what John the Baptist did—go to Christ as you see Him in the Gospels.

That is why, by the grace of God, the Gospels have been written. We cannot go see Christ in the flesh, but we can go to the Gospels and have a look at Him. And this is what we see: We are struck by the way He expounds the Scriptures in a way no one ever did before.

☙ A THOUGHT TO PONDER ☙

It is not understanding that is essential—it is accepting and submitting; it is giving yourself to Jesus Christ.

May 4

THOMAS

Except I see in his hands the print of the nails, and put my finger into the print of the nails, and thrust my hand into his side, I will not believe.

JOHN 20:25

As long as you reason and argue, you will never be satisfied. But the moment you see Him, your troubles will be resolved, and your answers will be given to you. The apostle Thomas is a perfect example of this.

We are familiar with the story of Thomas. After the death of Christ, the apostles were scattered. Then they met together, and when they were in an upper room, Christ appeared to them. Thomas was not with them then, but he joined the company later. They told him that the Lord had appeared among them, but Thomas would not believe it. He kept to the realm of reason and understanding. "No," he said, "I can't believe it, I cannot accept it—I must see Him for myself. I must put my hand into the print of the nails; I cannot believe this story."

But then later the Lord appeared in the room and said, "Where is that finger of yours, Thomas? Put it into My side." And Thomas broke down, as it were, and said that it was unnecessary. He fell at His feet and said, "My Lord and my God." Had he come to understand the resurrection? Of course he had not—he just knew that it was a fact.

So it is not a question of understanding—it is a question of the facts.

❧ A THOUGHT TO PONDER ☙

The moment you see Him, your troubles will be resolved, and your answers will be given to you.

From *The Heart of the Gospel*, pp. 24-25.

UNDERSTANDING CHRIST

*For the works which the Father gave me to finish, the same works
that I do, bear witness of me, that the Father hath sent me.*

JOHN 5:36

When you are faced with something that perplexes you about our
Lord, the first thing to do is always to start with the Lord Himself
and not with what He is doing. I am not surprised that people ask
the questions they do about Christ, because if they are not right
about His person, they will never understand His activities, and it
is really for this reason that they cannot understand His death. The
disciples only understood the meaning of His death after the resurrection; it was in the light of the resurrection that they knew He
was the Son of God, that they began to understand the meaning of
His death upon the cross. No one will ever understand the doctrine
of the cross unless he has grasped the doctrine of the person.

This, in effect, is what our Lord was telling John the Baptist in
Matthew 11:2-6: "John, you cannot understand what I am doing.
But are you trusting Me, do you really know who I am, are you
right about Me? You see, your question has led you to doubt Me in
other things. You have allowed the things I am not doing to raise a
query in your mind about My person. John, come back to the beginning—be right about Me. These are the things that I am doing.
Only the Messiah could do these things; here are the works that
authenticate Him. As I said to the people the other day, 'For the
works which the Father gave me to finish, the same works that I
do, bear witness of me, that the Father hath sent me'" (John 5:36).

❧ A THOUGHT TO PONDER ☙

When you are faced with something that perplexes you about our
Lord, the first thing to do is always to start with the Lord Himself
and not with what He is doing.

WHEN WE DON'T UNDERSTAND

All things work together for good to them that love God.
ROMANS 8:28

Our Lord's message to us is that we must trust Him absolutely and explicitly, even when we cannot understand. That, in effect, as we have seen, is what He was saying to John in Matthew 11:2-6. "I am doing the things you have heard reported of Me. But then you say, 'Why aren't You doing other things?' But if you really believe that I am the Messiah, the Son of God, cannot you leave it to Me? Even about this question of your being in prison and what your friends are saying about My not being concerned about you—John, if you know that I am who I am, cannot you trust Me there in prison itself?"

Faith means that I believe on the Lord Jesus Christ absolutely. Ah, we all have to learn this lesson. Even Paul had to pass this way. He had a thorn in the flesh, and he could not understand it. It seemed all wrong to him. He wanted to preach the Gospel, but the thorn was a hindrance to him. Three times he besought the Lord to remove it, but this was the answer he got: "My grace is sufficient for thee." "I am not taking out the thorn," said the Lord in effect, "but I will do something infinitely bigger. I will bless you with the thorn in your side. I assure you that even with the thorn I can do wonders through you." "Quite right," says Paul, "and I see that when I am weak, then I am strong, and I care about nothing except that I be right with You." The place that God would have us come to is the one in which we can say, "All things work together for good to them that love God" (Romans 8:28). "All things"—it doesn't matter what. "I have learned, in whatsoever state I am, therewith to be content" (Philippians 4:11).

✒ A THOUGHT TO PONDER ✒
Faith means that I believe on the Lord Jesus Christ absolutely.

From *The Heart of the Gospel*, pp. 51-52.

May 7

THE SOUL

*For what shall it profit a man, if he shall gain the whole world,
and lose his own soul?*

MARK 8:36

Our Lord always talked about one thing only. He had only one theme, and that was the soul of man. He kept on saying that there was something about the individual that was of priceless value. "For what shall it profit a man, if he shall gain the whole world, and lose his own soul?" It was as if He looked at His congregation and said to them, "You are always interested in things, in the world itself; but I am interested in that which is within you, which is called the soul. It will avail you nothing, though your whole world is put in order, if your soul is wrong with God." The soul—that was His constant theme. He persisted in dealing with it, and thereby He offended large numbers of people who listened to Him, people who were at first interested but who ended, like the people in John 6, by going home and walking no more with Him.

Think of many of the illustrations our Lord uses. Cannot you see that all of them are just illustrations about the soul? Look at Him in the country standing there with His followers beside the orchard. He seems to be very interested in fruit trees. He talks about them quite often and seems to know a lot about them. Yet He never lectured on horticulture and the mystery of life in the trees. He says in effect, "Do you see the trees of the orchard? They can be either good or bad, and you judge the tree eventually by the fruit that it bears. If it bears evil fruit, it is an evil tree. If it bears good fruit, it is a good tree. For 'by their fruits ye shall know them.' You have a soul within you, and it is like that tree in the orchard."

☙ A THOUGHT TO PONDER ☙
The soul—that was His constant theme.

From *The Heart of the Gospel*, p. 58.

THE OFFENSE OF CHRIST'S TEACHING

*For the Son of man is come to seek and
to save that which was lost.*

LUKE 19:10

What has offended mankind above everything else is the simplicity of our Lord's way of salvation. There is nothing that annoys people so much as the true doctrine of the cross, the doctrine of the blood of Christ and of the rebirth. Look at those people whom we read about in John 6. There they are; our Lord has said to them in essence, "I am the living bread. I am the bread of life. I have come down from heaven to give you new life that is life indeed." And it was that which made them go from Him and decide never to listen to Him again.

Let me put it again like this. If Christ had come and told us that the way of salvation was to consider a great, noble, and wonderful teaching and then to resolve to set out and do it, why, we would have liked it. Christ said in effect, "If man could save himself, I would never have come into this world. God," He said, "gave the people in past ages an opportunity of doing this. He gave them a law and told them when He gave it to them, 'Do that and it will save you; live that life and you will be righteous in My sight.'" If man could have saved himself, there would have been no need for the Son of God to come to earth. Indeed, His coming is proof that people cannot save themselves. Our Lord constantly said that, and that is what annoyed people so much. He said, "I have come to give My life as a ransom for many, for nothing but that could ever save those souls of yours and reconcile you to God. And," He said, "it is as simple as this: I have purchased your salvation—I offer it to you as a free gift."

⮞ A THOUGHT TO PONDER ⮜

If man could have saved himself, there would have been no need for the Son of God to come to earth.

May 9

UNBELIEF

If our gospel be hid, it is hid to them that are lost:
In whom the god of this world hath blinded the minds
of them which believe not.

2 CORINTHIANS 4:3-4

Let us consider what our Lord has to say about the terrible condition of unbelief. The first thing He tells us is that it is a definite mentality, a definite spirit. Unbelief is not a negative but an active thing. Of course, our tendency is to think of unbelief as just a negative condition in which a man does not believe, but according to the Bible that is an utter fallacy. Unbelief is terribly positive and active, a state and condition of the soul, with a very definite mentality. The Bible, indeed, does not hesitate to put it essentially like this: "Unbelief is one of the manifestations of sin; it is one of the symptoms of that foul disease." Or as the apostle Paul puts it in 2 Corinthians 4:3-4, "If our gospel be hid, it is hid to them that are lost: In whom the god of this world hath blinded the minds of them which believe not."

It is a terrible state and condition. Let me put it like this. It is not just a refusal to believe. That is how the devil foils us. He persuades modern unbelievers into thinking that they are unbelievers because of their great intelligence, their wonderful intellect and understanding. They think that people who are Christians are fools who have either not read or have not understood what they have read. The unbeliever thinks that he is in that state because of his scientific knowledge, and that it is in the light of these things that he refuses to believe. They rejoice in their great emancipation, that they have been delivered from the shackles of the Bible, and that they have been emancipated from this drug, this dope of the people that we call the Gospel. Poor things! They are unconscious slaves, and they do not know that they are victims.

✎ A THOUGHT TO PONDER ✍

They are unconscious slaves, and they do not know that they are victims.

From *The Heart of the Gospel*, pp. 85-86.

SODOM AND GOMORRAH

*If the mighty works, which have been done in thee [Capernaum],
had been done in Sodom, it would have remained until this day.
But I say unto you, That it shall be more tolerable for the land
of Sodom in the day of judgment, than for thee.*

MATTHEW 11:23-24

Sodom and Gomorrah were given an opportunity. Read the story in Genesis 19. But consider what the names of these cities suggest to us; Sodom has become a symbol of everything that is false and ugly in man as the result of the Fall. Sodom and Gomorrah suggest profligacy, born in the very gutters of sin, with marauders walking the streets with eyes that stand out in lasciviousness—those were the characteristics of the life there. Now what our Lord said in Matthew 11 was that the case of Capernaum and Chorazin and Bethsaida was worse than that of those Old Testament cities.

Now this can mean but one thing, which is that the judgment of all men and women is ultimately going to be in terms of their relationship to the Lord Jesus Christ. We are not told that the moral life of these cities was the same as that of Sodom and Gomorrah. We can be perfectly certain it was not; there were none of those evil men roaming the streets in their lusts. There was nothing like that at all, and yet they were worse than Sodom and Gomorrah! Why? Here is the answer: *He* had lived in Capernaum; He had walked its streets and made it His headquarters. Not only that, it was there that He had worked some of His most mighty and marvelous deeds. It was out of these cities that people like Peter and Andrew and Philip had come, and where our Lord had manifested His glory in a most signal manner. Yet these people went on living as if He had never come at all; that is the source of judgment.

ᔆ A THOUGHT TO PONDER ᔆ

The judgment of all men and women is ultimately going to be in terms of their relationship to the Lord Jesus Christ.

GOD'S REVELATION

. . . the world by wisdom knew not God, it pleased God by the
foolishness of preaching to save them that believe.

1 CORINTHIANS 1:21

Salvation is something that comes altogether from God. And when we put it like that, do we not see very clearly why it is that so many people reject it? The natural man dislikes the whole idea of revelation. Why? Because he is wise and prudent, so full of his own intellect and understanding. He boasts, "I am not going to be treated like a child. I have it within me and in my own power to arrive at any knowledge that I may desire." Revelation gives the lie to that.

But men and women do not like that, and Paul puts it like this in 1 Corinthians 1:21: When "the world by wisdom knew not God, it pleased God by the foolishness of preaching to save them that believe." Here is a great principle, and if we are wrong at this point, how can we be right anywhere else? The Gospel starts by proclaiming that it is a way of salvation. Its message is not something that man has thought of or achieved, but something that comes out of the mind of God. It is something that God shows and gives, that He has revealed; it is altogether from His side, and man contributes nothing to it.

Why is God's way of salvation a matter of revelation? One of the reasons why it must be revelation and not discovery is the greatness of God. "I thank thee, O Father, Lord of heaven and earth, that thou hast . . . revealed . . ." Oh, how easy it is to talk cleverly about God and to understand the philosophy of God, to have our religious arguments and discussions. But isn't half our trouble that we forget altogether who God is and what He is? From eternity to eternity, He is the Creator, the artificer, the sustainer of everything that is.

◆ A THOUGHT TO PONDER ◆

The Gospel is altogether from God's side, and man contributes nothing to it.

From *The Heart of the Gospel*, p. 112.

CHRIST IS CENTRAL

Thou hast hid these things from the wise and prudent, and
hast revealed them unto babes.

MATTHEW 11:25

How ridiculous it is for people to talk about arriving at God apart from our Lord! God has committed everything to Him. Christ is central; Christ is absolutely essential. He once put it in these words: "I am the way, the truth, and the life: no man cometh unto the Father, but by me" (John 14:6). This is the content of the revelation. He, Jesus of Nazareth, claimed that He was none other than the Son of God who had come to earth, and He said that He had done so because God had sent Him. Men and women had sinned against God and were therefore under His wrath; so God would have to punish their sin, and that would mean death and separation from God. So our Lord came, sent, He said, by God in order to deal with that problem.

So these, He says, are the things that have been "hid . . . from the wise and prudent, and . . . revealed . . . unto babes" (Matthew 11:25). Christ is the Son of God, and He has come into this world not only to teach and to work miracles. The real purpose of His coming was that He might die on the cross. God sent Him, says the author of the Epistle to the Hebrews, in order to "taste death for every man" (Hebrews 2:9). He said He came to bear the sins of mankind in His own precious body on the cross on Calvary's Hill. There He was punished for our sins. That is the message; that is the thing that "babes" have understood. These things are as simple as that, that God in Christ was making a way of salvation through the cross.

Therefore what have we to do? We have nothing to do but to believe that and to accept it as a free gift. For God's way of salvation is that all my sins and failure and shame have been put upon the Son and dealt with and punished.

❧ A THOUGHT TO PONDER ❧

God in Christ was making a way of salvation through the cross.

From *The Heart of the Gospel*, pp. 116-117.

KNOWING GOD

*No man knoweth the Son, but the Father; neither knoweth
any man the Father, save the Son, and he to whomsoever
the Son will reveal him.*

MATTHEW 11:27

Salvation brings me a knowledge of pardon and forgiveness, of reconciliation with God. Yes, but beyond all that, it gives me a knowledge of God.

Have you ever considered this text in that way? Have you ever seen the span and the ambit of the Gospel of Jesus Christ? Here it is. There is this little babe on the ground in his smallness and weakness and helplessness, yet the Gospel gives Him a knowledge of the Lord of heaven and earth, the Maker, the sustainer of everything that is. What a knowledge! Amazing! I, the pygmy creature of time, can know God the infinite, the absolute, and the eternal—and know Him as my Father—not as some great, mighty force away in the distant heavens, but as my Father.

Those who are interested in Greek words can examine the word for babies, used in Matthew 11:25, in the original and will find that it has a sense of sonship unfolding in it. That is what our Lord was saying: that we, though we have sinned, become in Him the sons of God, the heirs of heaven and of eternal and everlasting bliss.

What a way of salvation! May I say it with reverence—who but God could have thought of it? In such an astounding way, in our utter nakedness and helplessness He just draws back the veil and reveals it to us perfectly in Jesus Christ. He "of God is made unto us wisdom, and righteousness, and sanctification, and redemption" (1 Corinthians 1:30)—everything, a complete salvation. All you must do is to look at the Lord Jesus Christ and believe this record concerning Him. Surrender yourself to Him and accept the gift, and you will know the Lord of heaven and earth as your Father.

✍ A THOUGHT TO PONDER ✍

I, the pygmy creature of time, can know God the infinite, the absolute, and the eternal.

May 14

WRONG ASSUMPTIONS

There shall no man see me, and live.

EXODUS 33:20

We all start by assuming that our knowledge of God is all right, and if someone tells us that is the first problem, we feel it is almost insulting. This is surely the central cause of so many of our subsequent difficulties—namely, that we assume we know God, that we assume this great knowledge is something at which we start. We say, perhaps, that we know a certain amount of the teaching of our Lord Jesus Christ. Maybe we have enjoyed certain experiences— "Well, of course with regard to God, I have always believed in Him; I have always been in the position of a believer."

But my whole suggestion is that it is just there that we fail— and fail completely. Let me remind you of some of the statements that our Lord made with respect to this important matter. "No man hath seen God at any time; the only begotten Son, which is in the bosom of the Father, he hath declared him" (John 1:18)—revealed Him, manifested Him. "There shall no man," says God to Moses, "see me, and live" (Exodus 33:20). We think that we know everything about God and that there is no difficulty about our belief in God. My dear friend, ponder a statement like that—you have never seen God! No one can see God and live. God is incomprehensible to man; He is beyond him in His greatness and in His infinity. Consider what our Lord says in John 17:25: "O righteous Father, the world hath not known thee: but I have known thee, and these have known that thou hast sent me." There it is once more. He again makes the dogmatic statement that the world as it is, as the result of sin, does not know God, and never has.

☙ A THOUGHT TO PONDER ❧

The world as it is, as the result of sin, does not know God, and never has.

WHY JESUS CAME

He that hath seen me hath seen the Father.

JOHN 14:9

Christ came into this world in order that we might know God as our Father. So how does He reveal the Father to us? Well, I am just asking a question that introduces us to the four Gospels. Go back again to the New Testament, and quietly and simply read them with the idea in your mind that we are supposed to know God as Father. Ask yourself, do I know Him like that; have I ever known Him as Father? There in the Gospels you will find that *Christ revealed Him in His own life by living a spotless, sinless life*. At the end He turned to His accusers and said, "Can anybody point a finger at Me? Can you convict Me of any failure with regard to God or the law?" His life was unique; it was perfect. He revealed God by being what He was.

Then *He revealed God in His actions, His miracles*—raising people from the dead, healing the sick, giving sight to the blind. Take these things out of the New Testament and what is left? It is an essential part; it is God in the flesh. It is not difficult to expect miracles if God incarnate is here, and that is what He claims to be. Look at Him in the things He does.

Similarly, *He reveals the Father in His teaching*. He put it like this: "He that hath seen me hath seen the Father" (14:9). Just before the end, Philip said to Him, "Lord, show us the Father, and it sufficeth us" (John 14:8). In essence, "You say You are going to leave us. Please don't until You have revealed the Father to us. That is the one thing we want to know. We have had a vague belief in God, but we want to know Him as Father." In essence, our Lord answered, "Look at Me, Philip—look at My life and My actions. Look at Me, and if you do so and see Me truly, you have seen the Father."

☙ A THOUGHT TO PONDER ❧

It is not difficult to expect miracles if God incarnate is here.

From *The Heart of the Gospel*, pp. 127-128.

GOD'S JUDGMENT

. . . should not perish . . .

JOHN 3:16

Jesus taught about God the Father by showing God's wrath against sin. "But what about John 3:16?" asks someone. Listen to John 3:16, my friend. "For God so loved the world, that he gave his only begotten Son, that whoever believeth in him should not perish"—but apart from Him they would have perished; that is the only way to avoid perishing. Indeed, we also find in John 3 a statement that if a man does not believe, "the wrath of God abideth on him" (verse 36). Part of our Lord's teaching about the Father is that the Father is absolutely holy, that He hates sin and had pledged to destroy it and punish it with everlasting destruction. "Blessed," He said, "are the pure in heart: for they shall see God" (Matthew 5:8). No one else can see God because only the pure in heart could stand the sight of Him. To look at God is hell to a man unless he has been made pure in heart—". . . holiness, without which no man shall see the Lord" (Hebrews 12:14). So He revealed the character of the Father as a holy Father.

But Christ also told us about the Father's love and compassion. That is why, He tells us, He came into the world—it was because of the love of God. He shows us this same love and compassion in His life. That is why He worked His miracles, not simply to heal the people, but to reveal, to manifest, His glory and the love and compassion of God. He said in effect, "If you do not believe My words, then as I do these things, see the Father in Me." For this holy God is a God of love and compassion. As our Lord went about healing the sick and doing good, He told us that God is like that.

☙ A THOUGHT TO PONDER ❧

The Lord Jesus Christ revealed the character of the Father as a holy Father.

From *The Heart of the Gospel*, pp. 128-129.

"ALL THINGS"

All things are delivered unto me of my Father: and
no man knoweth the Son, but the Father.

MATTHEW 11:27

The Lord Jesus Christ made the following astounding claim for Himself: "All things are delivered unto me of my Father: and no man knoweth the Son, but the Father." Now let me try to reconstruct the whole situation. There is someone speaking. You look at Him and see He is a man. He is surrounded by a group of people who have attached themselves to Him and who have been following Him and listening to His teaching. They have been with Him as He has traveled back and forth in the ancient land of Palestine. They have seen the works that He performed, and there He is, as it were, a man speaking to men. But when He says, "All things," there is no limit to that word "all"; it is as all-inclusive as a word can be. So who is this person who is speaking?

He says that He is in a unique sense the Son of God. In John chapter 5 the Jews turned upon Him because He claimed God as His Father and said that He claimed equality with God. Now I feel that our real difficulty with the New Testament is that we are so familiar with these facts that we miss their extraordinary character. Our whole danger, is it not, is to fail to realize and remember that this is literal history. The fact of Jesus Christ is history, and what I am calling your attention to here is something that has actually happened. This person was on earth and was born in Bethlehem. He worked as a carpenter in Nazareth, and He told people that He was the Son of God in a way that no one else was.

❧ A THOUGHT TO PONDER ❧

He told people that He was the Son of God in a way that no one else was.

From *The Heart of the Gospel*, pp. 133, 135.

JESUS' UNIQUE RELATIONSHIP TO GOD

. . . no man knoweth the Son, but the Father.
MATTHEW 11:27

Our Lord claims that He is in a unique relationship to God in the matter of His knowledge of God. "No man," He says, "knoweth the Son, but the Father; neither knoweth any man the Father, save the Son." In other words, He looked at these people and said, "You see Me, but you do not really know Me. The only one who really knows Me is God, and I am the one, the only one, who really knows God. You pray, you speak to God, but you do not know God as I do." Nobody "hath seen God at any time," nor seen His shape. But Christ said that He had seen Him, and He claimed, as the Jews realized, an equality with God the Father. He put Himself side by side with God. Occasionally He withdrew the veil and gave a glimpse of that eternal, mystical relationship between the Father and Himself, and He claimed that He was in such an intimate relationship with God that all men were outside it. Here He is, the carpenter of Nazareth, and yet that is what He claims.

He stands there and tells these people, "Do you know that the whole of this world, the whole of time, the whole of history—heaven and earth and hell and all things—have been handed over to Me by God the Father?" That is His claim: a unique sonship, a unique relationship to God, and a unique relationship to this world. He stands there and says quietly that the whole world is in His hands. Never has the world seen or heard anyone who has claimed so much. Who is He, this babe of Bethlehem, this boy of Nazareth, this carpenter, this artisan, who claims that He is indeed the Son of God?

❧ A THOUGHT TO PONDER ❧

Christ claims a unique sonship, a unique relationship to God, and a unique relationship to this world.

From *The Heart of the Gospel*, pp. 135-136.

UNRECOGNIZED

*For had they known it, they would not have
crucified the Lord of glory.*

1 CORINTHIANS 2:8

Why is it that people fail to recognize Christ? For the fact is that those who were around Him, His own contemporaries, did not recognize Him. They did not believe the claim, for had they done so, they would have submitted themselves to Him at once. As Paul wrote to the Corinthians, the princes of this world did not know Him, "for had they known it, they would not have crucified the Lord of glory." They did not know Him. They heard the claim but said, "He is an impostor. Away with Him; crucify Him!"

Now I can understand someone saying, "If what you state is true, if this person is the Son of God, well, why is it that the whole world does not believe on Him and go after Him and submit to Him?" Our Lord answers that question. "No man," He says, "knoweth the Son." What does He mean? Let me explain. We are concerned with the mystery of the Incarnation, and it is that which causes men to stumble. Let no one imagine that this is something simple. There is a mystery in the Incarnation; there is a sense in which we can say quite honestly that had we been standing with the crowd when He was making this claim, we would have felt immediately and instinctively that there was something exaggerated. We would have felt that the claim that He was the one to whom all things had been committed, that He was the controller of the destinies of the universe, was impossible. There is this apparent contradiction. He was arrested in apparent weakness, and yet He said that all things were in His hands. That is why people found it difficult to believe His claim.

❧ A THOUGHT TO PONDER ❧

He was arrested in apparent weakness, and yet He said that all things were in His hands.

From *The Heart of the Gospel*, pp. 136-137.

INEVITABLE DEDUCTIONS

*He that honoureth not the Son honoureth not the Father
which hath sent him.*

JOHN 5:23

What has the Son of God done to me by coming into this world? What difference has He made? Now it seems to me that there are certain inevitable deductions, and here they are.

My relationship to God is determined solely and entirely and absolutely by Jesus Christ. If you tell me that you believe in God, I say to you that it is of no value if you do not believe in Christ. I say again with Martin Luther, "I know of no God save Jesus Christ." "He that honoureth not the Son honoureth not the Father which hath sent him." All things have been committed to Him. You cannot know God without Jesus Christ. "Neither knoweth any man the Father, save the Son, and he to whomsover the Son will reveal him" (Matthew 11:27). I cannot know God as my Father apart from the Son. I would have no forgiveness of sins if He, the Son of God, had not come and if He had not died for me on the cross. But because He has, I know my sins are forgiven. He and He alone can give me life anew; He imparts to me His own life, and He makes me a child of God. He came to do that, and He has done it.

My eternal destiny is determined solely by my relationship to Him. I assure you in the name of God and of the Bible that when you come to the great day of judgment—for it is coming; we all have to die and meet God—I solemnly assure you that you will have only one question to answer. You will not be asked about the good you have done, or about your learning and knowledge, or about your political party; none of these things will matter. There is only one question, which is: "What think ye of Christ?"

☙ A THOUGHT TO PONDER ❧

I cannot know God as my Father apart from Christ, the Son.

May 21

TRUE REST

*Come to me, all ye that labour and are heavy laden, and
I will give you rest.*

MATTHEW 11:28

The Gospel announces that rest is only to be found in a knowledge of God, because God has made us, and He has made us in such a way that we never can know rest apart from Him. The great Augustine of Hippo put that perfectly when he said, "Thou hast made us for Thyself, and our souls are restless until they find their rest in Thee."

You can scale the heights or plumb the depths, you can travel around the world, as many people have done, trying to find rest and peace, but you will never find it. God has so made us—and this is the glory and the dignity of man—that nothing can finally be made at rest until our souls are satisfied in God. And the world, I suggest to you, is an eloquent sermon on that particular theme. With all that we have in the modern world of wealth and culture and education and everything else, look at the picture of unutterable restlessness all around us. "There is no peace, saith my God, to the wicked" (Isaiah 57:21). There is no rest apart from a knowledge of God.

The Lord alone can give us this knowledge. "Come unto me, all ye that labour and are heaven laden, and I will give you rest. Take my yoke upon you, and learn of me" (Matthew 11:28-29). Notice the personal reference; all along He is pointing to Himself. Yes, but He is doing more than that—He is contrasting Himself with everybody else. His claim is that "Neither knoweth any man the Father, save the Son, and he to whomsover the Son will reveal him" (Matthew 11:27). He says that not only can He give us this knowledge of God, but that no one and nothing else can give us and create this knowledge in us.

✎ A THOUGHT TO PONDER ✐

"Thou hast made us for Thyself, and our souls are restless until they find their rest in Thee."

From *The Heart of the Gospel*, p. 162.

May 22

A RIGHT CONCEPTION OF GOD

Hallowed be thy name.

LUKE 11:2

When the disciples came to our Lord and said, "Lord, teach us to pray, as John also taught his disciples," He replied, "When ye pray say, Our Father which art in heaven, Hallowed be thy name" (Luke 11:1-2). You must start, said our Lord, with a right conception of God. Now is this not where we all tend to go astray? So often our initial error and trouble is that our ideas of God are so loose. Let us be quite frank and honest about this. Most of us, before we listen to Jesus Christ, rather feel that we are in a position even to criticize God: "Why should God . . . ? Why this? Why that?" We are, we think, the judges even where God is concerned. Now what our Lord tells us at the beginning is, "Put off thy shoes from off thy feet, for the place whereon thou standest is holy ground" (Exodus 3:5). Can you imagine God, can you picture Him? God is utterly and absolutely holy, so much so that we cannot imagine Him, eternal in His holiness and His absolute perfection.

That is what our Lord taught about God, and we must start there. We have to realize that if to know God is the first essential thing in rest and peace, we must begin by knowing something of His nature and character, and that is what our Lord always taught about Him.

Take His own attitude toward the Father. Look at the time He spent in prayer; observe the way in which He was always careful to say that He did nothing of Himself, that the works He did were those the Father had given Him to do, and that all the words He spoke were those that the Father gave Him.

❧ A THOUGHT TO PONDER ❧

You must start, said our Lord, with a right conception of God.

From *The Heart of the Gospel*, pp. 173-174.

May 23

THE PLACE OF THE MIND

Take my yoke upon you, and learn of me; for I am meek and lowly in heart: and ye shall find rest unto your souls.

MATTHEW 11:29

I am not suggesting that the Gospel is irrational, nor am I simply proclaiming that because it is miraculous and supernatural it is therefore unreasonable. Not at all! What I am saying is that we are here entering a realm that we cannot enter by reason alone. It is not unreasonable, but it transcends reason. It is not unreasonable for me to believe that when God acts, I cannot understand Him; and that is precisely what we are confronted with when we come to the Gospel of the Lord Jesus Christ.

Let no one imagine, therefore, that the teaching is that we just leave our intellects outside when we come into the house of God and abandon ourselves in a passive state to any feeling that may come or to any kind of emotion. Far from it! But we do say that when God does something, we must accept it as being supernatural and miraculous, and we must not, therefore, be surprised when we find that it is so.

We must believe and accept what God has done and then proceed to understand. To me the argument comes in this way: As a human being in this world I have been conscious of the need of rest. I have used my mind and my reason, I have listened to the world and its teaching and all its philosophies, but I find that they cannot give me rest and I am at the end of my tether. Then I am here confronted with a new offer that says, "Listen to this." I say it is reasonable to listen, and the moment I do so, I begin to find that what Christ has to say is indeed essentially different.

❧ A THOUGHT TO PONDER ❧

We are here entering a realm that we cannot enter by reason alone. It is not unreasonable, but it transcends reason.

OUTSPOKEN ABOUT SIN

It is better for thee to enter into life halt or maimed, rather than having two hands or two feet to be cast into everlasting fire.
MATTHEW 18:8

All talk about sin, say the self-expressionists, is utterly foolish, leading to self-repression, which is, they aver, the only sin. What used to be called sin is just expression of self, the greatest and the most vital possession that man has, they say. Not to sin, according to the old meaning of the term, is to do violence to the greatest gift he possesses. They plead, therefore, for the abolition of the word *sin* in its earlier associations. They deplore what they term the tragic spectacle of mankind shackled against its highest good by adherence to the warnings of the Bible, the Church, and the saints.

We can best consider this human view of life, and show its complete fallacy, by contrasting it with God's view as stated in the Bible. The teachings of our Lord and Savior, Jesus Christ, are outspoken against sin. He said, "Wherefore if thy hand or thy foot offend thee, cut them off, and cast them from thee: it is better for thee to enter into life halt or maimed, rather than having two hands or two feet to be cast into everlasting fire. And if thine eye offend thee, pluck it out, and cast it from thee: it is better for thee to enter into life with one eye, rather than having two eyes to be cast into hell fire" (Matthew 18:8-9).

Now there we are reminded of the way in which every conceivable view of life and of men is invariably dealt with somewhere or another in the Scriptures. Modern man is constantly flattering himself and suggesting to himself that certain of his ideas are quite new. But here again we find an illustration of a view that prides itself on its modernity dealt with completely and exhaustively in the Bible.

✒ A THOUGHT TO PONDER ✑
The teachings of our Lord and Savior, Jesus Christ, are outspoken against sin.

From *Truth Unchanged, Unchanging*, pp. 18-20.

THE NATURE OF SELF

And if thine eye offend thee, pluck it out, and cast it from thee:
it is better for thee to enter into life with one eye,
rather than having two eyes to be cast into hell fire.

MATTHEW 18:9

The modern cult of self-expression fails to realize the true nature of self. It talks much about giving expression to self, and yet we can show very easily that its very ideas concerning that self are false and do violence to man's true nature. Obviously, before expression must come definition; and our objection is not so much to the idea of self-expression per se as to the utterly false view of that self that is taken by so many today. The gospel answer to this modern cult is not a doctrine of repression, but rather a call to the realization of the true nature of the self. The clash between the biblical view and that of moderns comes out very clearly in the quoted lines above, especially in the emphasis that Christ places on the word *thee*. "If thine eye offend *thee* . . . cast it from *thee* . . . it is better for *thee* . . ."

The modern view does not differentiate between the self and the various factors that tend to influence the self, the various factors that the self uses in order to express itself. They claim that man in himself is but the result of these and their effects. Our Lord, on the other hand, draws that distinction very clearly and definitely in His emphasis on the word *thee*. That He does so is perhaps the real cause of all the modern confusion.

According to Christ, man is not a machine, nor is he an animal led and governed by whim. He is bigger than the body, bigger than tradition, history, and all else. For there is within man another element called the soul.

❧ A THOUGHT TO PONDER ❧

There is within man another element called the soul.

From *Truth Unchanged, Unchanging*, pp. 20-21, 24.

TRUE AND FALSE HAPPINESS

Blessed are they which do hunger and thirst after righteousness:
for they shall be filled.
MATTHEW 5:6

Man under the influence of alcohol may feel perfectly happy for the time being, but the question is, has he solved his problems? To place happiness before health and to regard it as the supreme good is to be guilty of a fundamental fallacy in the matter of standards.

Such unthinking procedure includes also the fallacy of failing to see that ultimately happiness depends upon health and is something that results from health. Any other type of happiness is negative and dependent only upon the absence of conditions that prevent happiness. However much we may strive to lessen our unhappiness, while there is disease, there can be no true happiness. Nothing is so fallacious, therefore, and so fatal to true happiness as to make ease and happiness ends in and of themselves.

When our Lord said, "Blessed are they which do hunger and thirst after righteousness: for they shall be filled" (Matthew 5:6), he did not say that they would be happy who hungered and thirsted after happiness. The blessedness, the happiness, the joy is something that will result from our seeking righteousness and from our becoming righteous. It is a by-product, an end-result. We are not to place blessedness or happiness in the supreme position. We are to seek righteousness, and, having found it, we shall then find ourselves to be happy and filled with blessedness.

What ultimately accounts for the failure of the false prophet to think clearly is the fact that he is deliberately determined to defend himself and to think well of himself. Pride is the root cause of the trouble. The view of the false prophet starts with the postulate that whatever else may be the cause of the troubles in life, it is not man himself.

❧ A THOUGHT TO PONDER ❧
The blessedness, the happiness, the joy is something that will result from our seeking righteousness and from our becoming righteous.

MISGUIDED ZEAL

I bear them record that they have a zeal of God,
but not according to knowledge.

ROMANS 10:2

The Jews were looking forward to the coming of the Messiah, but they did not recognize Him when He came. They who declared themselves anxious to be just with God were rejecting the one way whereby mankind can be justified before God.

To Paul there was but one explanation of that tragedy. He expressed it in the words, "I bear them record that they have a zeal of God, but not according to knowledge." He granted that their view was quite honest and quite sincere. The trouble with the Jews was not that they lacked sincerity, but rather that they trusted to it and, because of their reliance on it, neglected to consider the further light and knowledge that the Gospel could give them on the very object that they desired. Again their difficulty was not that they lacked fervor, but that they trusted to it and argued that because they were zealous they were therefore of necessity right. "They have a zeal of God, but not according to knowledge." Indeed, they rejected the knowledge the Gospel was offering them because of that very ardor. The conflict in their case was between zeal and knowledge, between sincerity and truth.

There can be no doubt at all but that these qualities—zeal and sincerity—are being exalted in our day precisely as they were by the Jews of old. Knowledge is being depreciated, almost despised. Clear, logical thinking and exact definitions are discounted. Doctrine and dogma are taboo and regarded as being almost the enemies of truth, and even good deeds are not given the prominence they had a few years ago.

∽ A THOUGHT TO PONDER ∾

These qualities—zeal and sincerity—are being exalted in our day precisely as they were by the Jews of old.

From *Truth Unchanged, Unchanging*, pp. 60-61.

THE SIMPLICITY OF THE GOSPEL

The light of the body is the eye: therefore when thine eye is single,
thy whole body also is full of light; but when thine eye is evil,
thy body also is full of darkness.

LUKE 11:34

There is nothing so disconcerting as a plain, direct gospel that, stripping away all mere decorations and embellishments and ignoring all nonessentials and make-believes, exposes the naked soul and flashes onto it the light of God. How much easier it is to appreciate the ceremony and ritual, to indulge in high-sounding, idealistic generalities, and to be busy with philanthropic actions. How much more gratifying to the natural self are these than to face the simple direct questions of the Word of God. Idealists and humanists are rarely, if ever, persecuted.

But leaving all that, let us consider positively the gospel view of life and the solution of the Gospel for the problems of life. That there is nothing so characteristic of it as its essential simplicity is seen most clearly perhaps if we look at it in the light of some words spoken by the Lord Jesus Christ. He said, "The light of the body is the eye: therefore when thine eye is single, thy whole body also is full of light; but when thine eye is evil, thy body also is full of darkness" (Luke 11:34).

If we work out the picture found in those words, we shall see plainly the simplicity of the Gospel. Our Lord says that what the eye is to the body in the matter of light, the soul is to man, and the individual man is to society. Thus we see that there is in man something vital and central. Man is not a mere collection and aggregate of parts. There is a center to his life called the soul, as vital to his life as the eye is to the body in the matter of light.

❧ A THOUGHT TO PONDER ☙

Our Lord says that what the eye is to the body in the matter of light, the soul is to man.

THE GOSPEL OF LIGHT

*I am the way, the truth, and the life: no man cometh unto
the Father, but by me.*

JOHN 14:6

Are we all doomed to perpetual blindness and darkness? There is but one hope. There is but one answer. There is but one cure. According to the Gospel, Jesus of Nazareth was the only begotten Son of God. He came down to earth because of the blindness of mankind, because man had been deluded by the god of this world. He came and brought that treatment that alone can avail. He has removed by His sacrificial, atoning death and His resurrection the stain of the guilt of sin. He has given new life and power to our diseased and paralyzed spiritual optic nerves. He enables us to see God, to behold the Father's face. And, looking at Him, the light of the eternal countenance irradiates our whole being.

He said, "I am the way, the truth, and the life: no man cometh unto the Father, but by me" (John 14:6). And that statement has been verified in countless thousands of experiences. He said that He was "the light of the world" (John 8:12) and that anyone who followed Him need no longer walk in darkness but will have "the light of life" (John 8:12). It is He alone who can reconcile us to God and enable us to see and to know God. The message of the Gospel therefore to this modern, distracted world is that in simplicity it has but to offer this prayer:

> *Holy Spirit, truth divine,*
> *Dawn upon this soul of mine.*
> *Word of God and inward light,*
> *Wake my spirit, clear my sight.*

The Gospel states with assurance that all who offer this prayer in sincerity and truth will be able to say with the apostle Paul that "the light of the knowledge of the glory of God in the face of Jesus Christ" (2 Corinthians 4:6) has shined into their hearts.

❧ A THOUGHT TO PONDER ❧

Jesus Christ alone can reconcile us to God and enable us to see and to know God.

From *Truth Unchanged, Unchanging*, pp. 103–104.

FACING GOD

How should man be just with God?

JOB 9:2

The most urgent, vital question confronting man is still the question asked of old by Job: "How should man be just with God?" Certainly there is a new setting to problems—whether they are economic, political, or educational; whether they deal with the shortage of houses or the proper treatment of strikes. But all these problems are temporary. Behind and beyond them all remains that unavoidable situation in which we shall be face to face with the eternal God, "the Father of lights, with whom is no variableness, neither shadow of turning" (James 1:17).

The ultimate problem for man is not himself, his happiness, or the conditions that surround him while he is here on earth. His ultimate problem is his relationship with God both in time and in eternity; and God is eternal, changeless, absolute. How foolish it is, therefore, to argue that modern man needs a new remedy or a new type of salvation rather than "the glorious gospel of the blessed God" (1 Timothy 1:11), which is to be found alone in our Lord and Savior, Jesus Christ.

Let us agree wholeheartedly with the modern man when he says that he believes always in having the best. The man who does not desire the best is a fool. Let us by all means have the best, whatever it may cost and whatever its source may be. Further, it is true to say that in many realms and departments of life the latest is undoubtedly the best. For example, the decline in the mortality rate in diseases like meningitis and pneumonia is truly astonishing. There can be no question at all but that in the treatment of the ills and diseases of the body, the latest is the best.

But can the same be said about the cure of the ills of the soul? Is there some magical potion that can be given to a man who is on his deathbed, who realizes his sinfulness?

❧ A THOUGHT TO PONDER ☙

The ultimate problem for man is his relationship with God.

From *Truth Unchanged, Unchanging*, pp. 120-123.

ONE CURE

Who his own self bare our sins in his own body on the tree,
that we, being dead to sins, should live unto righteousness:
by whose stripes ye were healed.

1 PETER 2:24

There is but one cure for the ills of man. When my conscience accuses me, there is but one thing I know of that can give me rest and peace. It is to know that Jesus of Nazareth, the Son of God, who bore my sins "in his own body on the tree," has forgiven me. It is to believe and to know that because He loved me and died for me, I am clear of accusation. Then, conscious as I am of my weakness and failure and my lack of power to live a life worthy of the name, I am again driven back to Him. It is only from Him and the power of the Holy Spirit that He imparts that I can be made more than a conqueror.

As I contemplate meeting my Maker and my eternal Judge, my only hope is that I shall be clothed with the righteousness of Jesus Christ and that He will take me by the hand and present me "fault-less before the presence of his glory with exceeding joy" (Jude 24). It is always and only in Christ that I find satisfaction. It is only in Him that my problems are solved. The world with all its methods cannot help me at the moment of my greatest need. But Christ never fails. He satisfies always and in every respect. The more I contemplate Him, the more do I agree with Charles Wesley when he said:

> *Thou, O Christ, art all I want;*
> *More than all in Thee I find!*

He still remains the only hope for individual man, the only hope for the whole world. Is the Gospel still relevant? It alone can deal with and solve the problems of man.

❧ A THOUGHT TO PONDER ❧
There is but one cure for the ills of man.

From *Truth Unchanged, Unchanging*, pp. 124-125.

June

WHEN GOD MOVES
IN REVIVAL

FROM

Revival

June 1

THE URGENT NEED FOR REVIVAL TODAY

*And when he was come into the house, his disciples asked him
privately, Why could not we cast him out? And he said unto them,
This kind can come forth by nothing, but by prayer and fasting.*

MARK 9:28-29

The church is so constituted that every member matters, and matters in a very vital sense. So I call attention to this whole subject [of revival] partly because I sense there is a curious tendency today for members of the Christian Church to feel and to think that they themselves can do very little, and so they tend to look to others to do all that is needed for them. This, of course, is something that is characteristic of the whole of life today. For instance, men and women no longer take exercise in sport as they used to. Instead, people tend to sit in crowds and just watch other people play. There was a time when people provided their own pleasure, but now the radio and television provide their entertainment and pleasure for them. And I fear that the tendency is even manifesting itself in the Christian Church. More and more we see evidence that people are just sitting back in crowds while one or two people are expected to do everything.

Now that, of course, is a complete denial of the New Testament doctrine of the Church as the Body of Christ, where every single member has responsibility and has a function and matters, and matters in a most vital sense. You can read the apostle's great expositions of that doctrine, for example in 1 Corinthians 12, where you find that he says that our less comely parts are as important as the more comely parts, that every part of the body is to function and is to be ready for the Master's use, and always to be usable.

Unless we as individual Christians are feeling a grave concern about the state of the Church and the world today, we are very poor Christians indeed.

✎ A THOUGHT TO PONDER ✎

The church is so constituted that every member matters, and matters in a very vital sense.

From *Revival*, p. 8.

HINDRANCES TO REVIVAL

And Isaac departed thence, and pitched his tent in the valley of
Gerar, and dwelt there. And Isaac digged the wells of water,
which they had digged in the days of Abraham his father;
for the Philistines had stopped them after the death of Abraham:
and he called their names after the names by which
his father had called them.

GENESIS 26:17-18

This incident in the life of Isaac has much to teach us in our consideration of the whole question of revival. The picture is one of Isaac in trouble, in a difficulty. If you read the context, you will find that he had been living in another part of the country, and God had blessed him in a very striking manner. So much so that Isaac had become the object of envy of those who were living round and about him, and they had forced him to move. "And Abimelech said unto Isaac, Go from us; for thou art much mightier than we" (Genesis 26:16). And so Isaac was compelled to move with his family and all his servants, possessions, and belongings. Then he came to the valley of Gerar and decided that he would dwell there.

Of course, the moment he arrived he was confronted by an urgent and a very desperate need—the need of water. I do want to emphasize that because this was the need for something that is absolutely essential to life, in addition to being essential to well-being. He was not merely confronted by the problem of seeking some beautiful spot where he might pitch his tent or erect some kind of dwelling-place for himself. He was not looking for entertainment or for luxuries; he was not looking for any kind of accessory to life. The whole point of the story is that he was looking for something that is an absolute essential and without which life cannot be maintained at all.

I emphasize that because the first thing that we must realize about the situation we are in today is its desperate character.

✎ A THOUGHT TO PONDER ✎
The first thing that we must realize about the situation we are in today is its desperate character.

REDISCOVERING THE CENTRAL TRUTHS OF THE GOSPEL

Nevertheless the foundation of God standeth sure.
2 TIMOTHY 2:19

Without a single exception it is the rediscovery of the cardinal doctrines of the Christian faith that has led ultimately to revival. There is always a preliminary to revival. It appears to come suddenly, and in a sense it does. But if you look carefully into the history, you will always find that there was something going on quietly, there was a preliminary, a preparation unobserved by people. And the preparation, invariably, has been a rediscovery of these grand and glorious central truths.

Take, for instance, the history of the Protestant Reformation. It was only after Martin Luther had suddenly seen the grand truth of justification by faith alone that the Protestant revival came. It was getting back to that truth, in the epistles to the Galatians and the Romans, that prepared the way for the outpouring of the Spirit. It happened in this country and in every country where the Reformation spread.

That also happened in the eighteenth century. There you had that deadness. Bishop Butler wrote his book *The Analogy of Religion*, and the "Boyle lectures" were started in an attempt to counter this rationalism, but it availed nothing. Then suddenly the revival seemed to come. Whitefield, the Wesleys, and others like them appeared. Yes, but how did revival come through these men? Well, the story is well-known. What really made it possible for John Wesley to have the experience he had in Aldersgate Street, when his heart was "strangely warmed" by the Holy Spirit, was something that happened three months earlier. He had the experience in Aldersgate Street on May 24, 1738, but in March 1738 his eyes had been opened to the truth of justification by faith only. The famous conversation, on the journey between London and Oxford, between Peter Bülow and Wesley was all about justification by faith alone. It was only after he had seen that, and it had gripped him, that the Holy Spirit came upon him and began to use him.

❧ A THOUGHT TO PONDER ❧
There is always a preliminary to revival.

From *Revival*, pp. 35-36.

IS THE LORD JESUS CHRIST CENTRAL?

In whom we have redemption through his blood,
the forgiveness of sins.

EPHESIANS 1:7

If the Lord Jesus Christ is not crucial, central, vital, and occupying the very center of our meditation and our living, thinking, and praying, we have no right to look for revival. And yet, if you go and talk to many people, even in the church, about religion, you will find that they will talk to you at great length without ever mentioning the Lord Jesus Christ. I am never tired of putting it like this, because it is something that I am so familiar with in my experience as a pastor. People come and talk to me about these things, and I put my question to them. I say, "If you had to die tonight, how would you feel?"

"Oh," they say, "I believe in God."

"All right," I reply, "what will you say when you stand in the presence of God? What are you relying on?"

"Well," they say, "I have always tried to live a good life, I have done my best, I have tried to do good."

"But nevertheless you have sinned, haven't you?"

"Oh yes, I have sinned."

"So," I ask, "what do you do about your sin? What will you say to God, in the presence of God, about your sin?"

"Well," they say, "I believe God is a God of love."

"And how does that help you?"

"Well," they say, "I believe that if I acknowledge my sin to God and then ask Him to forgive me, He does forgive me, and I am relying upon that."

The point I am making is that they do not even mention the name of the Lord Jesus Christ. They seem to think that they can go to God directly without the Lord Jesus Christ at all. There is a great deal of so-called Christianity that is quite Christ-less.

❧ A THOUGHT TO PONDER ❧

If the Lord Jesus Christ is not occupying the very center of our meditation, we have no right to look for revival.

From *Revival*, pp. 45-46.

THE BAPTISM OF THE HOLY SPIRIT

And they were all filled with the Holy Ghost, and began to speak
with other tongues, as the Spirit gave them utterance.

ACTS 2:4

I take it by definition that a revival means the outpouring of the Spirit of God, the Spirit of God coming in power upon a person or a number of persons at the same time.

But there are some who, while not dismissing this as hysteria, seem to me to be guilty of quenching the Spirit, because they argue like this: "The baptism of the Holy Spirit is what happens to every man when he is born again, when he is regenerated. So we are all baptized with the Spirit—we have all received this baptism." Now remember, they are talking about the thing that is described in the second chapter of Acts. And they say, "Yes, that was the baptism of the Holy Spirit. But we all get that now, and it is unconscious, we are not aware of it; it happens to us the moment we believe and we are regenerated. It is just that act of God that incorporates us into the Body of Christ. That's the baptism of the Spirit—God's pouring out His Spirit upon the Church, baptizing the Church afresh with His Holy Spirit, a baptism of power. And since it has happened to all of us, we must not ask for it."

Or the argument is put another way. It is taught that what happened on the Day of Pentecost happened once and forever, that it cannot be repeated, and therefore it is wrong for us to pray that the Holy Spirit should be poured forth. They say, "God, on the Day of Pentecost, did pour forth His Spirit upon the Church. And the Holy Spirit has been in the Church ever since. So," they teach, "it is actually wrong to pray for an outpouring of God's Spirit." It is not surprising that as that kind of preaching has gained currency, people have stopped praying for revival, and the Church is as she is today.

❧ A THOUGHT TO PONDER ❧

Revival is the outpouring of the Spirit of God.

From *Revival*, pp. 50-52.

June 6

ENTHUSIASM

Quench not the Spirit.
1 THESSALONIANS 5:19

A characteristic of dead orthodoxy is a dislike of enthusiasm. If you like it in more biblical terms, I could put it like this: It is to be guilty of quenching the Spirit. To dislike enthusiasm is to quench the Spirit. Those who are familiar with the history of the Church, and in particular with the history of revivals, will know that this charge of enthusiasm is the one that has always been brought against people who have been most active in a period of revival.

This has been a common accusation throughout history. Read, for instance, the stories of the men of the eighteenth century. A charge that George Whitefield constantly had to answer and rebuff at the hand of bishops was this charge of enthusiasm. They said, "Look here, we're not objecting so much to your doctrine—it is the way you are preaching it, it is the way you are doing it." John Wesley was constantly charged in the same way, even by his own mother, Susannah Wesley. Why could he not preach like everybody else? What was he so excited about? Why all this disturbance? Susannah Wesley was a very godly woman, but she could not understand this son of hers, who suddenly had become an enthusiast. One of the things that comes out very clearly as you read the literature of the eighteenth century in terms of the Christian Church is that this charge was constantly brought forward.

So, then, we must look at this subject because clearly this opposition to what is called enthusiasm can be one of the greatest hindrances to revival. And it is the particular danger of people who are in a state of dead orthodoxy. As I understand the matter, there are two great principles laid down in the New Testament for our help and guidance. The first principle is that everything must be done "decently and in order" (1 Corinthians 14:40). But there is another statement: "Quench not the Spirit" (1 Thessalonians 5:19).

∽ A THOUGHT TO PONDER ∽

To dislike enthusiasm is to quench the Spirit.

June 7

PSEUDO-INTELLECTUALISM

Despise not prophesyings.
1 THESSALONIANS 5:20

Some people are so afraid of emotionalism that there is an absence of a true and a healthy and a God-given emotion among them.

What is this all due to? I believe it is due to a pseudo-intellectualism, a false sense of what is respectable, and I am profoundly convinced that this may be one of the greatest hindrances to revival. You see, we pride ourselves on our learning.

One of the greatest intellects that this world has ever known was the apostle Paul. But look at him as he is moved by a grand sweep of emotion. He starts off on a point, but suddenly he names Christ, and he is lost. He forgets what he is saying, and he bursts into magnificent eloquence. And then he comes back to his point again. Disorder, if you like, inconsistencies—use your own term. Yes, but it is the glory of the man; this giant intellect, who could be moved by the truth, was moved to tears.

As George Whitefield was preaching about the glories of grace and salvation, tears were pouring down his cheeks, and those who listened to him were weeping too. It is true of all these men; yet *we* may be so hard and so intellectual and so controlled. This is not a plea for emotionalism, which I have denounced—it is a plea for emotion. God save us from being so afraid of the false that we quench the Spirit of God and become so respectable and so pseudo-intellectual that the Spirit of God is kept back, and we go on in our dryness and aridity and in our comparative futility and helplessness and uselessness. Let us approximate a little more closely to the Church as she is depicted in the pages of the New Testament. "Quench not the Spirit," "despise not prophesyings," but at the same time "prove all things; hold fast that which is good."

☙ A THOUGHT TO PONDER ❧
This is not a plea for emotionalism—it is a plea for emotion.

SPIRITUAL INERTIA

Because thou sayest, I am rich, and increased with goods, and
have need of nothing; and knowest not that thou art wretched,
and miserable, and poor, and blind, and naked . . .
REVELATION 3:17

There are what you may call the heights and depths of the Christian life—the possibilities open to the Christian in this present world. And you find that not only in the Scriptures, but as you read the biographies of the saints, as you read the stories of what happens to people in a time of revival, you find yourself reading of people who have realized these possibilities.

There is a story of an old Puritan who had an experience once when he was walking over a mountainside. Suddenly the Lord Jesus Christ came to him, and gave him manifestations of Himself. And this man said that he learned more during that one brief experience than he had learned in fifty years of reading, studying, and meditation. That is always a possibility.

You find it again as you read the history of revival. You hear of people talking about communications and about their dealings with God and with the Lord Jesus Christ, the realizations of His presence, the manifestations of His love; of being almost overwhelmed by a sense of the nearness of the Lord Jesus Christ, of being filled with a sense of God's glory and of His love.

Why do we not know these things? It is because we are so like the people in the church at Laodicea. This is what is said to them by the risen Lord: "Because thou sayest, I am rich, and increased with goods, and have need of nothing; and knowest not that thou art wretched, and miserable, and poor, and blind, and naked" (Revelation 3:17). And that is the condition of the Church today.

✍ A THOUGHT TO PONDER ✍

You hear of people being almost overwhelmed by a sense of the nearness of the Lord Jesus Christ.

From *Revival*, pp. 84-85.

June 9

A REVIVAL'S OVERWHELMING CHARACTER

That all the people of the earth might know the hand of the LORD, that it is mighty: that ye might fear the LORD your God for ever.
JOSHUA 4:24

A revival is something that, when it happens, leads people to say, as the townspeople said in Jerusalem on the Day of Pentecost, "What is this? What is it?" It is something that comes like a tornado. It is almost like an overflowing tide; it is like a flood. Astounding things happen, and of such a magnitude that men are left amazed, astonished.

Let me give you an illustration that is one of the most lyrical and one of the most wonderful. There was a preacher in Scotland three hundred years ago by the name of John Livingstone of Kilsyth. John Livingstone and a number of others had been spending Sunday night after the services in prayer. Monday morning came, and John Livingstone had been asked to preach. He was out in the fields meditating, and suddenly he felt that he could not preach, that the thing was beyond him and that he was inadequate. And he felt like running away. But suddenly the voice of God seemed to speak to him, not in audible language, but in his spirit, telling him not to do that and that God did not work in that way, and it made him feel that he must go back. He preached, he tells us, on Ezekiel 36. And he said, "I preached for about an hour and a half. Then," he said, "I began to apply my message," and as he was beginning to apply it, suddenly the Spirit of God came upon him, and he went on for another hour in this application. And as he did so, people were literally falling to the ground, and in that one service five hundred people were converted.

That is the kind of thing that happens in a revival. And poor John Livingstone says that kind of thing only happened to him on one other occasion.

☙ A THOUGHT TO PONDER ☚
Revival is almost like an overflowing tide; it is like a flood.

From *Revival*, pp. 115-116.

THE PURPOSE OF REVIVAL

. . . as the LORD your God did to the Red sea, which he dried up
from before us, until we were gone over: That all the people
of the earth might know the hand of the LORD, that it is mighty:
that ye might fear the LORD your God for ever.

JOSHUA 4:23-24

Why does God send revival from time to time? The first reason given in Joshua 4:24 is this: "that all the people of the earth might know the hand of the LORD, that it is mighty." God does this thing from time to time, God sends revival, blessing, upon the Church in order that He may do something with respect to those who are outside Him. He is doing something that is going to arrest the attention of all the people of the earth. Here, we must always realize, is the chief reason for ever considering this matter at all. This is my main reason for calling attention to this whole subject of revival and for urging everybody to pray for revival, to look for it, and to long for it. This is the reason—the glory of God.

You see, Israel alone represented God and His glory. All the other nations of the world were pagan; they had their various gods, and they did not believe in or worship the God of Israel. But God had chosen Israel. He had made a nation for Himself in order that through them, and by means of them, He might manifest His own glory and that they might bear this testimony to all the nations of the world. That was the real function of the children of Israel, and the other nations were watching them and were ready always to scoff at them and to ridicule them. Whenever the nation of Israel was defeated, the other nations would say, "Where is their God? Where is His power?"

☙ A THOUGHT TO PONDER ❧

God sends revival to arrest the attention of all the people of the earth.

THE EFFECTS OF REVIVAL

*And they were all amazed, and were in doubt, saying one
to another, What meaneth this? Others mocking said,
These men are full of new wine.*

ACTS 2:12-13

What effect does revival have, especially on those who are outside
God's people? It is meant to let all the nations of the world know that
"the hand of the LORD, that it is mighty," as is clear from the book
of Joshua. But the question arises at once, does it have that effect?
Are all convinced by it? Acts 2 gives us an answer to that question
that is of very great value to us and should be of urgent concern to
all who are looking for and longing for revival. Here at any rate is
a possible reaction. And we find it not only here, but elsewhere in the
Bible. As we read the history of the Church and of revival throughout the centuries, we find that this kind of thing is constantly
repeated. We read, "And they were all amazed, and were in doubt,
saying one to another, What meaneth this?"

You remember how the Holy Spirit was poured out upon the disciples and others with them, 120 people, there in the upper room.
And as the result of this mighty outpouring of the Spirit that came
upon them, they began to speak in other tongues, and undoubtedly
there were many other similar phenomena as well. All this was
noised abroad, and the people gathered together from everywhere,
and observing and hearing this they said, "What meaneth this?"
They were amazed, some doubted, and "Others mocking said, These
men are full of new wine." Now there, you see, is a reaction on the
part of certain people to this mighty phenomenon that takes place
when God pours forth His Spirit. This is a reaction that is due, as
we are told here so plainly in the context, to certain phenomena
that may sometimes accompany revivals.

✒ A THOUGHT TO PONDER ✒

They were amazed, some doubted, and "Others mocking said, These
men are full of new wine."

June 12

THE DAY OF PENTECOST

And it shall come to pass afterward, that I will pour out my spirit
upon all flesh; and your sons and your daughters shall prophesy,
your old men shall dream dreams, your young men shall see
visions: and also upon the servants and upon the handmaids
in those days will I pour out my spirit.

JOEL 2:28-29

See in Acts 2 what happened on the Day of Pentecost to the disciples themselves, these apostles and the other people. Something so extraordinary happened that to certain people standing there they appeared to be drunk. They said, "This is nothing but drunkenness—this is sheer madness." And this charge of madness has often been brought forward. But then consider the apostle's explanation of these remarkable phenomena.

He says, "This is that which was spoken by the prophet Joel." This is what Joel said would happen. "And it shall come to pass afterward, that I will pour out my spirit upon all flesh." The Spirit had been *given* before, but He had not been *poured out* before. Previously, a man here, and another man there; now, "I will pour out." It will be something overwhelming; it will be something *en masse*, as it were. "I will pour out my spirit upon all flesh; and your sons and your daughters shall prophesy, your old men shall dream dreams, your young men shall see visions: and also upon the servants and upon the handmaids in those days will I pour out my spirit."

This happened to the mill girls in Northern Ireland. Poor girls who had been brought up in poverty and penury, who were ignorant and had had practically no education, suddenly began to prophesy. They displayed amazing knowledge and were able to speak in an unusual manner. Does it not rather look as if the prophet Joel had anticipated this and prophesied that it was going to happen? Young men, young women, visions, dreams, prophecies, old men dreaming dreams—"That is what is happening," said Peter.

☙ A THOUGHT TO PONDER ☙
It will be something overwhelming; it will be something *en masse*.

From *Revival*, pp. 143-144.

TRANCES

I was in a trance.

ACTS 22:17

We read in Acts 10:10-12 that the apostle Peter was upon a certain housetop and that he was in a trance, and that in this trance he had a vision of a sheet sent down from heaven full of various beasts. Again we read in Acts 16 that the apostle Paul wanted to go and preach in Asia, but the Spirit prohibited him. He than wanted to go to Bithynia, but the Spirit would not let him. And then he had a vision in the night of the man of Macedonia, with his cry for help. We also read in Acts 22 that he says, "I was in a trance."

Let us be careful lest, with our scientific friends, we be found to deny the Scriptures. When the Spirit comes upon a man, he may be in a trance. Then you have only to read 1 Corinthians 12—14 to see that there were all kinds of phenomena in the church of Corinth, and the apostle had to instruct them and guide them and restrain them and tell them that everything must be done decently and in order. There, then, is the testimony of the Scripture.

What then is our attempt at an explanation, and what are our conclusions? Let me put them in a series of propositions to you. Does it not seem clear and obvious that in this way God is calling attention to Himself and His own work by unusual phenomena? There is nothing that attracts such attention as this kind of thing, and it is used of God in the extension of His kingdom to attract, to call the attention of people. I am sure there is that element.

But second, we must never forget that the Holy Spirit affects the whole person. Man reacts as a whole. And it is just folly to expect that he can react in the realm of the spiritual without anything at all happening to the rest of him—to the soul and to the body.

❧ A THOUGHT TO PONDER ❧
The Holy Spirit affects the whole person.

THE FIRST STAGE IN REVIVAL

And the Lord said unto Moses, Depart, and go up hence, thou and the people . . . for I will not go up in the midst of thee; for thou art a stiffnecked people: lest I consume thee in the way.

EXODUS 33:1, 3

God's reply to Moses is in effect, "I have given this promise to these people, that they shall go to that land of promise, that land of Canaan, which is flowing with milk and honey. And, therefore, I tell you now, you lead them up. *You* take them to the land of promise. In view of what they have done, I am no longer coming up with you."

That, then, is the position. And what is of such great interest to us is the reaction of Moses and the Church to this. This is always the first stage in revival. You see the position they were in—their sin, God's pronouncement, God's judgment upon it. And the first stage, the first step, in revival is, as we see here, a realization of the position.

These people who had rebelled and turned their backs on God, who had blasphemed His name and had criticized His servant Moses, who had caused Aaron to make the calf and had worshiped it, and who had sinned, suddenly they were stopped short. They realized something, at any rate, of the situation they were in. Now obviously this is a matter of final importance. There is no hope of revival apart from this. It is an awakening to the situation. It is an awareness of the implications of what God has said: "He is going to withdraw His presence from us, and He has done so. The cloud has disappeared. The pillar of fire is no longer in evidence. God said He would withdraw, and God has withdrawn." There is a consciousness and a realization of His displeasure. I defy you to read the history of the revivals—you will find at once that without a single exception this always happens.

❧ A THOUGHT TO PONDER ❧

The first step in revival is a realization of sin.

From *Revival*, pp. 152-153.

FORSAKING SIN

And when the people heard these evil tidings, they mourned: and no man did put on him his ornaments. For the LORD had said unto Moses, Say unto the children of Israel, Ye are a stiffnecked people: I will come up into the midst of thee in a moment, and consume thee: therefore now put off thy ornaments from thee, that I may know what to do unto thee. And the children of Israel stripped themselves of their ornaments by the mount Horeb.

EXODUS 33:4-6

We have not repented truly until we have done that. It means that having had this profound realization of our sinfulness, especially in His sight, our one desire now is to do everything we can that is well pleasing in His sight. And that means forsaking sin and doing His commandments: "Put off thy ornaments"—and the children of Israel stripped themselves of their ornaments. Yes, it was these ornaments that had led to their downfall. These were like the things out of which the golden calf had been made. And they hated the very thought of the whole thing. God says, "Strip yourselves of them." And they stripped themselves.

You have only to read Christian biographies and the story of revivals to see exactly what I mean. There is always this stripping. Men and women are aware that they have been doing things they should not do. Not very harmful things perhaps in and of themselves, but they stand between them and God, so they must go. Ornaments vanish. The people strip themselves. And they give themselves to God in a new consecration and in a new dedication.

This, I say again, is the very essence of repentance. But we realize that we must act. We have to take some steps. Every one of us has to be stripped of something. When a man realizes his sinfulness and sees that the state of the Church is due to the fact that he and others like him are so sinful, a true repentance will lead each one to such an examination.

✒ A THOUGHT TO PONDER ✑

The people give themselves to God in a new consecration and in a new dedication.

From *Revival*, pp. 159-160.

REVIVAL OFTEN STARTS WITH ONE PERSON

And Moses took the tabernacle, and pitched it without the camp,
afar off from the camp, and called it the Tabernacle of the
congregation . . . which was without the camp.

EXODUS 33:7

Here is profound teaching. This Tabernacle was a kind of tent that Moses set up in the middle of the congregation, in the middle of the camp of Israel, where he and others would pray, a "tent of meeting" where people might go together to meet with God. The tent of meeting—it is such a significant and such a wonderful term. The Nonconformist fathers generally referred to their places of worship as meeting houses, and it is a good old term. You see, it is a place not so much where people meet with one another, though that is included, but the essential meaning is this—the place where they meet with God.

It is important that we should understand that Moses was clearly led to take this peculiar action. He took this Tabernacle out of the center of the camp and put it outside, far off from the camp. This was an action taken by Moses himself. And I must pause with that, because you will always find as you read the history of these movements of the Spirit in the long story of the Christian Church that generally the very first thing that happens, and which eventually leads to a great revival, is that one man, or a group of men, suddenly begin to feel this burden, and they feel the burden so much that they are led to do something about it.

Martin Luther, a very ordinary kind of monk, suddenly became aware of this burden. And it so burdened him that he was led to do something about it. Just one man, and through that one man, God sent that mighty movement to the Church.

⚘ A THOUGHT TO PONDER ⚘

Generally one man suddenly begins to feel this burden, and he feels the burden so much that he is led to do something about it.

From *Revival*, pp. 162-163.

DRAWING ASIDE

*And Moses took the tabernacle, and pitched it without the camp,
afar off from the camp, and called it the
Tabernacle of the congregation.*

EXODUS 33:7

Moses set the Tabernacle up outside the camp—"afar off from the camp." Now here is the point at which I am most liable to be misunderstood, but it is here, and it is part of the teaching. There is invariably, in the history of every revival, this drawing aside. Let us not forget that the camp of Israel was then the Church of God. In the Old Testament the nation of Israel was the Church in the wilderness. This is the Church we are talking about, and yet you see what Moses did? He took this tabernacle from the midst of the Church as it were and put it up outside, "afar off from the camp."

No revival that has ever been experienced in the long history of the Church has ever been an official movement in the Church. That is a strong statement, is it not? But I repeat it. No revival that the Church has ever known has ever been an official movement. You read of the great precursors of the Protestant Reformation, people like Wycliffe, Jan Hus, and others. It was always unofficial, and the officials did not like it. It was the same with Martin Luther. Nothing happened in Rome. No; it happened just to this monk in his cell. And so it has continued to happen.

Even after the reformation of the Church of England, there were men who began to feel dissatisfied, and they began to follow this pattern and do the self-same thing. That is the origin of Puritanism. Then you are all probably familiar with the story of Methodism in its various branches. The two Wesley brothers and Whitefield and others were members of the Church of England. But they did not begin to do something in the Church of England but formed what they called their Holy Club, outside the camp.

✎ A THOUGHT TO PONDER ✎

No revival that has ever been experienced in the Church has ever been an official movement in the Church.

CONSECRATION

*And Moses took the tabernacle, and pitched it without the camp,
afar off from the camp, and called it the Tabernacle of the
congregation. And it came to pass, that every one which sought
the LORD went out unto the tabernacle of the congregation,
which was without the camp.*

EXODUS 33:7

There is another element in revival that I must emphasize. It is clear
that in putting the Tabernacle outside the camp, Moses had another
motive and a very important one. It is this whole idea of consecration. Moses felt that this could not be done in the midst of the camp.
The camp had become unclean, and he deliberately took the
Tabernacle out, "afar off from the camp." It was a very deliberate
action. But by doing it, he said in effect, "We must do this thing in
God's way; we must get out of the impurity and this sinful atmosphere. We must get together here instead." Yes, that is consecration. That is, if you like, the call to holiness.

I am suggesting to you that the history of every revival brings out
this same factor in exactly the same way. What is it that has happened to these men whom God has used? Take any one of them,
and you will find almost invariably that their first concern has not
been the state of the Church—it has been the state of their own souls.
It has been the holiness of God. The Methodists said, "We must meet
to study the Scriptures together, we must pray together, and we
must live methodically in everything." Methodists, yes; but what
they were searching for was holiness. And that has always been
God's way. One man or a number of men suddenly become awakened to their distance from God, to the fact that they are in a far
country. And their first concern is to be holy as God is holy, and to
come into His presence, and to know His glory.

❧ A THOUGHT TO PONDER ❧

Their first concern has not been the state of the Church—it has
been the state of their own souls.

From *Revival*, pp. 168-169.

LOOKING ON

And it came to pass, when Moses went out unto the tabernacle,
that all the people rose up, and stood every man at his tent door,
and looked after Moses, until he was gone into the tabernacle.
EXODUS 33:8

I am rather interested in what we are told about the remainder of the people. They say that Moses and one or two individuals used to go out of the camp to the Tabernacle to pray. In Exodus 33:8 we read, "And it came to pass, when Moses went out unto the tabernacle, that all the people rose up, and stood every man at his tent door, and looked after Moses, until he was gone into the tabernacle."

There is something very wonderful about this. All they did was to look on with interest. They were aware that something was happening, but they did not know what it was, and they did not understand it. They did not go out of the camp with Moses into the tent of meeting with God and pray and intercede. All they knew was that Moses had taken the tent outside the camp and that he and certain others periodically visited it. So they just stood at their tent doors, watching Moses as he went and talking about him, wondering what he was doing and what exactly was happening. Now the appalling thing is that the right place for the tent was in the midst of the camp. But it was not there.

As you read the history of the Church, you will find this repeated. At first just a few people feel the call and separate themselves, and then the others begin to say, "What is happening to so and so? Have you heard about this man or that woman?" They stand at their tent doors, and they look on. They have a feeling that something is happening. But they do nothing at all. Oh, if we wait until the whole Church moves, revival will never happen.

❧ A THOUGHT TO PONDER ☙

If we wait until the whole Church moves, revival will never happen.

A DEEPER KNOWLEDGE OF GOD

. . . that I may know thee.

EXODUS 33:13

Moses was not content with a mere knowledge of the fact that he was accepted by God and that he was in God's care. He knew that, but he was not content with it; he wanted more. "That I may know thee," said Moses. He wanted a personal knowledge of God. He wanted a direct knowledge of God.

And here is something that you will find in the lives of all the great saints of God in the Church throughout the ages. The first thing that happens to them is that they themselves feel this desire for a deeper knowledge of God. They begin to feel a hunger and thirst for something bigger and something deeper. They are no longer content with what I may call the ordinary condition of the Church. They want something extraordinary, something unusual.

Let me give you some lines from a hymn that seem to me to put it very well indeed.

> *Speak, I pray thee, gentle Jesus;*
> *Oh, how passing sweet, thy words,*
> *Breathing o'er my troubled spirit,*
> *Peace, which never earth affords.*

And then it goes on to say:

> *Tell me thou art mine, O Savior;*
> *Grant me an assurance clear. . . .*
> WILLIAM WILLIAMS

That is the thing. He knows that the Savior loves him. But you see what he wants:

> *Tell me thou art mine, O Savior.*

Only the man who knows the Savior's love asks Him for that. Here is a man asking for something special, something unusual, something additional.

❧ A THOUGHT TO PONDER ❧

They feel a desire for a deeper knowledge of God.

From *Revival*, pp. 177-178.

THE PRAYER FOR POWER

Now therefore, I pray thee, if I have found grace in thy sight,
show me now thy way, that I may know thee, that I may find
grace in thy sight: and consider that this nation is thy people.
And he said, My presence shall go with thee, and I will give thee
rest. And he said unto him, If thy presence go not with me,
carry us not up hence.

EXODUS 33:13-15

In Moses' prayer he prayed for power. God said to Moses, "My presence shall go with thee, and I will give thee rest." And Moses said to God, "If thy presence go not with me, carry us not up hence."

This prayer for power is always in evidence in the history of the Church prior to revival. This is the end of which the intercessors always become most conscious, and there are many reasons for this. The first, of course, was the Israelites' awareness of the magnitude of the problem confronting them, the strength of the enemy that they were going to meet, the powerful nations in the land of promise—the Amalekites and others—and the tremendous task of occupying a land. Here they were, just a kind of nomadic people traveling along like this, and they were going to settle a land and conquer it and make their homes there. And suddenly they became aware of the immensity of the problem.

I have to emphasize this because to me there is nothing so tragic about our position today as the obvious failure of so many people to realize the magnitude of the problem that confronts us. If we only realized the magnitude of the problem, there would be no need to urge prayer for revival. But our eyes seem to be shut. "Everything is going well," we say. "Look at the reports. Marvelous. Look at the activities. Is all not well?"

✎ A THOUGHT TO PONDER ✐

Prayer for power is always in evidence in the history of the Church prior to revival.

From *Revival*, p. 180.

SPECIAL AUTHENTICATION

*For wherein shall it be known here that I and thy people have
found grace in thy sight? is it not in that thou goest with us?
so shall we be separated, I and thy people, from all the people
that are upon the face of the earth.*

EXODUS 33:16

Moses prayed for a special authentication of the Church and her
mission. This is the message of Exodus 33:16. You can hear him
argue. "Wherein," he said—"For wherein shall it be known here
that I and thy people have found grace in thy sight? is it not in that
thou goest with us? so shall we be separated, I and thy people, from
all the people that are upon the face of the earth."

In other words, this is a prayer that the Church should be as
she is meant to be. The Church is meant to be separate. The Church
is meant to be unique. "Now," said Moses to God, "I am asking
for this something extra, because I am concerned. Here are we, Thy
people. How are all the other nations to know that we really are
Your people? They are looking on at us; they are laughing at us,
mocking us, and jeering at us; they are ready to overwhelm us. Now
I am asking for something," said Moses, "that will make it
absolutely clear that we are not just one of the nations of the world,
but that we are Thy people, that we are separate, unique, altogether
apart."

The prayer for revival, then, is the prayer that the Church may
again become like that. And my argument is that nothing but some
unusual outpouring of the Spirit of God can do that. What is needed
is something that cannot be explained in human terms. What is
needed is something that is so striking and so extraordinary that it
will arrest the attention of the whole world. That is revival.

✎ A THOUGHT TO PONDER ✐

This is a prayer that the Church should be as she is meant to be.

From *Revival*, pp. 182-183.

June 23

WHAT TO PRAY FOR IN REVIVAL

*Searching what, or what manner of time the Spirit of Christ
which was in them did signify, when it testified beforehand the
sufferings of Christ, and the glory that should follow.
Unto whom it was revealed, that not unto themselves, but
unto us they did minister the things, which are now reported
unto you by them that have preached the gospel unto you with
the Holy Ghost sent down from heaven.*

1 PETER 1:11-12

Consider God's unusual attestation, this indication that the Church is His, that it is His power that is within her, that she is unique, that this is not of men. A man can preach without the Holy Spirit. We need the demonstration of the Spirit and of power. "The Holy Ghost [was] sent down from heaven"—the descent of power, this uniqueness, this special manifestation of the presence and of the power of God. That is always the most urgent petition in the mouths and on the lips of those who see the position as it is and who see the need of revival—"Authenticate Thy word. Lord God, let it be known beyond a doubt that we are Thy people. Shake us!" I do not ask Him to shake the building, but I ask Him to shake us.

It is clear that revival is nothing that man can produce or organize; it is plain that it is an act of God. God authenticating His people, their work, and their message, and saying, "Yes, these are My people. And I am doing something in their midst that I never will do among anyone but My own people." Are we clear that the prayer for revival is not the prayer for regular blessing on the work—we must always go on doing that—it is the prayer for the unusual on top of it, in addition to it, something special, something that authenticates God and His work among His people.

✎ A THOUGHT TO PONDER ✎

Revival is nothing that man can produce or organize; it is an act of God.

From *Revival*, pp. 185-186.

THE REAL REASONS FOR REVIVAL: THE GLORY OF GOD

And the LORD said unto Moses, I have seen this people, and, behold, it is a stiffnecked people: Now therefore let me alone, that my wrath may wax hot against them, and that I may consume them: and I will make of thee a great nation. And Moses besought the LORD his God, and said, LORD, why doth thy wrath wax hot against thy people, which thou hast brought forth out of the land of Egypt with great power, and with a mighty hand?

EXODUS 32:9-11

You see Moses' concern? He is concerned about the name—that is, the reputation and the glory—of God. And that is the point he is making here. "This nation," he says, "is Thy people." He is saying, in effect, that God's honor and God's glory is involved in this situation. They are, after all, His people; they have claimed that, He has given indications of that, and He has brought them out of Egypt in a marvelous and a miraculous manner. He has brought them through the Red Sea. Is He going to leave them here in the wilderness? What will the Egyptians say? What will the other nations say? Has He failed? He promised them great things. Can He not execute them? Can He not bring them to fulfillment?

Moses is suggesting to God that His own glory, His own honor, is involved in this whole situation. Now you will find this plea endlessly in the Psalms. You will find it constantly in the prophets. Their prayer to God is, "for Thine own name's sake," as if to say, "We have no right to speak, but for the sake of Thine eternal honor." Moses thus had a concern for and was jealous about the name and the glory of God. And here he is asking God, for His own sake, to do this extra, this special, thing.

❧ A THOUGHT TO PONDER ☙

Moses was concerned about the name and the glory of God.

From *Revival*, pp. 188-189.

THE REAL REASON FOR REVIVAL: THE HONOR OF THE CHURCH

Yet now, if thou wilt forgive their sin . . .
EXODUS 32:32

The second real reason for revival—and it must always come in the second place, never in the first—is a concern about the honor of the Church itself. In Exodus 33 there is nothing more wonderful than the way in which Moses shows his concern for the Church, which was then the nation of Israel. God had been giving Moses some wonderful intimations of His loving interest in him, but Moses is not content with that. Moses does not merely seek personal blessings. He wants to make sure that the children of Israel, as a whole, are going to be involved in this blessing.

He is given again a wonderful example of that in Exodus 32, one of the most glorious passages in the Old Testament. "And it came to pass on the morrow, that Moses said unto the people, Ye have sinned a great sin: and now I will go up unto the LORD; peradventure I shall make an atonement for your sin. And Moses returned unto the LORD, and said, Oh, this people have sinned a great sin, and have made them gods of gold. Yet . . ." It is as if he breaks down and cannot speak any longer. He is in great agony of soul. "Yet now, if thou wilt forgive their sin— . . ." He pauses and then he is able to speak: "and if not, blot me, I pray thee, out of thy book which thou hast written" (Exodus 32:30-32). "I do not want to go on living," he says in essence, "if You are not going to include them in the blessing."

God had said, "I am going to blot out this people—I am going to make a nation out of you."

"No," says Moses, "blot me out as well. I do not want to go on without them."

Oh, this is true intercession. The man is concerned about the state of the whole Church.

❧ A THOUGHT TO PONDER ❧
Moses is concerned about the state of the whole Church.

From *Revival*, pp. 191-192.

THE REAL REASONS FOR REVIVAL: OUTSIDERS

For wherein shall it be known here that I and thy people have found grace in thy sight? is it not in that thou goest with us? so shall we be separated, I and thy people, from all the people that are upon the face of the earth.

EXODUS 33:16

The third reason Moses gives for revival is his concern about the heathen who are outside: "For wherein shall it be known here [in the wilderness, where we are] that I and thy people have found grace in thy sight? is it not in that thou goest with us? so shall we be separated, I and thy people, from all the people that are upon the face of the earth."

We have considered the three motives in praying for revival. For the name and the honor and glory of God and for the sake of the Church that is His. Yes, and then for the sake of those people who are outside, who are scoffing, mocking, jeering, laughing, and ridiculing. "Oh, God," say His people one after another, "arise and silence them. Do something so that we may be able to say to them, 'Be still, keep silent, give up.'"

"Be still, and know that I am God" (Psalm 46:10). That is the prayer of the people of God. They have their eye on those who are outside. Moses is praying for these people, that they may be stopped short and apprehended and may develop an interest in which God is leading them and is directing them. This should make us ask, therefore, whether we are concerned at all about these people who are outside. It is a terrible state for the Church to be in when she merely consists of a collection of very nice and respectable people who have no concern for the world.

☙ A THOUGHT TO PONDER ☙
It is a terrible state for the Church to be in when she has no concern for the world.

"AS ON US AT THE BEGINNING"

And the Spirit bade me go with them, nothing doubting. Moreover
these six brethren accompanied me, and we entered into the man's
house: And he showed us how he had seen an angel in his house,
which stood and said unto him, Send men to Joppa, and call for
Simon, whose surname is Peter; who shall tell thee words,
whereby thou and all thy house shall be saved. And as I began to
speak, the Holy Ghost fell on them, as on us at the beginning.

ACTS 11:12-15

Notice that Peter says the Holy Ghost fell on Cornelius and his
household "as on us at the beginning." He said in essence, "The
same thing happened to them as happened to us on the Day of
Pentecost." In other words, the baptism of the Holy Ghost took
place on the Day of Pentecost, but it also took place later upon
Cornelius and his household. That is exactly Peter's argument:
"Then remembered I the word of the Lord, how that he said, John
indeed baptized with water; but ye shall be baptized with the Holy
Ghost. Forasmuch then as God gave them the like gift"—the same
gift, you see—"as he did unto us, who believed on the Lord Jesus
Christ; what was I, that I could withstand God?" And he repeats
the same argument in Acts 15.

So, then, I do trust we are clear about this and see that we really
must cease to say that what happened on the Day of Pentecost happened once and for all. It did not; it was simply the first of a series.
I am ready to admit that you cannot repeat the first. But that is
nothing; what matters is the thing that happened. And the thing
that happened at Pentecost happened later in exactly the same way
while Peter was preaching to Cornelius and his household. The Holy
Ghost fell upon them as He had fallen upon those people in the
upper room in Jerusalem.

☙ A THOUGHT TO PONDER ☙

The Holy Ghost fell upon them as He had fallen upon those people
in the upper room.

From *Revival*, p. 200.

WHAT HAPPENS IN REVIVAL? PART 1

And when the day of Pentecost was fully come, they were all with one accord in one place. And suddenly there came a sound from heaven as of a rushing mighty wind, and it filled all the house where they were sitting.

ACTS 2:1-2

Consciousness of a power and of a presence is sometimes physical, as it was here in the "sound . . . of a rushing mighty wind." It is not always physical, but it has often been so in revivals. But what believers are always conscious of is the sudden awareness of a glorious presence in their midst, such as they have never known before—a sense of power and a sense of glory.

It may be accompanied by phenomena, as it was here: "cloven tongues like as of fire," speaking with tongues. These things are not always repeated. Sometimes this sense of power and glory is so great that people are prostrated to the ground by reason of it. As you hear of people literally fainting when they suddenly get a piece of good news that they have not expected, so when men and women experience this glorious presence, sometimes it is too much for their physical frame. We must not stay with these things, but they do emphasize the sense of God, the presence and the presidency of the Holy Ghost.

In any record of great men of the Church who have given an account of how they have passed through times of revival, you will always find that what they experience is that they no longer merely have a belief in God—God has become a reality to them. God has come down, as it were, into their midst. In revivals the meeting is sometimes taken out of the hands of whoever may have been in charge, and the Holy Ghost begins to preside and to take charge, and everybody is aware of His presence and His glory and His power. That is what happened on the Day of Pentecost. That is what happens, in some measure and to some extent, in every revival that the Church has ever known.

✍ A THOUGHT TO PONDER ✍

They no longer merely have a belief in God—God has become a reality to them.

WHAT HAPPENS IN REVIVAL? PART 2

And they were all filled with the Holy Ghost, and began to speak
with other tongues, as the Spirit gave them utterance.

ACTS 2:4

In a revival the Church is given great assurance concerning the truth. She does not have to investigate the truth or set up a commission to look into it. She is given an absolute certainty about it. That is the thing that comes out so clearly in the story in Acts. Take these men, these apostles. You remember how a few weeks before, after the crucifixion, they were very shaken and most uncertain. They had come to a belief in the Lord Jesus Christ, and they had come to see that He was the Messiah; but then He was crucified, and they were shattered and confused in their minds.

You will find, in the last chapter of John's Gospel, that they were just talking to one another when Peter suddenly said, "I will go fishing. I must do something to relieve this; it is too miserable; it is impossible." And the others said, "We will go with you."

You cannot imagine a more dejected picture. They were shaken and uncertain about everything. And then the Lord appeared to them, and He taught them. Ah, yes, this certainly put them in a better condition. But it was only after what happened to them on the Day of Pentecost that they were filled with assurance and understanding and immediately began to speak to the people about the wonderful works of God. Never again was there any doubt; never again was there any difficulty about understanding.

Take Peter himself; look at the sermon that he preached on that occasion. He was absolutely certain and assured. That is something that is absolutely universal in times of revival.

❧ A THOUGHT TO PONDER ❧

Never again was there any doubt; never again was there any difficulty about understanding.

From *Revival*, pp. 204-205.

WHAT HAPPENS IN REVIVAL? PART 3

*And they, continuing daily with one accord in the temple, and
breaking bread from house to house, did eat their meat with
gladness and singleness of heart, praising God, and having
favour with all the people.*

ACTS 2:46-47

The next thing I notice is that the Church is filled with great joy
and a sense of praise. Read again the terms used toward the end of
Acts chapter 2. "And they, continuing daily with one accord in the
temple, and breaking bread from house to house, did eat their meat
with gladness and singleness of heart, praising God, and having
favour with all the people." Now that is how the Christian Church
is meant to be. Great joy, great praise to the Lord Jesus Christ and
to God, glorying in this great salvation, in the new life they have
received, and in this sense of heaven.

It is but the simple pattern of what has been repeated so frequently when God has poured out His Spirit upon the Church. I
never tire of quoting something I remember reading in the journals
of George Whitefield. He was preaching on one occasion in
Cheltenham, England, and he said, "Suddenly the Lord came down
amongst us." Do we know anything about that? Do we believe in
that sort of thing or that it is possible? Now George Whitefield,
even at his worst, was probably the greatest preacher this country
[England] has ever known. But there were variations, even in his
ministry. On this occasion he was surprised himself. There he was,
preaching and having a very good service, when suddenly he knew
that the Lord had come down among them. That is the wonderful
thing, and it resulted in great joy, praise, and thanksgiving. When the
Church is in a state of revival you do not have to exhort people to
praise—you cannot stop them, they are so filled with God.

✎ A THOUGHT TO PONDER ✎

When the Church is in a state of revival you do not have to exhort
people to praise—you cannot stop them.

July

THE KINGDOM OF GOD

FROM

The Kingdom of God

AND

Why Does God Allow War?

PREACHING

Now after that John was put in prison, Jesus came into Galilee,
preaching the gospel of the kingdom of God.

MARK 1:14

The word *preaching* came in this way. When a son and heir was born to the emperor, a proclamation was made, and the word that was used for that very process was the word translated "preaching." It was an announcement; it happened when the heir was born, when he came of age, and at his accession to the throne or to the imperial power. So what we are told here is that when John the Baptist was put in prison, Jesus came into Galilee announcing, proclaiming, heralding. It was the particular work of the herald to do this very thing.

The word *preaching* is interesting, therefore, because it at once conveys this notion and idea. A herald does not make an uncertain announcement or get up and blow his trumpet and say, "Listen, we do not quite know what's happening or what is going to take place, but—well, we hope that something is going to happen!" That is not heralding! No; the herald has a definite, specific message, and that is why he gets up and blows his trumpet. "Listen," he says, "I have something to tell you." Now that is the term that is used here about what our Lord did. It is also the term that is used about what the apostles did afterwards, and it is the word that has been used about preaching in the Christian Church ever since.

So you see we start with a note of certainty, issued from the Imperial Palace. That was the first word uttered, not just a man getting up and saying, "Well, my opinion is that before long there will be an announcement." No! He stood up with a bit of paper in his hand and said, "Issued by the Imperial Palace at such and such a time, we have the honor to inform you . . ." That is it. Preaching—the very word carries with it the whole notion of authority, an absolute unequivocal statement.

✎ A THOUGHT TO PONDER ✎

Jesus came into Galilee announcing, proclaiming, heralding.

From *The Kingdom of God*, pp. 11-12.

July 2

ANNOUNCING THE PLAN

We speak the wisdom of God in a mystery, even the hidden wisdom, which God ordained before the world unto our glory.
1 CORINTHIANS 2:7

Christian preaching announces a plan and a purpose. "Where do you find that?" asks someone. Well, look at Mark 1:14: "Now after that John was put in prison, Jesus came into Galilee, preaching the gospel of the kingdom of God, and saying, The time is fulfilled." The Bible says that God had made this plan even before the foundation of the world itself. The apostle Paul says in 1 Corinthians 2:7, "We speak the wisdom of God in a mystery, even the hidden wisdom, which God ordained before the world unto our glory." That is it. That is the essence of this proclamation that is being made, the essence of Christian preaching. It does not say to us, "There is truth in that uncharted ocean—get out onto it, take your soundings, try to get your bearings, try to find out. Yes, you have discovered a little bit! You may go for weeks and find nothing; months, years pass, then just another little glimmer. But at last . . . ah, it won't happen in your time; it will happen perhaps in your grandchildren's, or it may be even longer than that. But go on, it is marvelous, keep on."

No! Christian preaching is the exact opposite to that. The message of the Bible is not to urge us to try to find truth; it is to ask us to listen to the truth, to God's truth. For its whole point is to say that God, knowing Himself, knowing man, knowing everything, has devised and schemed a plan whereby men and women can be delivered out of their failure and sin and can be made citizens and worthy citizens of God's kingdom. This is God's plan!

We are also told that God made this plan known. "God . . . hath in these last days spoken unto us by his Son" (Hebrews 1:1-2).

❧ A THOUGHT TO PONDER ☙

The message of the Bible is to ask us to listen to the truth, to God's truth.

From *The Kingdom of God*, pp. 14-15.

GOD ACTING IN HISTORY

We do hear them speak in our tongues the wonderful
works of God.

ACTS 2:11

God's plan is carried out by His acting in history. This is a vital point. Christianity is not primarily teaching; it is a recorded history. Christianity is not urging men to think and to try to delve into the mystery and to discover the truth about God. It says, "Listen, this is what God has done." Is that not what happened on the Day of Pentecost in Jerusalem? Is that not what the people said about the apostles when they began to speak with other tongues? "What is this?" they said. "We do hear them speak in our tongues"—what?— "the wonderful works of God." Not the thoughts of God but the works of God, the things that God has done.

And that is the message of Christianity. Here it is: "Now after that John was put in prison" (Mark 1:14); that is a fact of history, an event in time, just as Julius Caesar landed in Britain in 55 B.C. So at a given point in time John the Baptist was thrown into prison, and at that moment Jesus came into Galilee, preaching the Gospel of the kingdom of God and saying, "The time is fulfilled." "Listen to Me," He said, "it has happened, it has come." Now what does this mean? It means that your salvation and mine depends not upon our thoughts, nor upon our discovery of truth, but entirely and utterly upon something that has literally happened in this world almost two thousand years ago.

So we preach to this atomic age, and this is what we say—not "Come and join us on the unchartered ocean, and help us take soundings in order that we may arrive ultimately." No; we say, "Look back, look back; go back two thousand years, to the first century. Listen: 'When John was thrown into prison Jesus came and said . . .'" That is it. In other words, our salvation depends not upon our understanding but upon what God has done in Christ.

✎ A THOUGHT TO PONDER ✎

Our salvation depends not upon our understanding but upon what God has done in Christ.

July 4

ENTERING GOD'S KINGDOM

*. . . not imputing their trespasses unto them . . . For he hath
made him to be sin for us.*

2 CORINTHIANS 5:19, 21

You cannot live in God's kingdom unless you are a worthy citizen.
How, then, can you enter? Christ is the answer. This is the Good
News, that He bore our sins "in his own body on the tree, that we,
being dead to sins, should live unto righteousness" (1 Peter 2:24).
Here is the message: "God was in Christ, reconciling the world
unto himself, not imputing their trespasses unto them. . . . For he
hath made him to be sin for us, who knew no sin; that we might be
made the righteousness of God in him" (2 Corinthians 5:19, 21).
And thereby by dying on the cross, He has opened the gateway into
the kingdom, and He says, "Today is the day of salvation—enter in."
"Come unto me, all ye that labour and heavy laden, and I will give
you rest" (Matthew 11:28).

"The time is fulfilled" (Mark 1:15). The time promised so long
ago has arrived; the kingdom of God has drawn near, has come. He
says, "I am the King; come unto Me just as you are." Thank God you
do not have to put yourself right first; you do not have to understand
the profundity first; you do not have to set out on some great quest.
You may have to die very soon, and your question is, "How can I
stand before God? How can I know that I am going to heaven and
eternal bliss?"

And this is the answer: "The time is fulfilled; the kingdom has
come." The King is the Lord Jesus Christ, and He loved you so much
that He died for you and your sins, and all He says to you is,
"Repent, think again, believe My message." Repent and believe the
Gospel; acknowledge your folly and your sin, your shame, and your
helplessness. Stop making inquiries; stop setting out with your great
intellect to understand. Simply believe.

∾ A THOUGHT TO PONDER ∾
"I am the King; come unto Me just as you are."

From *The Kingdom of God*, pp. 23-24.

AN ALTOGETHER DIFFERENT TEACHING

Therefore take no thought, saying, What shall we eat? or,
What shall we drink? or, Wherewithal shall we be clothed?

MATTHEW 6:31

The Gospel seems to come as a challenge to us and as a condemnation of what we have habitually believed. Our Lord puts it like this. He says in Matthew 6:31, "Therefore take no thought, saying, What shall we eat? or, What shall we drink? or, Wherewithal shall we be clothed?" and then in verse 32, "For after all these things do the Gentiles seek." Now we must remember that He was preaching to Jews, to people who had received their Old Testament Scriptures, who regarded themselves as the people of God, and who were concerned about God and about righteousness. And the division of the ancient world to them, was, of course, Jews and Gentiles—those who had received this religion and those who had not.

And that is an equally appropriate classification in our day and age and generation. "The Gentiles" are those who do not know the revelation; they are people who trust to their own thoughts and their own ideas, who live as if God has never been pleased to reveal anything at all concerning Himself. So the division is as appropriate now as it ever has been; and the point I am making is that our Lord emphasizes the great fact that what He teaches is altogether different from everything that has ever been thought by man or conjured up in man's mind or imagination.

This, again, is a very important preliminary point that we must never lose sight of. The Christian position, the Christian way of life, is not only slightly different from every other—it is *essentially* different; it is something that stands out alone and unique and apart.

✎ A THOUGHT TO PONDER ✐

The Christian position stands out alone and unique and apart.

From *The Kingdom of God*, pp. 28-29.

A TOTALITARIAN DEMAND

Taste and see that the LORD is good.

PSALM 34:8

Christianity is a way of life. And it is a way of life that demands a total commitment; it is, if you like, a totalitarian demand. It does not merely ask that we consider it and say, "Oh yes, I can take on that teaching; that's a good emphasis there, I'll add that!" No; it is not something to be applied as we think and when and where. Jesus says, "Seek ye first."

In other words, let me put it like this: Men and women will never know the truth of Christianity or the blessings that it can give until they have given themselves to it. You can examine Christianity from the outside, but you will never know it, you will never get it. "If any man will do his will," says our Lord, "he shall know of the doctrine whether it be of God" (John 7:17).

Here is a great fundamental principle about this way of life: "Taste and see that the LORD is good" (Psalm 34:8). You will never know that the Lord is good until you have tasted Him, until you have tried Him. So many of us are like a man standing in an orchard, and there he looks at an apple tree or a pear tree, and he examines it at a distance. Somebody says, "You know, that has a most wonderful flavor. If only you would try it, you would say that it is the most wonderful fruit you've ever tasted in your life." But the man looks on, and he is not quite satisfied; he is not convinced, and he can argue and stay there for as long as he likes, but he will never know the fruit until he takes it and puts it in his mouth and bites it and proves it. "Taste and see that the LORD is good."

A theoretical examination of Christianity will never bring us anywhere. Our Lord always calls for a committal.

❧ A THOUGHT TO PONDER ❧

Christianity is a way of life that demands a total commitment.

From *The Kingdom of God*, pp. 31-32.

CLOTHES AND DURATION OF LIFE

*Which of you by taking thought can add one cubit
unto his stature?*

MATTHEW 6:27

There is this matter of clothing. "What shall we put on? How shall we appear before people?" The way to be happy is to impress people with your beauty or your greatness or this or that; your elegance! And immediately everybody looks at you with admiration; so you are perfectly happy, and you put your head on your pillow at night with great contentment; you have achieved your objective. Money, food, drink, clothing—these are the things, says our Lord, for which people live.

In other words, you see, He says that the tragedy of life is due to the fact that men and women are living and are thinking as if they were only bodies. The thought, the attention, the planning, the scheming, the thinking are all in the realm of the body. People conceive of themselves as if they were but animals. That is what animals do—they eat and drink and so on, and so do men and women. These are the things they talk about; as you see a peacock preening himself, so does a man and so does a woman. What they put on, the impression they make—they live for these things, says our Lord, and hence all the troubles.

And, of course, there is this other priority that He mentions, and that is the extension of your life in this world. He puts it in these words: "Which of you by taking thought can add one cubit unto his stature?" (Matthew 6:27). What that really means is, "Which of you by taking thought can add one inch, as it were, to the duration of your life?" But that is what people are interested in— to prolong life, and all the care and the thought and the attention that they put into that! I am not saying this is wrong. Certainly thank God for medicine, for the extension of life; but, says our Lord, do you make that your priority?

❧ A THOUGHT TO PONDER ❧

The tragedy of life is that men and women are living and are thinking as if they were only bodies.

From *The Kingdom of God*, pp. 34-35.

RIGHT THINKING

It is he that hath made us, and not we ourselves.

PSALM 100:3

Get right in your thinking about yourself; then think of yourself in your relationship to God. And the moment you do so, you will realize that you are utterly dependent upon Him. "It is he that hath made us, and not we ourselves." Our times and our breath are in His hand. God brought us into being, and He could end it in a moment. We, none of us, control life; God controls it all. But men and women do not stop and think about that. They say, "What shall I put on tonight? How shall I dress tomorrow?" They may be dead before tomorrow! But they do not think of that. The whole of life, for them, is without God; He does not enter into their calculations.

That is why the world is as it is, says our Lord. If only all men and women believed in God, they would all humble themselves before Him. If only the whole world believed in God, there would be no preparation for war, there would be no jealousy and envy and rivalry, because all men and women would be bowing before Him and worshiping Him and living to His glory and His praise. But because they do not, they set themselves up as gods, and they worship themselves. So there are barriers between nations. "I am going to be bigger," says one; so he makes a bigger bomb. "I will make a bigger one!" says the other. And up and up and up we go, and we get worse. "Whence come wars and fightings among you? Come they not hence, even of your lusts . . .? Ye ask, and receive not," says the apostle James (James 4:1, 3).

You will never satisfy your god, and so, according to the Bible, we get all the troubles in the world—individual troubles and collective troubles, national troubles and international troubles! All this rivalry is because we are not living as under the eye of an almighty God.

❧ A THOUGHT TO PONDER ❧

If only all men and women believed in God, they would all humble themselves before Him.

"An Uncertain Sound"

*For if the trumpet give an uncertain sound, who shall
prepare himself to the battle?*

1 CORINTHIANS 14:8

The apostle Paul says to the Corinthians, "If the trumpet give an uncertain sound, who shall prepare himself to the battle?" If the sound is uncertain, then we shall add to the confusion. And that is why nothing is more important than that we should be perfectly clear in our minds as to what this Christian message really is. What does Christianity offer to people; what is it? How can we become Christians? These are the questions that we must answer.

Furthermore, what makes this terrible confusion so utterly inexcusable, of course, is that we have an open Bible before us, and we have it in a language that we can understand. If we had no Bible but merely some oral tradition, then there would be some excuse for the confusion. Or if we only had the Bible in a language that we could not understand, again there would be considerable excuse. But that is not our position at all. So why is there any confusion? And there is only one answer to that question. It is because men and women, instead of taking the message as it is in the Bible, are imposing their own message upon it. They are approaching it with their philosophies, their theories, their ideas, and their attempts to understand; and they are bypassing what is stated in this Book that is open before them in a language that all can understand.

So my plea is that in all honesty, apart from anything else, we must come back to the Bible. Here are the documents of the early Church; here are the records of how Christianity came into being, of what the Church taught at the beginning and something of what happened as the result of that. In particular we must come back to the words and to the teaching and the message of the Lord Jesus Christ Himself.

❧ A Thought to Ponder ❧
We must come back to the Bible.

From *The Kingdom of God*, p. 50.

THE KINGDOM OF GOD, PART 1

*And when he was demanded of the Pharisees, when
the kingdom of God should come, he answered them and said,
The kingdom of God cometh not with observation.*

LUKE 17:20

"The kingdom of God cometh not with observation." So, then, how does it come? What are the forms of the kingdom of God?

The kingdom of God comes, and came, with the very presence and power manifested by the Lord Jesus Christ Himself. There is a wonderful illustration of that in Luke 11:14-20: "And he was casting out a devil, and it was dumb. And it came to pass, when the devil was gone out, the dumb spake; and the people wondered. But some of them said, He casteth out devils through Beelzebub the chief of the devils. And others, tempting him, sought of him a sign from heaven. But he, knowing their thoughts, said unto them, Every kingdom divided against itself is brought to desolation; and a house divided against a house falleth. If Satan also be divided against himself, how shall his kingdom stand? because ye say that I cast out devils through Beelzebub. And if I by Beelzebub cast out devils, by whom do your sons cast them out? therefore shall they be your judges. But if I with the finger of God cast out devils, no doubt the kingdom of God is come upon you."

Now that is what I mean. The kingdom of God came when the Son of God was in this world. The kingdom of God is a manifestation of the power of God, a manifestation of the fact that God is superior to the elements of nature, that He is superior also to the devils and to everything that is evil. The kingdom of God is God's reign, and when Christ was here on earth, and when He worked His miracles and manifested His marvelous powers, He said, "This is the kingdom of God."

◈ A THOUGHT TO PONDER ◈

The kingdom of God is God's reign.

From *The Kingdom of God*, pp. 56-57.

THE KINGDOM OF GOD, PART 2

*The wolf also shall dwell with the lamb, and the leopard lie down
with the kid; and the calf and the young lion and the fatling
together; and a little child shall lead them.*

ISAIAH 11:6

The kingdom of God will come with great external pomp and glory,
and Christ will come to reign, to judge, and to set up His everlasting kingdom.

Let me give you Christ's own words: "Then answered Peter and
said unto him, Behold, we have forsaken all, and followed thee; what
shall we have therefore? And Jesus said unto them, Verily I say unto
you, That ye which have followed me, in the regeneration when the
Son of man shall sit in the throne of his glory, ye also shall sit upon
twelve thrones, judging the twelve tribes of Israel" (Matthew 19:27-
28). That is it. The Son of Man will come and sit in the throne of
His glory. This is "the regeneration," He says, and this is the great
message about the visible form of the kingdom that is to come. It
means that when all the elect have been gathered in, the Son of God
will return again into this world. He will set up the judgment throne,
and He will judge the whole world in righteousness. All who do
not believe in Him will be consigned to everlasting punishment with
the devil and all the evil angels, and they will be banished out of
His sight.

Then the whole world, the cosmos, will be purged of all evil.
Nature is now "red in tooth and claw," but it will not be so then:
"The wolf also shall dwell with the lamb, and the leopard lie down
with the kid; and the calf and the young lion and the fatling together;
and a little child shall lead them" (Isaiah 11:6). This is "the regeneration," and it is coming. Sin and evil will be banished; there will
be a realm of glory, and He will sit upon His throne in that glory, and
all who have believed in Him will be with Him forever and ever.

✒ A THOUGHT TO PONDER ✑
The cosmos will be purged of all evil.

From *The Kingdom of God*, pp. 60-61.

ENTERING THE KINGDOM

And he said unto me, It is done. I am Alpha and Omega,
the beginning and the end.
REVELATION 21:6

We must realize that Christ brings us into His kingdom by dying for us, by bearing our sins in His own body, by being made the Lamb of God for us; that He bears our punishment, and that He is our only way of deliverance and salvation. You believe it and you say:

> *Just as I am, without one plea*
> *But that Thy blood was shed for me,*
> *And that Thou bid'st me come to Thee,*
> *O Lamb of God, I come.*
> CHARLOTTE ELLIOTT

In other words, it means that you make an absolute, total surrender; you cast yourself entirely into His hands. You deny yourself, you take up your cross, and you follow Him. And if you do these things, the kingdom of God is within you. You have entered the kingdom, and the kingdom has entered you; you see that He is everything to you, and you are nothing. You see that Christ is "the Alpha and the Omega, the beginning and the end." "He is the lily of the valley: the bright and morning star. He is the fairest of ten thousand to my soul."

> *Thou, O Christ, art all I want;*
> *More than all in Thee I find.*
> CHARLES WESLEY

You just give yourself to Him and acknowledge Him as the Son of God and your personal Savior and Lord. Your one desire is to know Him, to be near Him, and to follow Him in order that you may be in glory with Him in the final regeneration when He comes at the end of time.

✒ A THOUGHT TO PONDER ✒

Your one desire is to know Him.

From *The Kingdom of God*, pp. 66-67.

A FALSE VIEW OF THE KINGDOM

The Pharisee stood and prayed thus with himself, God,
I thank thee, that I am not as other men are, extortioners, unjust,
adulterers, or even as this publican.

LUKE 18:11

Let me touch on an aspect of a false view of the kingdom of God. I refer to those who confuse Christianity with a kind of morality only. There are so many people who think of Christianity as if it were but a collection of vetoes and prohibitions and restraints. That was the trouble there in Rome. You should not eat this, you should not eat that, and all those other observances. And there they were, experts about these particular things. "No," says the apostle; "Christ did not come from heaven to earth for that reason; that's not Christianity!"

And we can interpret that at the present time in this way: It is to think that you make yourself a Christian by the way in which you live; that if you do not do certain things you are a Christian, but that if you do them, then you are not. So you do not do these things, and then, of course, you can criticize others; you can feel that you are better than they are, and so you look down upon them. That was the trouble with the Pharisee we read about in Luke 18: "I thank God I am not like other men. I fast twice in the week; I give a tenth of my goods to the poor. How good I am! Not like this miserable publican, this sinner fellow!" But that is not the kingdom of God; that is the precise opposite. But how common this idea is! How many people think of Christianity today as something that is purely negative, something that always makes demands of you, that tells you that if you are going to be a Christian you have got to stop this, that, and the other. And it goes no further and never tells you what Christianity gives you. So Christianity is confused with morality.

✎ A THOUGHT TO PONDER ✐

Christianity is confused with morality.

A JUDGMENT

Yea doubtless, and I count all things but loss for the
excellency of the knowledge of Christ Jesus my Lord:
for whom I have suffered the loss of all things, and
do count them but dung, that I may win Christ.

PHILIPPIANS 3:8

The apostle Paul was very proud of his achievements, all he had accomplished as Saul of Tarsus. But when he saw Christ, all he could say was, "I do count them but dung." "From him that hath not shall be taken away even that which he hath." He will arrive at the bar of eternal judgment with nothing at all, just his own miserable, sinful self—naked, empty, forlorn, and hopeless—and he will go on living like that forever and ever.

This word is a judgment. Do you have this vital thing or do you not? "But what can I do?" asks someone. "I see now that I am a fool. I hadn't realized that it was a mystery. I thought I knew what Christianity is, but I see now that it means being reconciled to God, being right for the judgment and for eternity. I know nothing about it—how can I get it?"

It is quite simple. Instead of shutting your eyes in blind prejudice, open them and pay attention to the message. Come as a little child, as a pauper. Come as you are, not to criticize, not to be clever, not to justify yourself; come and acknowledge that you have nothing. "Except ye be converted," says our Lord, "and become as little children, ye shall not enter into the kingdom of heaven" (Matthew 18:3). You need the simplicity of a little child. You need, in other words, an acknowledgment of your sin, of your utter failure. You have to come saying, "I am nothing. I have nothing. God have mercy upon me, a sinner."

☙ A THOUGHT TO PONDER ☙
You have to come saying, "I am nothing. I have nothing. God have mercy upon me, a sinner."

From *The Kingdom of God*, pp. 103-104.

POWER

For the kingdom of God is not in word, but in power.
1 CORINTHIANS 4:20

The apostle Paul tells us that whatever the kingdom of God may be, it is a power. Let us be clear about this. The Christian message is the proclamation of, and a history of, the greatest power that has ever entered into this world. There has been nothing that has so changed and affected the course of history and the lives of individuals as much as this message.

That is why we must always be careful to emphasize the fact that we are not concerned here primarily with a philosophy, but with a history. Jesus Christ dominates history; even the numbering of our years is acknowledged by His birth. He is, indeed, the biggest factor and the biggest power that history has ever known. The cross of Christ "towers o'er the wrecks of time."

There is no doubt but that Christianity is the most powerful influence that has ever entered into the life of the whole world. It has changed communities as well as changing men and women. How easy it would be to recount the story of some of the great revivals that have taken place in the history of the Christian Church. The great historian Lecky did not hesitate to say that what saved Britain from what was experienced by France at the time of the French Revolution was the evangelical or the so-called Methodist Revival of the eighteenth century. The effect of that revival is incalculable. It not only changed individuals but also whole communities. It gave people an interest in education, and schools came into being. It produced Sunday schools; it gave a stimulus to hospitals and medical care; it led to the reform of the poor law. All these things came out of that mighty visitation of the Spirit of God. Christianity is a power.

❧ A THOUGHT TO PONDER ❧
Whatever the kingdom of God may be, it is a power.

FACING DEATH

Henceforth there is laid up for me a crown of righteousness.
2 TIMOTHY 4:8

The kingdom of God gives us power even to look into the face of death and to smile at it. We go out of this world in triumph and in joy. Consider what Paul says; this is power, this is not just a talker, nor just a man who has been writing all his life. Here is a man who has known the power; so he says, "I have fought a good fight, I have finished my course, I have kept the faith: Henceforth there is laid up for me a crown of righteousness, which the Lord, the right-eous judge, shall give me at that day: and not to me only, but unto all them also that love his appearing" (2 Timothy 4:7-8).

So what about it? Have you known all this? This is Christianity; this is the kingdom of God, the power of God! Here, then, are the questions that we must ask ourselves. Do I know anything about this power of God? Is it obvious to those who live with me that the power of God is in me? Does my life show it? Are other people influenced by what they see? Can I say, "I am not ashamed of the gospel of Christ: for it is the power of God unto salvation to every one that believeth" (Romans 1:16)?

Has God made you anew? Do you know there is a new nature in you? If not, you are not a Christian; you are outside the king-dom of God, whatever your knowledge, whatever your interest may be. A Christian is a new creation born of the Spirit, born from above, born again—"not in word, but in power" (2 Corinthians 4:20). Have you known this? If you have, I need not exhort you to praise God! If you have not, then go to Him; tell Him you are dead and lifeless. Cry, "God have mercy upon me, a sinner."

❧ A THOUGHT TO PONDER ☙

A Christian is a new creation born of the Spirit, born from above, born again.

From *The Kingdom of God*, p. 119.

A WOULD-BE FOLLOWER

And he said unto another, Follow me. But he said, Lord,
suffer me first to go and bury my father.

LUKE 9:59

Here is someone whom our Lord invites to follow Him. "He said to another, Follow me. But he said, Lord, suffer me first to go and bury my father. Jesus said unto him, Let the dead bury their dead: but go thou and preach the kingdom of God" (Luke 9:59-60). Our Lord challenged him and said, "Follow me!" And the man, you remember, responded by saying, "All right, I am coming, but 'suffer me first to go and bury my father.'"

What is the principle here? Well, our Lord is teaching this man the urgency of entering the kingdom of God at once, without a moment's delay. You must be right in your understanding of it, and then you must enter it immediately. Now let us be clear about that. Our Lord's statement sounds terrible, does it not? On the surface it sounds as if He was refusing this man permission to go home to bury his poor father who was dying. But it does not mean anything of the sort. If this man's father had been ill and had died, the son would not be with the Lord. The Jews were strict about this.

The question was that this young man says, "Yes, I am going to be a Christian, but not just now. I will be a Christian later on, when I have time. I am very busy at the moment. I am at the top of the ladder. I have great success ahead of me. I am beginning in my profession, or in my trade, or in my industry. Not yet! Oh, I like this teaching! I believe it is right; but I cannot do anything about it now."

✎ A THOUGHT TO PONDER ✎

Our Lord is teaching this man the urgency of entering the kingdom of God at once, without a moment's delay.

THE LIFE OF THE SOUL

Jesus said unto him, Let the dead bury their dead:
but go thou and preach the kingdom of God.

LUKE 9:60

Some men and women can see that there is truth in the Christian message, but they are troubled by it and say, "Yes, of course that is what I really must do—but not yet." Take the prayer of Saint Augustine. He was not Saint Augustine when he prayed it; he was a brilliant philosopher, but he was troubled. He was listening to the preaching of Ambrose, that great preacher in Milan, and he was disturbed by it. He knew it was right and that he was wrong, but he was living with his mistress. And here, you see, is the fight and the conflict. He knew what was right; so he offered this prayer: "Lord, make me chaste: but not yet."

Do you know something about that? "I want to be good, but I also want to have this other thing. 'Suffer me first . . .'" How many have done this! "Let me make my name first. I do not believe in some of the things I am doing, but they have to be done, and once I have got on, then I will be a thorough Christian. I really will!" And so our Lord confronts this man immediately and shows him that he is all wrong, and He puts it in a very striking manner: "Let the dead bury their dead: but go thou and preach the kingdom of God."

Christ says in effect, "The kingdom of God is for live people, not for dead ones. I am not in this world to deal with matters like that. They are all right; there is nothing wrong with a man looking after his aged parents and burying them; but you know, that is not the first thing in life. The first thing in life is the soul! The men and women in My kingdom are alive, awakened to the fact of the soul and its eternal destiny and its relationship to God."

❧ A THOUGHT TO PONDER ☙
The first thing in life is the soul!

SO NEAR AND YET SO FAR

Thou art not far from the kingdom of God.

MARK 12:34

If people are not sure whether they are Christians or not, then I take leave to suggest that they are not. The Christian, according to the New Testament, is someone who can say something like this: "I was—I am." That is how the apostle described the Corinthians, was it not? He said, "And such were some of you!" They had been drunkards, adulterers, fornicators, etc. "But," he says, "you are not like that now—'But ye are washed, but ye are sanctified, but ye are justified in the name of the Lord Jesus, and by the Spirit of our God'" (1 Corinthians 6:11). The apostle Peter used exactly the same terminology: "Which in time past were not a people, but are now the people of God: which had not obtained mercy, but now have obtained mercy" (1 Peter 2:10). That is it!

There are variations in people's relative positions with respect to this kingdom. Our Lord said about one of the scribes who came to him, "Thou art not far from the kingdom of God." He did not say that about everybody, but He did say it about him. So outside the kingdom people can be in one of many, many positions.

There are people who have never given it a thought, who have never read the Bible and are not interested in it—they do not know its barest elements. They are not interested in God, in the Lord Jesus Christ, or in the soul, and they live the kind of life that we can see all around us.

Although there are different positions occupied by men and women outside the kingdom of God, in the last analysis they do not matter at all. There is no advantage in being "not far from the kingdom." "But," you reply, "do you mean to say that the person who is at the very door has no advantage over the one who is, as it were, at the other end of the world?" Precisely! And that is where the devil deludes so many.

✎ A THOUGHT TO PONDER ✎

There is no advantage in being "not far from the kingdom."

From *The Kingdom of God*, pp. 176-178.

BORN AGAIN

Jesus answered and said unto him, Verily, verily, I say unto thee,
Except a man be born again, he cannot see the kingdom of
God. . . . Verily, verily, I say unto thee, Except a man be born of
water and of the Spirit, he cannot enter into the kingdom of God.

JOHN 3:3, 5

When our Lord says, "Ye must be born again," He throws down the gauntlet. He says in effect, "It is all right; I know what you are going to say, but you need not say it—it is all wrong—you must be born again." "Verily, verily"—"truly, truly." Whenever He uses that formula He is always saying something of unusual seriousness and of deep import. He says, "Verily, verily, I say unto thee, Except a man be born again, he cannot see the kingdom of God."

This is the crucial phrase, the key phrase of Christianity: "born again"! Some people say it should be translated "born from above." Others say it should be translated "born anew." I think that they are probably nearest to the truth who say that undoubtedly our Lord was speaking to Nicodemus in Aramaic, that the Greek is a translation from the Aramaic, and that then our English is a translation from the Greek. But the original was probably Aramaic, and there it means "except a man has another birth, he will never see the kingdom of God." It is the same thing. "Born again," "another birth," "born from above," "born of the Spirit"—take any of the terms you like.

This is the great New Testament doctrine, and what it means, negatively, is that Christianity is not just an addition to something you already have. Christianity, in other words, is not something that you and I, as we are, can take up; all that is contradicted here. Before we can become Christians we need an entirely new start.

◆ A THOUGHT TO PONDER ◆
This is the crucial phrase, the key phrase of Christianity: "born again"!

From *The Kingdom of God*, pp. 193-194.

GOD IS JUDGE

*Whose voice then shook the earth: but now he hath promised,
saying, Yet once more I shake not the earth only, but also heaven.*
HEBREWS 12:26

What does the writer to the Hebrews mean when he says, "Whose voice then shook the earth: but now he hath promised, saying, Yet once more I shake not the earth only, but also heaven. And this word, Yet once more, signifieth the removing of those things that are shaken, as of things that are made, that those things which cannot be shaken may remain" (Hebrews 12:26-27)? Well, he is here contrasting the old dispensation with the new. He is writing to Hebrew Christians, and he is reminding them how the law was given to them by God through Moses on that great and famous occasion on Mount Sinai. He says, "Look back at that, consider that," and he gives them this tremendous description of it.

He says, "For ye are not come unto the mount that might be touched, and that burned with fire, nor unto blackness, and darkness, and tempest, And the sound of a trumpet, and the voice of words; which voice they that heard entreated that the word should not be spoken to them any more: (For they could not endure that which was commanded, and if so much as a beast touch the mountain, it shall be stoned, or thrust through with a dart: And so terrible was the sight, that Moses said, I exceedingly fear and quake:)." But you have not come to that, he says; "But ye are come unto mount Sion, and unto the city of the living God, the heavenly Jerusalem, and to an innumerable company of angels, to the general assembly and church of the firstborn, which are written in heaven"—and notice!—"and to God the Judge of all" (Hebrews 12:18-23).

Here is the great basic theme of the whole of the Bible. I must listen to it because I am moving every day I live nearer and nearer to a final judgment. "God the Judge of all"!

❧ A THOUGHT TO PONDER ❧
Every day I move nearer and nearer to a final judgment.

HOLY HANDS

I will therefore that men pray every where, lifting up holy hands,
without wrath and doubting.
1 TIMOTHY 2:8

There are conditions that govern the activity called prayer. One condition is that we are to lift up "holy hands." We are not now concerned about the question of posture in prayer, nor to indicate that the Jews generally stood and held up their hands to God when they prayed. We shall not tarry with the fact that it was a Jewish custom to wash their hands before they took part in an act of worship. That was merely the external symbol used to emphasize the principle that the apostle is anxious to stress.

The clean hands, the "holy hands," are indicative of and represent a holy character. That must ever be the first question in any approach to God. "Holiness, without which no man shall see the Lord" (Hebrews 12:14). "Thou [God] art of purer eyes than to behold evil" and cannot "look on iniquity" (Habakkuk 1:13). There is nothing that is so utterly contrary to the whole teaching of the Bible as the assumption that anyone at any time without any conditions whatsoever may approach God in prayer. Indeed, the first effect of sin, and the main result of the Fall, was to break the communion that obtained between God and man. Man, by sin, has forfeited his right approach to God, and indeed were he left to himself he never would approach God. But God in His wondrous grace has made a way for man to approach Him. That is the explanation of all the teaching concerning offerings and sacrifices in the Old Testament, as it is also the explanation of the ceremony of the Tabernacle and the Temple and the Aaronic priesthood. Without these things men could not approach God. We can commune with Him only in this way and according to His dictates. There is no access otherwise.

✍ A THOUGHT TO PONDER ✍

We can commune with God only according to His dictates.

From *Why Does God Allow War?* pp. 25-26.

"WITHOUT WRATH"

I will therefore that men pray every where, lifting up holy hands,
without wrath and doubting.

1 TIMOTHY 2:8

The second condition about prayer laid down by the apostle Paul is "without wrath." It is most important that we should realize the exact meaning of this word "wrath." It does not mean what is usually suggested to us by the common usage of that word. It does not mean so much anger or the expression or manifestation of anger as an unloving disposition—not a violent outburst of temper, but rather a settled condition of ill will and resentment. Here the emphasis is not upon the way in which a man regards God and approaches Him, but on the way in which he approaches and regards his fellowmen, his neighbors. Added to this, perhaps, is the whole question of a man's spirit—not only his actions, but also his outlook and his attitude toward others and toward life. How vitally important this is! And how tragically we all tend to fail at this point.

Often there is a feeling of resentment in our hearts even against God while we are praying to Him. We feel that we have a real grudge and a genuine complaint. We feel that we have been wronged. And yet we feel that we are dependent upon God; so we ask Him for favors. We feel that He is against us, that He is not fair to us, and yet in that state and condition we ask Him to bless us, and we expect Him to do so. God says to the children of Israel, "This people . . . honoreth me with their lips, but their heart is far from me" (Matthew 15:8).

This same spirit also shows itself in our attitude toward our fellows. If we have enemies, we must not hate them, but love them. The rule is, "love your enemies." "Without wrath."

✎ A THOUGHT TO PONDER ✐

The emphasis is not upon the way in which a man regards God, but on the way in which he regards his fellowmen.

From *Why Does God Allow War?* pp. 28-30.

July 24

"WITHOUT DOUBTING"

I will therefore that men pray every where, lifting up holy hands,
without wrath and doubting.

1 TIMOTHY 2:8

The third condition about prayer is described as "without doubting," or if you prefer it, "without disputing." The reference is not to disputing with others, but to disputing with oneself. It denotes a state of wavering and uncertainty or perhaps even a state of actual intellectual rebellion.

The doubt may express itself in many different ways. It may be doubt with respect to the very being of God, doubt, to use the words of the author of the Epistle to the Hebrews, as to whether "he [God] is." Then there is often doubt with respect to what we may call the power or the possibility of prayer, as to whether anything can happen or even does happen, in a word whether there is any point in our praying at all.

As a result of these doubts, it often comes to pass that prayer is nothing but some desperate adventure or doubtful experiment in which we engage. We find ourselves in a difficult position or face to face with some dire need. We more or less "cry out in the dark," on the possible chance that it may succeed and we may be delivered.

Unless we observe this third condition, prayer is useless. We must approach God believing "that he is, and that he is a rewarder of them that diligently seek him" (Hebrews 11:6). The men whose prayers have been answered have always been those who knew God, those who have trusted Him most thoroughly, those who have been most ready to say at all times and in all circumstances, "Thy will be done," assured as they were of His holy and loving purpose. There must be no doubt, no disputing, no desperate experiments, but rather a calm and unhurried resting upon and in God and His perfect will.

❧ A THOUGHT TO PONDER ☙

The men whose prayers have been answered have always been those who knew God.

From *Why Does God Allow War?* pp. 30-32.

July 25

WHY DOES GOD ALLOW WAR?

From whence come wars and fightings among you? come they not hence, even of your lusts that war in your members?

JAMES 4:1

As I contemplate human nature and human life, what astonishes me is not that God allows and permits war, but the patience and the long-suffering of God. "He maketh his sun to rise on the evil and on the good, and sendeth rain on the just and on the unjust" (Matthew 5:45). He suffered the evil, perverse ways of the children of Israel for centuries; and now for nearly two thousand years He has patiently borne with a world that in the main rejects and refuses His loving offer, even in the Person of His only-begotten Son. The question that needs to be asked is not, Why does God allow war? but rather, Why does God not allow the world to destroy itself entirely in its iniquity and its sin? Why does He in His restraining grace set a limit to evil and to sin, and a bound beyond which they cannot pass?

Oh, the amazing patience of God with this sinful world! How wondrous is His love! He has sent the Son of His love to our world to die for us and to save us; and because men cannot and will not see this, God permits and allows such things as war to chastise and to punish us, to teach us and to convict us of our sins, and above all to call us to repentance and acceptance of His gracious offer. The vital question for us therefore is not to ask, Why does God allow war? The question for us is to make sure that we are learning the lesson and repenting before God for the sin in our own hearts and in the entire human race that leads to such results. May God grant us understanding and the true spirit of repentance, for His Name's sake.

✎ A THOUGHT TO PONDER ✎

As I contemplate human nature and human life, what astonishes me is not that God allows and permits war, but the patience and the long-suffering of God.

From *Why Does God Allow War?* pp. 100-101.

AN ALL-INCLUSIVE PROMISE

And we know that all things work together for good to them that love God, to them who are the called according to his purpose.

ROMANS 8:28

Let us look at the all-inclusiveness of the promise—"all things work together for good." It is generally agreed that the "all things" has special reference to trials and tribulations. Here is one of the most remarkable claims ever made for Christianity. Here is certainly the boldest justification of God's ways to man.

Let us observe what this verse says. Perhaps we shall best be able to grasp its significance if we approach it along the negative route. We see clearly that, as Christians, we are not promised an easy time in this world. Our Lord Himself in His teaching told the disciples that they would have tribulations and trials and sufferings. And in the same way Paul teaches that "unto you it is given in the behalf of Christ, not only to believe on him, but also to suffer for his sake" (Philippians 1:29). The Christian's view of life and of the world is realistic, not romantic. He does not avoid troubles and problems. Neither does he try to minimize the seriousness and the greatness of the troubles and problems. The glory of the Gospel is that it faces the whole situation without shirking anything, and yet shows the way out.

Some of the older versions bring out this feature in our text very clearly by adding the word "God" to "all things work together for good"—i.e., that "God works all things together for good to them who love him." And that is undoubtedly what the apostle teaches. These trials are not to be ignored; neither are they without any explanation whatsoever. God uses them to our advantage in order to bring His own great purposes to pass. "And we know that all things work together for good to them that love God, to them who are called according to his purpose." That is the ultimate justification of God's ways; that is the ultimate answer to all our questions as to why God allows certain things to happen.

✺ A THOUGHT TO PONDER ✺

God uses our trials to our advantage in order to bring His own great purposes to pass.

From *Why Does God Allow War?* pp. 116-117, 119.

July 27

LIMITATION TO THE PROMISE

And we know that all things work together for good to them that love God, to them who are the called according to his purpose.

ROMANS 8:28

We now note what we might call the limitation to this promise. "And we know that all things work together for good *to them that love God, to them who are called according to his purpose.*" In the original that is emphasized by placing "to them that love God" at the commencement of the sentence. "We know that to them that love God all things work together for good."

The promise is definitely limited. It is not universal as to the people included. The popular idea of the love of God is the very antithesis of this. That idea says that He is regarded as promising to bless all in exactly the same way. That He does so in His providential dealings with mankind in general is true. But following that, there is a great fundamental division and distinction everywhere in the Bible between the saved and the unsaved, between those who have entered into a covenant relationship with God in salvation through Jesus Christ and those who have not, or, to use the words of our text, "those who are the called" and those who have not been called.

Salvation is the result of the operation of special grace, and there are special promises to those who have received this grace. The Gospel has but one word to speak to those who do not believe on the Lord Jesus Christ. It is to exhort them to repent and to believe. It holds out to them no special promises until they have done so. Indeed it threatens them with disaster. It does not tell them that "All things work together for good" for the reason that it tells them that they are "condemned already." Special promises and comforts and consolations are not to be obtained directly. They are the consequences and results of salvation. They are offered only to those who "love God."

❧ A THOUGHT TO PONDER ❧
Salvation is the result of the operation of special grace.

From *Why Does God Allow War?* pp. 119-121.

The Mechanism of the Promise

And we know that all things work together for good to them that
love God, to them who are the called according to his purpose.

ROMANS 8:28

We must look at what I choose to call the mechanism of the promise—the way in which it works. The apostle says that "all things
work together for good to them that love God, to them who are
the called according to his purpose." He says that we "know" this,
that it is something that is well-known and acknowledged, something that to the Christian is self-evident. How is this so? The answer
is partly doctrinal and partly a matter of experience.

The doctrinal answer starts at the end of our text—"to them
who are the called according to his purpose." It continues at the
end of the chapter. We know that all things work together for good
to believers because their whole position is dependent upon God and
His activity. Our salvation is God's work. Listen to the argument:
"For whom he did foreknow, he also did predestinate to be conformed to the image of his Son, that he might be the firstborn among
many brethren. Moreover whom he did predestinate, them he also
called: and whom he called, them he also justified: and whom he justified, them he also glorified" (verses 29-30). There is nothing accidental or fortuitous or contingent about God's work. It is all planned
and worked out from the beginning right until the end. In our experience it comes to us increasingly, but in the mind and purpose of
God, it is all already perfect and entire. Nothing can frustrate it.

But it is not merely a matter of high doctrine. There is a fact
that confirms it all: "he that spared not his own Son, but delivered
him up for us all, how shall he not with him also freely give us all
things?" Is God, who actually delivered up His only Son to that cruel
death on Calvary's cross for us, likely to allow anything to stand
between us and His ultimate purpose for us? Impossible.

❧ A Thought to Ponder ❧

There is nothing accidental or fortuitous or contingent about God's
work.

From *Why Does God Allow War?* pp. 122-123.

THE REALM OF EXPERIENCE, PART 1

And we know that all things work together for good to them that love God, to them who are the called according to his purpose.

ROMANS 8:28

But God be thanked, we can also answer the question with regard to the mechanism of this glorious promise in an experimental manner, from the realm of experience. That our text is true is the universal testimony of all the saints whose histories are recorded both in the Bible and in the subsequent history of the Christian Church. The ways in which this promise works out are almost endless; but the principle that is common to them all is that there is but one ultimate good—the knowledge of God and the salvation of our souls. Holding that in mind, we see that trials and tribulations work out in the following ways:

They awaken us to the fact of our overdependence on earthly and human things. Quite unconsciously, oftentimes we become affected by our surroundings, and our lives become less and less dependent upon God, and our interests become more and more worldly. The denial of earthly and human comforts and joys often awakens us to the realization of this in a way that nothing else can do.

Our trials also remind us of the fleeting nature of our life here on earth. How easy it is to "settle down" in life in this world and to live on the assumption that we are here forever. We all tend to do so to such an extent that we forget "the glory which shall be revealed" (verse 18), and that, as we have shown, should be the frequent theme of our meditation. Anything that disturbs this sloth and reminds us that we are but pilgrims here therefore stimulates us to "set your affection on things above" (Colossians 3:2).

❧ A THOUGHT TO PONDER ❧

There is but one ultimate good—the knowledge of God and the salvation of our souls.

From *Why Does God Allow War?* pp. 123-124.

July 30

THE REALM OF EXPERIENCE, PART 2

And we know that all things work together for good to them that love God, to them who are the called according to his purpose.

ROMANS 8:28

In the same way, *great crises in life show us our weakness, helplessness, and lack of power.* Paul illustrates that in Romans 8. "We know not what we should pray for as we ought." In a time of peace and of ease we think that we can pray, that we know how to pray. We are assured and confident, and we feel that we are living the religious life as it should be lived. But when trials come, they reveal to us how weak and helpless we are.

That, in turn, drives us to God, and makes us realize more than ever before our utter dependence upon Him. This is the experience of all Christians. In our folly we imagine that we can live in our own strength and by our own power, and our prayers are often formal. But troubles make us fly to God and cause us to wait upon Him. God says of Israel through Hosea, "In their affliction they will seek me early" (Hosea 5:15). How true that is of all of us. To seek God is always good, and afflictions drive us to do so.

But all this is mainly from our side. Looking at it from the other side, we can say that *there is no school in which Christians have learned so much of the loving, tender care of God for His own as the school of affliction.* While all is well with us, in our self-satisfaction and self-contentment we shut God out of our lives; we do not allow Him to reveal to us His solicitude for us even in the details of our lives. It is only when we are troubled that we "know not what we should pray for as we ought" and that we begin to realize that "the Spirit . . . maketh intercession for us with groanings which cannot be uttered."

☙ A THOUGHT TO PONDER ❧

There is no school in which Christians have learned so much of the loving, tender care of God for His own as the school of affliction.

From *Why Does God Allow War?* pp. 124-125.

THE WONDERS OF HIS GRACE

And he said unto me, My grace is sufficient for thee:
for my strength is made perfect in weakness. Most gladly therefore
will I rather glory in my infirmities, that the power of Christ
may rest upon me. Therefore I take pleasure in infirmities,
in reproaches, in necessities, in persecutions, in distresses for
Christ's sake: for when I am weak, then am I strong.

2 CORINTHIANS 12:9-10

It is to those who were in the depths that the sense of the presence of God has been most real and the realization of His sustaining power most definite.

The widow of a German Moravian bishop told me that the universal testimony of all the Christians in Germany who had suffered untold hardships on account of their faith was, in her experience, that they would have missed none of these things, that indeed they thanked God for them. By these things they had been awakened to a realization of the poverty of their Christian lives and experiences; by these things also they had had their eyes opened to "the wonders of His grace."

That is but their modern way of expressing what the psalmist puts thus: "It is good for me that I have been afflicted; that I might learn thy statutes" (Psalm 119:71).

It is also but the re-echo of Paul's reaction to the verdict, "My grace is sufficient for thee: for my strength is made perfect in weakness," which led him to say, "Most gladly therefore will I rather glory in my infirmities, that the power of Christ may rest upon me. Therefore I take pleasure in infirmities, in reproaches, in necessities, in persecutions, in distresses for Christ's sake: for when I am weak, then am I strong" (2 Corinthians 12:9-10). If we but love God and submit ourselves to Him, that most certainly will be our experience; for again I would remind you that "all things work together for good to them that love God, to them who are the called according to his purpose."

A THOUGHT TO PONDER

By these things they had been awakened to a realization of the poverty of their Christian lives.

From *Why Does God Allow War?* pp. 125-126.

August

KNOWING AND
SERVING GOD

FROM

God the Father, God the Son

GENERAL REVELATION

Because that which may be known of God is manifest in them;
for God hath showed it unto them. For the invisible things of
him from the creation of the world are clearly seen,
being understood by the things that are made, even his eternal
power and Godhead; so that they are without excuse.

ROMANS 1:19-20

According to the Bible, God has revealed Himself in two main ways. The first is what we call *general revelation*; the other, obviously, is *special revelation*. So first let us look at general revelation. What is this? The Bible tells us that God has revealed Himself, in general and first, through *creation and nature*. Paul made a most important declaration on this subject to the people of Lystra. He said, "[God] left not himself without witness, in that he did good, and gave us rain from heaven, and fruitful seasons, filling our hearts with food and gladness." Immediately before that, Paul had said, "God . . . made heaven, and earth, and the sea, and all things that are therein" (Acts 14:17, 15).

The other classic statement on that same point is to be found in Acts 17:24: "God that made the world and all things therein, seeing that he is Lord of heaven and earth, dwelleth not in temples made with hands." Again, you find the same thing stated in Romans 1:19-20: "Because that which may be known of God is manifest in them; for God hath showed it unto them. For the invisible things of him from the creation of the world are clearly seen, being understood by the things that are made, even his eternal power and Godhead; so that they are without excuse"—another momentous passage. All those statements remind us that God, after all, has left His marks, His imprints, in nature and creation; they are "the works of his hands" (Psalm 111:7). "The heavens declare the glory of God" (Psalm 19:1).

Everything that has been made is in itself a revelation of God. That is the first definition of general revelation.

✎ A THOUGHT TO PONDER ✎
Everything that has been made is in itself a revelation of God.

From *God the Father, God the Son*, pp. 13-14.

PROVIDENCE AND HISTORY

*Because that, when they knew God, they glorified him not as God,
neither were thankful; but became vain in their imaginations,
and their foolish heart was darkened. Professing themselves
to be wise, they became fools.*

ROMANS 1:21-22

You get the same type of revelation [as seen in creation and nature] in what is commonly called *providence*: the ordering of things in this world, their maintenance, their sustenance, and the fact that everything keeps on going and continues in life.

How is all this explained? Well, ultimately it is a question of providence. Through the ordering of providence, the seasons, the rain and the snow, and the fructification of crops are all manifestations of God.

The third aspect of general revelation is *history*. The whole history of the world, if we could but see it, is a revelation of God.

But now we have to say that in and of itself general revelation is not sufficient. It ought to be sufficient, but it is not. And that, it seems to me, is Paul's argument in Romans 1:20, where he says, "They are without excuse." The evidence is there, but that has not been enough. Why? Because of sin. If men and women were not sinners, by looking at the miracles and the works of God in creation, in providence and in history, they would be able to arrive, by a process of reasoning, at God. But because of their sin, they do not; they deliberately turn their backs upon doing so. That is the great argument in the remainder of Romans 1. Paul says, "Because that, when they knew God, they glorified him not as God, neither were thankful; but became vain in their imaginations, and their foolish heart was darkened. Professing themselves to be wise, they became fools" (verses 21-22). And he goes on to say that they began to worship the creature rather than the Creator.

❧ A THOUGHT TO PONDER ❧

The whole history of the world, if we could but see it, is a revelation of God.

From *God the Father, God the Son*, pp. 14-15.

SPECIAL REVELATION

I will take away mine hand, and thou shalt see my back parts:
but my face shall not be seen.

EXODUS 33:23

We ask, Is there any hope for us? And the answer is to be found in the second type of revelation of which the Bible speaks, and that is what we call *special revelation*. And the special revelation that we find in the Bible has a very distinct and definite object, which is to reveal to us the character of God, the nature of God, and especially the character and nature of God as they are revealed in His saving grace.

Now the Bible makes a unique claim at this point: It claims that it and it alone gives us this special knowledge of God. The Bible claims for itself that it is the record of God's special revelation of Himself and of all His gracious and saving purposes with respect to men and women. The great message of this book from beginning to end is God revealing Himself. It is not the great religious quest of mankind. No; it is the great eternal God drawing back the veil and giving an insight into and a knowledge of Himself and of His great and gracious purposes. That is the subject matter of the Bible.

God has been pleased to reveal Himself through what are called theophanies—manifestations of God, the various appearances of God. This happened to Moses: "And it shall come to pass, while my glory passeth by, that I will put thee in a clift of the rock, and will cover thee with my hand while I pass by: and I will take away mine hand, and thou shalt see my back parts: but my face shall not be seen" (Exodus 33:22-23). God said in effect, "You cannot see Me face to face, for no man can see Me in that sense and live. Nevertheless, I will reveal My glory to you." Moses saw the glory of God; he saw the back parts of God passing by.

❧ A THOUGHT TO PONDER ❧

The Bible claims for itself that it is the record of God's special revelation of Himself.

From *God the Father, God the Son*, pp. 15-16.

August 4

How Is the Bible Inspired?

*All scripture is given by inspiration of God, and is profitable
for doctrine, for reproof, for correction,
for instruction in righteousness.*

2 TIMOTHY 3:16

What is meant by *inspiration*? When we say that the Bible is divinely inspired, what exactly do we mean? I start with a negative. We do not mean that certain portions of the Bible are inspired and that others are not. There are some people who think that. There are, they say, portions and particular statements and teachings, especially those concerned with the Lord Jesus Christ, that are inspired. But, they say, the historical books and various other sections are not inspired. Now that is *not* what we mean when we say that the Bible is divinely inspired.

Neither do we mean simply that the men who wrote the Bible were writing in an exalted or creative way. When a poet produced a masterpiece, you have often heard people say that the poet was "inspired." But we do not mean that the writers of the books of the Bible were inspired in that way when they came to write these books. Others say they regard inspiration as just meaning that the ideas that were given to the writers were inspired. That is true, of course, but we mean much more than that. Neither does it mean that the books—the writings as such—are the product of human origin onto which the divine breath or *afflatus* has come.

So what do we mean? We mean that the Scriptures are a divine product breathed out by God. Inspired really means "God-breathed." We mean that God breathed these messages into men and through them, and these Scriptures are the result of that divine action. We believe that they were produced by the creative breath of Almighty God. Put in a simpler form, we mean that everything we have in the Bible has been given by God to man.

❧ A Thought to Ponder ❧
The Scriptures are a divine product breathed out by God.

From *God the Father, God the Son*, pp. 23-24.

VERBAL INSPIRATION

I will raise them up a Prophet from among their brethren,
like unto thee, and will put my words in his mouth; and
he shall speak unto them all that I shall command him.

DEUTERONOMY 18:18

The particular words used in the Bible are divinely inspired. I shall try to demonstrate to you that the Bible claims for itself what is called *verbal inspiration*. It is not merely that the thoughts are inspired, not merely the ideas, but the actual record, down to the particular words. It is not merely that the statements are correct, but that every word is divinely inspired.

Verbal inspiration means that the Holy Spirit has overruled and controlled and guided the writers of the Bible, even in the choice of particular words, in such a way as to prevent any error, and above all to produce the result that was originally intended by God.

The Bible makes specific claims in this matter of inspiration. Take, for instance, certain terms that the Bible uses of itself, such as *Scripture*. That designates "holy writings"; not ordinary writings but special ones—holy writings.

Let us take a more specific claim. Take that great prophecy, which is very crucial in this matter, spoken by Moses and recorded in Deuteronomy 18:18: "I will raise them up a Prophet from among their brethren, like unto thee, and will put my words in his mouth; and he shall speak unto them all that I shall command him." All the prophets of the Old Testament make this claim. They do not say that they suddenly decided to write; they say, "The word of the Lord came . . ." (see, for example, Ezekiel 1:3; Hosea 1:1; Jonah 1:1), and they tell you exactly when it came. They were called, they were commissioned, and the word was given to them. So they are constantly saying something like, "Thus saith the Lord." That is their claim.

☙ A THOUGHT TO PONDER ❧

It is not merely that the statements are correct, but that every word is divinely inspired.

From *God the Father, God the Son*, pp. 24-26.

OUR LORD AND SCRIPTURE

Think not that I am come to destroy the law, or the prophets:
I am not come to destroy, but to fulfil. For verily I say unto you,
Till heaven and earth pass, one jot or one tittle shall in no wise
pass from the law, till all be fulfilled.

MATTHEW 5:17-18

The most vital testimony about the authority of the Bible that we must adduce is the testimony of the Lord Jesus Christ Himself. Read your Gospels, and notice the way in which He constantly quotes the Old Testament. Notice the way in which He assumed that it is authoritative, that it puts a matter beyond argument and beyond any dispute whatsoever. He just says, "It is written," and that is final (see, for example, Luke 19:46; John 6:45). He obviously accepted the Old Testament *in toto* as authoritative, final, and supreme.

There are also certain specific statements that He made: "Think not that I am come to destroy the law, or the prophets: I am not come to destroy, but to fulfil. For verily I say unto you, Till heaven and earth pass, one jot or one tittle shall in no wise pass from the law, till all be fulfilled" (Matthew 5:17-18). And in a sense that is the whole of the Old Testament—Moses and the prophets. "I am not come to destroy, but to fulfil." Then you will find Him, for example, saying, "And he answered and said unto them, Have ye not read, that he which made them at the beginning made them male and female" (Matthew 19:4). That quotation alone is sufficient to show that our Lord regarded what we read in the early chapters of Genesis as being authoritative for the whole question of man and woman and their appearance in the world. So if you begin to play fast and loose with the authority of the Scriptures and with the verbal inspiration of the Scriptures, you are of necessity involved in difficulties about the person of the Lord Himself.

❧ A THOUGHT TO PONDER ☙

The most vital testimony about the authority of the Bible is the testimony of the Lord Jesus Christ Himself.

THE AUTHORITY OF THE BIBLE

*If he called them gods, unto whom the word of God came, and
the scriptures cannot be broken . . .*

JOHN 10:35

Moses, the prophets, and the Psalms—Christ accepted it all and asked the disciples to consider its teaching concerning Himself. And He expounded it to them. I refer to John 10:35, where He tells us, "If he called them gods, unto whom the word of God came, and the scriptures cannot be broken . . ." So in the last analysis our authority for our understanding of inspiration is to be found in the Lord Jesus Christ Himself. That was His view of the Scriptures.

Now I know there are many who want to ask a question at this point. What about the various differences, what about certain discrepancies, and so on? Well, there is a very comforting answer to all that. There are, as we have them in our versions, certain things that we simply cannot explain, and it is our business to say that quite readily and frankly. But let me hasten to add that most of these so-called difficulties and discrepancies that the critics bring forward can be explained; indeed, most of them have been explained. Many of them have been explained in the last few years as a result of archaeology and further linguistic understanding of the Scriptures.

Still, there are a certain few differences that remain, but it is significant that they are never with respect to doctrine or historical facts. It is a matter of figures or something that is comparatively unimportant and can be explained quite readily—the mistake, perhaps, of a copyist or of some translator. There is nothing that in any way interferes with vital, essential doctrine. So what we affirm and state is this: The original documents, as first given, are inerrant and infallible.

Finally, you cannot prove to anybody that the Bible is uniquely and divinely inspired. Ultimately people have to be enlightened by the Holy Spirit.

✒ A THOUGHT TO PONDER ✒
The original documents, as first given, are inerrant and infallible.

THE EXTENT OF REVELATION

For now we see through a glass, darkly; but then face to face: now
I know in part; but then shall I know even as also I am known.
1 CORINTHIANS 13:12

There are certain things in the Scriptures about which we cannot speak with finality. There are certain things about which equally good and capable men and women are not agreed and cannot agree. When we come to such matters, surely it is our business to say that we do not know. We cannot prove them, and we are content to wait until we arrive in glory, and all things are made plain and clear to us. At the moment we see and understand only in part, "through a glass, darkly." Our knowledge is not full. It is not final. Let us be content with the revelation that is given.

But there are certain doctrines about which we are and must be absolutely final, and they are the doctrines that are essential to the way of salvation. I am not referring to the mechanism of salvation. When you come to that, you find good people often differing. I accept that. I am prepared to say, "I believe this, and I am not prepared to believe that." And another man says, "All right—as long as we both agree about the way of salvation." But there must be no disputing about the person of Christ, about the miraculous and the supernatural, about Christ's substitutionary death upon the cross, and about His literal, physical resurrection. There is no argument here. This is final; this is absolute.

But with regard to all other matters, where we cannot be final and absolute, let us be sympathetic. Let us be tolerant. Let us admit our inability to prove, and let us together enjoy the great salvation in which we all participate and look forward to the day when the hidden things shall be made plain, and we shall know even as we are already known.

❧ A THOUGHT TO PONDER ❧
Our knowledge is not full. It is not final. Let us be content with the revelation that is given.

August 9

THE EXISTENCE OF GOD

In the beginning God created the heaven and the earth.

GENESIS 1:1

We say we want to worship God and to know Him; so the first thought that comes to our minds is the existence of God, because, as we all know full well, there are many people who tell us they do not believe in it. It is not so much that we are concerned with them and their arguments as that, from our own standpoint, it is essential that we should be clear in our thinking about this subject.

The Bible does not argue about the existence of God—it declares it. The Bible does not give us any proofs of the existence of God—it assumes it. Take that opening phrase of the Bible. Genesis does not start by saying, "Well, by the following proofs we establish the existence of God, and because He was existent, we establish that at the beginning He created . . ." Not at all! "In the beginning God created . . ." It just states His existence and His being.

Some theological books present a number of "proofs" of the being and existence of God. There is the so-called cosmological argument, which is an argument from nature: Every effect has a cause. Then there is the argument from order and design, called the teleological argument, which says that everything leads up to something—that is clearly evident. Then there is the moral argument, which concludes that our awareness of good and bad, our sense of right and wrong, point to the existence of a moral God.

Now what the Bible teaches about such arguments is that they can never create faith. They are useful in a negative sense, but they will never lead to faith; and according to the Scriptures, no one can believe in God without faith, without the inward work of the Holy Spirit that leads to faith.

☙ A THOUGHT TO PONDER ❧

The Bible does not argue about the existence of God—it declares it.

From *God the Father, God the Son*, pp. 48–49.

KNOWING GOD

*For my thoughts are not your thoughts, neither are your ways
my ways, saith the LORD. For as the heavens are higher than
the earth, so are my ways higher than your ways, and
my thoughts than your thoughts.*

ISAIAH 55:8-9

Is it possible to know God? Here I have to introduce a term, a big
and yet vital word. The Bible teaches what is called the *incompre-
hensibility of God.* It means that God cannot finally be comprehended or understood by human beings. It means that we can read
around the doctrine of God and try to grasp it with our minds, but
by definition God is incomprehensible; we can never know Him in
the ultimate, final, and complete sense. "For my thoughts are not
your thoughts, neither are your ways my ways, saith the LORD. For
as the heavens are higher than the earth, so are my ways higher
than your ways, and my thoughts than your thoughts." Read about
this also in Romans 11:33 and 1 Timothy 6:16. God dwells in that
light that no one can approach. God in His eternal and absolute
being is incomprehensible.

Yet we see that though God is finally incomprehensible, He is
nevertheless knowable; He cannot be comprehended, but, thank
God, He can be known. Let us be clear about this. There are those
who would have us believe that God cannot be known in His real
being, that He can only be known in His dealings with men and
women. But that is a position that is quite wrong when you bring it
into the light of biblical teaching. The knowledge that we have of
God's being will never be anything but a partial knowledge, but
though it is partial, it is nevertheless real; though it is not complete,
it is true knowledge, enough to lead us to glorify Him. And we have
this knowledge of God because it has pleased God Himself to give
it to us.

❧ A THOUGHT TO PONDER ❧
Though God is incomprehensible, He is nevertheless knowable; He
cannot be comprehended, but He can be known.

THE ATTRIBUTES OF GOD

*Before the mountains were brought forth, or ever thou hadst
formed the earth and the world, even from everlasting to
everlasting, thou art God.*

PSALM 90:2

We will now consider some of the attributes of God. And by attributes I mean some of the perfections of God, or to put it another way, some of the virtues of God. Peter says in his first epistle, ". . . that ye should show forth the praises of him who hath called you out of darkness into his marvellous light" (2:9). That is it. The Christian is meant to show forth the attributes of God—the perfections, the excellencies of God.

Here is another definition of God's attributes: They are the things about God, certain aspects of His great and glorious eternal nature, that He has been pleased to reveal to us, and that, in a measure, we can lay hold of. All sorts of classifications have been suggested. Some have said that the division should be into the natural attributes of God and the moral attributes of God—that is, into attributes that belong to God in and of Himself and those that have a kind of moral implication. Well, it does not matter very much what we may call them. I would suggest some classification like this: first, the attributes of absolute personality that belong to God, and second, the moral attributes of God.

God is a personality in an absolute sense. Now, what are the attributes that belong to His personality? They are, of course, expressive of His eternal being, and the first one, therefore, that we have to note is the *eternity* of God, and with it the *immutability* of God. God is without beginning and without ending; He is everlasting. You will find a great statement of that in Psalm 90: "Before the mountains were brought forth, or ever thou hadst formed the earth and the world, even from everlasting to everlasting, thou art God" (verse 2). You will find it in the same way in Psalm 102. His eternity is something that we just assert and at which we wonder.

✎ A THOUGHT TO PONDER ✎

The Christian is meant to show forth the attributes of God—the perfections, the excellencies of God.

From *God the Father, God the Son*, pp. 59-60.

GOD'S OMNISCIENCE

*Great is our LORD, and of great power: his understanding
is infinite.*

PSALM 147:5

Another of God's great attributes is His omniscience. God knows
all things, and His knowledge is always absolute knowledge. It is
perfect knowledge, a complete knowledge of everything.

There are very many statements of this, of course, in the
Scriptures. Take, for instance, Psalm 147:5: "His understanding is
infinite." Then in Proverbs 15:3 we read, "The eyes of the LORD
are in every place, beholding the evil and the good."

The Bible tells us quite a lot in detail about this knowledge, this
omniscience of God. For instance, it tells us about God's knowledge of nature: "He telleth the number of the stars; he calleth them
all by their names" (Psalm 147:4). But let me give you another example. Do you remember those tender words of our Lord in which He
tells us that not a single sparrow falls to the ground without our
Father's knowing it (Matthew 10:29)? Everything in the realm of
nature is known by God. It is quite inconceivable to us, but the
Bible asserts this is true of God. Look up into the heavens on a
starry night and see all that multiplicity of stars. He knows them,
every one, and He has a name for every one. There is nothing in
creation but that God knows it in that intimate and personal sense.

But we are obviously more interested in God's knowledge of us
and of our human experience. Psalm 139 is very eloquent here. The
psalmist says, "Thou knowest my downsitting and mine uprising,
thou understandest my thought afar off" (verse 2). My very thought!
He knows all about me. "Thou compassest my path and my lying
down, and art acquainted with all my ways" (verse 3). Indeed, he
goes further in verse 4 and says, "For there is not a word in my
tongue, but, lo, O LORD, thou knowest it altogether." What an exact
and detailed knowledge God has of us!

❧ A THOUGHT TO PONDER ❧

God knows all things, and His knowledge is always absolute knowledge.

From *God the Father, God the Son*, p. 63.

GOD'S OMNIPOTENCE

. . . him who worketh all things after the counsel of his own will.
EPHESIANS 1:11

Another of God's attributes is His omnipotence. God is all-powerful. The omnipotence of God is that by which He brings to pass everything He wills. The omnipotence is the will of God being put into operation. How often we read in the Bible about the will of God. For example, Paul writes of "him who worketh all things after the counsel of his own will." What is the will of God? It is the final ground of everything, of all existence. It is the final explanation of everything that has ever happened or everything that will happen. And the Bible teaches that the will of God is sovereign; in other words, it is not determined by anything but by God Himself. It is the expression of His Lordship, His absolute being.

But remember, His will is never arbitrary. It is never exercised except in perfect harmony with all the other attributes of God's great and glorious being. It is the same God who is glorious and wonderful. It is the same God who is love and compassion and mercy. We must not divide these things, though we distinguish them for the purposes of thought and understanding.

Furthermore, you will find that the will of God expresses itself in two main ways. He declares certain things that He Himself is going to do; that is called the *decretive will* of God. He also prescribes certain things for us to do; that is the *prescriptive will* of God. The terms are not of great importance, but constantly in the Bible you see these two aspects of God's will. God tells us what He Himself is going to do, and He gives commands to us about what we are to do.

✺ A THOUGHT TO PONDER ✺

The omnipotence of God is that by which He brings to pass everything He wills.

From *God the Father, God the Son*, pp. 66-67.

August 14

GOD'S POWER

. . . his mighty power, which he wrought in Christ,
when he raised him from the dead.
EPHESIANS 1:19-20

God's power is endless. He is omnipotent. "Is any thing too hard for the LORD?" God asked Abraham (Genesis 18:14), and the angel Gabriel said to Mary, "For with God nothing shall be impossible" (Luke 1:37). His might, His power, His strength are endless. The Bible is full of this! He made everything out of nothing; He spoke and it happened. He said, "Let there be light: and there was light" (Genesis 1:3). He sends His frosts and His snow. Read the Psalms, and you will find that they glory in the endless power of God.

This sovereign will and power of God have been manifested most of all, and most clearly, in three ways: in creation, in salvation, and in providence. And I suppose there is no greater manifestation of the power of God than the one to which Paul refers in the first chapter of Ephesians: ". . . his mighty power, which he wrought in Christ, when he raised him from the dead."

This idea of omnipotence is staggering! There are many things we do not understand about the will of God. But we are not meant to understand them; we are meant to look at them with reverence and awe and worship. We are meant to realize that there would be no hope for us at all were it not for the omnipotence of God. I say with reverence, nothing less than the omnipotence of God could save a single soul. But thank God, He is omnipotent, and we are saved by the power of God in and through the Lord Jesus Christ.

The glory of God is the biblical way of describing God's greatness, His splendor, His majesty. We read of the glory of God filling the Temple (1 Kings 8:11) and of the glory of God being manifested in dimmed vision to certain people. This means they had some conception of the greatness, the splendor, the majesty, the might of His being.

❧ A THOUGHT TO PONDER ❧
Read the Psalms, and you will find that they glory in the endless power of God.

From *God the Father, God the Son*, pp. 67-68.

THE HOLINESS OF GOD

Be ye holy; for I am holy.
1 PETER 1:16

God's moral attributes are, in a sense, communicable. Something corresponding to them is to be found in men and women. What are these? Well, first we must mention the holiness of God. What is holiness? I think we almost inevitably tend to deal with it in negative terms, and we define it as meaning that God is entirely separate from and apart from sin. Holiness primarily means separation—separation from evil.

But, of course, holiness is also something positive. It is absolute purity. The Bible teaches us everywhere that God is holy, and a part of the manifestation of this holiness is His hatred of sin and His separation from sin, from the sinner and from all that is evil.

Let me give you certain outstanding examples and illustrations of the Bible's teaching on this. God has revealed His holiness by granting visions of Himself to certain people. There is the great case of Moses, in Exodus 33 and in other places, where God appeared, as it were, to Moses, and Moses was overwhelmed by the sense of His holiness. The same thing happened to Job, to Isaiah, and to Ezekiel. Anyone who has ever come anywhere near to God has always been impressed by His absolute holiness.

The Bible teaches this in certain terms that it uses; it refers to God as "the Holy One" (Isaiah 40:25), and we have God's injunction, "Be ye holy; for I am holy" (1 Peter 1:16), which is a specific, explicit statement of God's holiness.

I suppose if you were to be asked to say where the Bible teaches the holiness of God most powerfully of all, you have to go to Calvary. God is so holy, so utterly holy, that nothing but that awful death could make it possible for Him to forgive us. The cross is the supreme and the sublimest declaration and revelation of the holiness of God.

❧ A THOUGHT TO PONDER ☙

The cross is the supreme and the sublimest declaration and revelation of the holiness of God.

From *God the Father, God the Son*, pp. 69-71.

GOD'S RIGHTEOUSNESS

He that believeth on the Son hath everlasting life: and
he that believeth not the Son shall not see life;
but the wrath of God abideth on him.

JOHN 3:36

Another moral attribute of God that the Bible emphasizes is the righteousness or the justice of God. Now this follows, of course, inescapably, from the holiness of God. What is righteousness? Well, it is holiness manifested in God's dealings with us. I think that is as good a definition as you can get. Or you can look at it like this: It is that quality in God that always reveals God as doing that which is right. It is that in God which makes Him incapable of doing anything that is wrong. Righteousness and justice are the carrying out of God's holiness and the expression of it in the government of the world.

A further definition still is that the righteousness of God is God's love of holiness, and the justice of God is God's abomination of sin. And I think that is the definition that most commends itself.

Now the righteousness and the justice of God, of course, are revealed almost everywhere in the Scriptures. The wrath of God is taught in both the Old and New Testaments. Our Lord Himself taught it; one of the cardinal doctrines of the whole Bible is that God has a hatred of sin, which He expresses in His wrath. If anyone does not believe, says John, then "the wrath of God abideth on him" (John 3:36). We are all by nature, says Paul, "the children of wrath" (Ephesians 2:3).

But God's righteousness and justice are not only manifested in His wrath. He reveals the same qualities in forgiving our sins. Having prepared the way of forgiveness, if we conform to it, the justice of God comes in, and by His justice God forgives us. And God prepared the way of forgiveness by providing propitiation for our sins—and this is the most remarkable thing of all.

❧ A THOUGHT TO PONDER ☙

Righteousness is holiness manifested in God's dealings with us.

From *God the Father, God the Son*, pp. 72-73.

GOD'S FAITHFULNESS

God is faithful, by whom ye were called unto the fellowship of his Son Jesus Christ our Lord.

1 CORINTHIANS 1:9

Another moral attribute of God is God's faithfulness. What does it mean? When you say that God is faithful, you mean that He is one upon whom you can safely lean. It means one on whom you can absolutely rely, one upon whom you can depend, one upon whom you can secure yourself, without ever being in doubt that He will suddenly let you go.

The Bible has some glorious statements about this. It tells us about the faithfulness of God who always keeps His promises and never breaks His covenants. It tells us that God will always fulfill every word that has ever gone out of His mouth (Isaiah 55:11). It tells us that God will always faithfully and certainly defend and deliver His servants at all times of trial, testing, and conflict. It tells us that God can be relied upon to confirm and to establish all whom He has called, guarding them from the evil one and keeping them and guiding them until His purposes are fulfilled in them.

Listen to one great statement of all that: "God is faithful, by whom ye were called unto the fellowship of his Son Jesus Christ our Lord" (1 Corinthians 1:9). Whatever else may happen, whatever may be going wrong, Paul tells those people to be sure of this— God is faithful. Again he says, "And the very God of peace sanctify you wholly; and I pray God your whole spirit and soul and body be preserved blameless unto the coming of our Lord Jesus Christ" (1 Thessalonians 5:23). Then notice, "Faithful is he that called you, who also will do it" (verse 24). This is absolutely certain: Nothing can frustrate His plans; nothing can make Him forego what He has promised; nothing can cause Him to change what He has purposed with respect to you.

❧ A THOUGHT TO PONDER ❧
God is one upon whom you can safely lean.

From *God the Father, God the Son*, pp. 76-77.

GOD'S ETERNAL DECREES

*According as he hath chosen us in him before the foundation of
the world, that we should be holy and without blame
before him in love.*

EPHESIANS 1:4

God's manner or method of working is what is commonly called
the doctrine of the eternal decrees of God. These are the things that
God determined and ordained before He had done anything at all.
We must approach this subject with an open mind, seeking and
searching for the teaching of Scripture.

There are certain things that our finite minds will not be able to
reconcile with one another. Here I must introduce the word *antinomy*. What is an antinomy? It is a position in which you are given two
truths that you yourself cannot reconcile. There are certain final
antimonies in the Bible, and as people of faith we must be ready to
accept that. When somebody says, "Oh, but you cannot reconcile
those two," you must be ready to say, "I cannot. I do not pretend to
be able to. But I believe what I am told in the Scriptures." For example, I know the Bible tells me that man, in a sense, is a free agent,
and on the other hand that God's eternal decrees govern everything.

In the light of the nature and character of God, the doctrine of the
eternal decrees must follow as an utter, absolute necessity. Because
God is who and what He is, He must work in the way in which He
does work. From eternity God has had an unchangeable plan with
reference to His creatures. The Bible is constantly using phrases such
as "before the foundation of the world" (see Ephesians 1:4).

God's plan comprehends and determines all things and events
of every kind that come to pass. If you believe that God has determined certain ends, then you must believe that He determines everything that leads to those ends. The doctrine of the eternal decrees of
God says that all things are ultimately determined and decreed by
Him.

☙ A THOUGHT TO PONDER ☞

From eternity God has had an unchangeable plan with reference to
His creatures.

From *God the Father, God the Son*, pp. 93, 95-96.

ORDAINED TO ETERNAL LIFE

*And when the Gentiles heard this, they were glad, and
glorified the word of the Lord: and as many as were ordained
to eternal life believed.*

ACTS 13:48

The salvation of men and women, and of certain of them in particular, was determined by God before the foundation of the world. He does this entirely according to His own good will and His grace. Read Matthew 11:25-26: "At that time Jesus answered and said, I thank thee, O Father, Lord of heaven and earth, because thou hast hid these things from the wise and prudent, and hast revealed them unto babes. Even so, Father: for so it seemed good in thy sight." And in John 6:37 we read, "All that the Father giveth me shall come to me." In verse 44 our Lord says, "No man can come to me, except the Father which hath sent me draw him." In Acts 13:48 we read, "And as many as were ordained to eternal life believed."

Above all, realize that if you are a child of God, it is because God has determined it, and what He has determined about you is certain and safe and sure. Nothing and no one can ever take you out of His hands or make Him forego His purpose in respect to you. The doctrine of the eternal decrees of God before the foundation of the world has decreed this! He knew me. He knew you. And our names were written in the Lamb's Book of Life before the world was ever made, before you and I or anybody else ever came into it.

Let us bow before His Majesty. Let us humble ourselves in His holy presence. Let us submit ourselves to the revelation that He has so graciously been pleased to give.

❧ A THOUGHT TO PONDER ❧

Nothing and no one can ever take you out of God's hands or make Him forego His purpose in respect to you.

GOOD ANGELS

. . . as the angels of God in heaven.
MATTHEW 22:30

We must see what we are told about good angels. We are told that they dwell in heaven. We are to be "as the angels of God in heaven," our Lord says. The statement in Matthew 18:10 reads, ". . . their angels do always behold the face of my Father which is in heaven." It is clear, therefore, that the dwelling-place, the place of existence, of these good angels is in heaven around the throne of God.

What is the business or purpose of these good angels? We are told that they spend their time adoring God and the Lamb. We read in Revelation 5 that they are singing His praise and worshiping Him and adoring Him. That is what they delight in. That is what, as it were, they live for.

There is something else that the angels are very busy doing. I have never read this next point without having a still more glorious understanding of my salvation. We are told that they spend a good deal of their time looking into this question of our salvation. Let me give you my authority. Peter, talking about our salvation, says, "which things the angels desire to look into" (1 Peter 1:12). It is something so marvelous and so wonderful that these created angelic spirits, always in the presence of God, are, as it were, looking on at this thing that is most astonishing to them and that surpasses everything else.

The angels not only behold the face of God, they are not only looking into salvation, but they are looking at us. In 1 Corinthians 11:10 Paul uses these words: "For this cause ought the woman to have power on her head because of the angels." A woman should have her head covered to show that she is under the authority of the man; and in addition to that, Paul says, she should be covered because of the presence of the angels. In other words, when Christians gather together in prayer, the angels of God are present.

✎ A THOUGHT TO PONDER ✐
Good angels spend their time adoring God and the Lamb.

From *God the Father, God the Son*, pp. 109-110.

ANGELIC REVELATIONS

Are they not all ministering spirits, sent forth to minister for them who shall be heirs of salvation?

HEBREWS 1:14

Another function of the angels is to reveal God's purposes. It was through angels that God revealed to Abraham His purpose with regard to Sodom and Gomorrah (Genesis 18), and He revealed His will to Jacob more than once in the same way. Gideon also was told God's purpose for him through an angel, and in the New Testament Zacharias was told about the birth of his son, who became known as John the Baptist, through an angel that appeared to him when he was in the Temple. It was an angel who told Joseph that he need not worry about the condition of his espoused wife Mary. It was an angel also who told him to flee to Egypt, and an angel who told him to come out of Egypt.

But I would say that the most comforting and the most wonderful aspect of this teaching is what we are told in the Scriptures of the way in which God uses angels to bless and to care for His own people: "Are they not all ministering spirits, sent forth to minister for them who shall be heirs of salvation?" (Hebrews 1:14). What is the greatest function of the angels? It is to minister to you and to me—to minister to the "heirs of salvation."

It seems to me from this biblical teaching that I am entitled to say that the angels are used by God with respect to us and to our salvation. For example, in the account of the conversion of Cornelius in Acts 10, we are told that as Cornelius was praying one day an angel suddenly appeared to him and began to give him a preview, as it were, of his own salvation and to tell him what he should do in order that his salvation might be realized.

✎ A THOUGHT TO PONDER ✎
God uses angels to bless and to care for His own people.

August 22

THE NAMES OF THE DEVIL

Wherein in time past ye walked according to the course of this world, according to the prince of the power of the air, the spirit that now worketh in the children of disobedience.

EPHESIANS 2:2

What does the Bible tell us about the devil? First of all, let us consider some of the names that are applied to him in the Scriptures. He is referred to as "Satan," and the word *Satan* means "adversary." He is also referred to as "the devil," and *devil* means "slanderer." He is also described as "Beelzebub," which means that he is the prince of the devils. He is described as "Apollyon" and as "the angel of the bottomless pit." He is called "the prince of this world" and "the god of this world." He is described as "the prince of the power of the air, the spirit that now worketh in the children of disobedience" (Ephesians 2:2). He is referred to as "the dragon," as a lion, as "Lucifer, that old serpent," and, perhaps one of the most significant names of all, as "the evil one."

Now you will often find in the New Testament that whereas in the *King James Version* the word "evil" is sometimes used, it is probably true to say that it should be "the evil one." Sometimes you will find "wicked" when it should be "the wicked one." There are those who say that when we pray, "deliver us from evil" (Matthew 6:13), it should be, "deliver us from the evil one." And when John, in the last chapter of his first epistle, says that the "whole world lieth in wickedness," he is undoubtedly saying that the whole world lies in "the wicked one" (1 John 5:19).

In the same way in John 17 when our Lord prays in His high-priestly prayer, "I pray not that thou shouldest take them out of the world, but that thou shouldest keep them from the evil," it should be translated "from the evil one" (verse 15). It is a most important term—the evil one.

◆ A THOUGHT TO PONDER ◆

The devil is referred to as "Satan," and the word *Satan* means "adversary."

THE DEVIL IS A PERSON

*Ye are of your father the devil, and the lusts
of your father ye will do.*

JOHN 8:44

The second thing that the Bible tells us about the devil is that he is a person. This is most important at the present time, because it has been the fashion for at least a century not to believe in the devil as a person. This is true not only of those who are unbelievers but also of many who call themselves Christians. They say they believe in the power of evil or an evil influence or a kind of lack in us, but they have a feeling that to believe in a personal devil is to be very much behind the times. But that is thoroughly unbiblical, because the Bible teaches us that the devil is a person.

For myself, there is one proof that is more than sufficient in and of itself, and that is the accounts we have in the Gospels of the temptations of our Lord. Now obviously our Lord's temptations came from somewhere, and when people say that temptation to evil is something that arises solely from within and from a certain lack of power or positive qualities in us, they have no explanation to offer for the temptations of our Lord. It was a person who tempted our Lord, and our Lord addressed him as such; it was the devil who spoke to Him, and He spoke to the devil (Luke 4:1-13)—not an influence, but a person. Furthermore, we find the same thing in the book of Job in the first chapter, where the devil appears quite clearly as a person and addresses God. And God addresses him.

The biblical teaching is in no doubt at all about this. Our Lord, turning to certain Jews one day, said to them, "Ye are of your father the devil, and the lusts of your father ye will do" (John 8:44). How often you find the phrase, "the wicked one"—for example, "then cometh the wicked one" (Matthew 13:19).

⮜ A THOUGHT TO PONDER ⮞

It was a person who tempted our Lord, and our Lord addressed him as such.

From *God the Father, God the Son*, p. 117.

THE CREATION OF THE WORLD

Through faith we understand that the worlds were framed by the word of God, so that things which are seen were not made of things which do appear.

HEBREWS 11:3

We are not given a fully detailed account or philosophy of creation, and yet we claim that the account that we are given is wholly accurate. The Bible claims that it is from God. We read in Hebrews 11:3, "Through faith we understand that the worlds were framed by the word of God, so that things which are seen were not made of things which do appear." God gave an account of the creation to Moses or someone else; so it is not man's ideas or theories. The biblical account does not, however, claim to explain everything.

Second, we must be clear about what creation means. It has been defined as "that free act of God whereby He . . . in the beginning brought forth the whole visible and invisible universe without the use of pre-existing materials, and thus gave it an existence distinct from His own and yet always dependent on Him" (Berkhof).

Now, we hold to that as against other theories that have been put forward. There are those who believe that matter itself is eternal, while others believe in the spontaneous generation of matter and its spontaneous development. Other views are that God simply worked to form matter that already existed or that matter is just an emanation of the divine substance. Pantheism teaches that matter is but a form of God—that it *is* God. On the other hand, those who believe in dualism say that God and matter are eternal, while some teach that the world was produced by an antagonistic spirit, another god or demiurge.

But the biblical doctrine is clear: God made everything out of nothing. The world has a distinct existence, but it is always dependent upon God. "By him," says Paul, "all things consist" (Colossians 1:17).

❧ A THOUGHT TO PONDER ❧
The biblical doctrine is clear: God made everything out of nothing.

From *God the Father, God the Son*, pp. 127-128.

PROVIDENCE

He taketh away the heart of the chief of the people of the earth,
and causeth them to wander in a wilderness where there is no way.

JOB 12:24

What exactly do we mean by *providence*? I cannot think of a better definition or description than this: "Providence is that continued exercise of the divine energy whereby the Creator upholds all His creatures, is operative in all that transpires in the world, and directs all things to their appointed end."

Notice how Psalm 104 puts it in verses 28-30: "That thou givest them [animals of the earth] they gather: thou openest thine hand, they are filled with good. Thou hidest thy face, they are troubled: thou takest away their breath, they die, and return to their dust. Thou sendest forth thy spirit, they are created: and thou renewest the face of the earth." Now God does not create these animals of the earth constantly. What He does is to keep life, to preserve what He has already created.

We are also told that God's providence is exercised over the affairs of nations. You will find that in Job 12:24: "He taketh away the heart of the chief of the people of the earth, and causeth them to wander in a wilderness where there is no way."

We are also told that God providentially governs a man's birth and his lot in this world. We read in 1 Samuel 16:1, "And the LORD said unto Samuel, How long wilt thou mourn for Saul, seeing I have rejected him from reigning over Israel? Fill thine horn with oil, and go, I will send thee to Jesse the Bethlehemite: for I have provided me a king among his sons." And Paul says about himself in Galatians 1:15-16, "But when it pleased God, who separated me from my mother's womb, and called me by his grace, to reveal his Son in me, that I might preach him among the heathen . . ."

✒ A THOUGHT TO PONDER ✐

The Creator is operative in all that transpires in the world and directs all things to their appointed end.

From *God the Father, God the Son*, pp. 143-144, 147.

THE COVENANT OF GRACE

I will take you to me for a people, and I will be to you a God.
EXODUS 6:7

God has made certain promises. So what is the great central promise that He has made in the covenant of grace? He has promised to be a God unto man. That is the great promise: "I will be to you a God." Do you see the importance and significance of this? God had been the God of Adam, but Adam sinned against Him and fell; he became the slave of Satan and broke the connection with God. And the remarkable and astounding thing is that God turned to man and assured him in the covenant of grace that He had a way whereby He could still be a God to man. "I will take you to me for a people, and I will be to you a God" (Exodus 6:7).

Make a note of that because as you go through the Scriptures you will find that this great promise is repeated time and time again. You will find it in Jeremiah 31:33; 32:38-40. You will find it in Ezekiel 34:23-25; 36:25-28; 37:26-27. You will find it in 2 Corinthians 6:16-18 and in Hebrews 8:10 and, in a marvelous way, in Revelation 21:3 where we read: "Behold, the tabernacle of God is with men, and he will dwell with them." That is the final state. So you see that is the very essence of God's promise in the covenant of grace—that what had been broken by sin and the Fall was going to be restored. And the supreme blessing therefore, the ultimate blessing, the blessing of blessings, is that God is my God, and that I have a right to say, "*my* God." And the whole of salvation is included in that.

How often do we tend to define salvation in terms other than that? Yet the greatest thing a human being can ever say since the Fall is this: "God is my God."

✎ A THOUGHT TO PONDER ✐
The greatest thing a human being can ever say since the Fall is this: "God is my God."

From *God the Father, God the Son*, pp. 226-227.

THE COVENANT OF GRACE IN THE OLD TESTAMENT

*And I will put enmity between thee and the woman,
and between thy seed and her seed; it shall bruise thy head,
and thou shalt bruise his heel.*

GENESIS 3:15

What are the ways in which the covenant of grace was dispensed under the old dispensation? Well, you go first of all to Genesis 3:15. If you are interested in the technical term, it is generally called the *protevangel*. In other words, there is a kind of foreshadowing of the whole Gospel in Genesis 3:15.

Now to me this is one of the most fascinating and thrilling things anyone can ever encounter. Here is this great book; we divide it up, and we call it the Old Testament and the New Testament, and we all know what we mean by that. But, you know, if we were to be strictly accurate we would not describe it in that way. The real division of the Bible is this: first, everything you get from Genesis 1:1 to Genesis 3:14; then everything from Genesis 3:15 to the very end of the Bible. What you have up until Genesis 3:14 is the account of the creation and of God's original covenant of works with man and of how that failed because man broke it. Beginning with Genesis 3:15 you get the announcement of the Gospel, the covenant of grace, the way of salvation, and that is the whole theme of the Bible until you come to the last verse of the book of Revelation. That is the real division of the Bible.

But, of course, we talk about the Old Testament and the New Testament because we want to emphasize the two main ways in which this one great covenant of grace has been administered, and here it is beginning in Genesis 3:15. Now the whole of the Gospel is in that verse. It is there in this almost cryptic form, in this very underdeveloped form, but it is there.

❧ A THOUGHT TO PONDER ❧

There is a kind of foreshadowing of the whole Gospel in Genesis 3:15.

THE PROTEVANGEL

*And I will put enmity between thee and the woman,
and between thy seed and her seed; it shall bruise thy head,
and thou shalt bruise his heel.*

GENESIS 3:15

What does God tell us in Genesis 3:15? Well, first of all that He was going to put enmity between the serpent and the woman and her seed. Hitherto there had been no enmity between them; but the serpent had beguiled Eve, so they were very friendly together, and the woman was now under the dominion of the devil. Had God not done something, that would have been the end of the story. But God came in and said, "Now I am going to break that friendship; you were meant for friendship with Me, not with the devil. So I am going to put enmity between you and the devil, and between the devil and you." This was the first announcement of salvation. Man cannot be saved while he is a friend of the devil and an enemy of God. He must be a friend of God; therefore he must become an enemy of the devil.

The second thing, therefore, that is implied is that God was going to give man power and grace to fight the devil. Man had already been defeated by him and was his slave. Man must have help and strength, and God promised him that. God promised to be on man's side in this fight against the enemy. He applied the promise also to the "seed"—"between thy seed and her seed." That is most important. It was not a temporary promise given there in Eden; it was to continue until it had achieved its ultimate purpose.

You notice also that God said that the quarrel was to go on not only between the woman and her seed and the devil, but also between the seed of the woman and the seed of the serpent. So humanity can be divided into the seed of God and of Christ and the seed of the devil, and there is a fight between them—all announced in Genesis 3:15.

❧ A THOUGHT TO PONDER ❧
Man cannot be saved while he is a friend of the devil.

From *God the Father, God the Son*, pp. 228-229.

August 29

ONE COVENANT OF GRACE

I will be their God.

GENESIS 17:8

Consider the new disposition of the covenant of grace—the word "new" simply means a new administration of the same covenant. Let us remind ourselves of God's purpose in this covenant of grace. Through sin and the Fall men and women lost their knowledge of God—they were estranged from Him, and God's purpose of redemption was to bring us back to know Him. The working out of the new economy of this covenant has been done in and through our Lord and Savior Jesus Christ. It is important, first of all, that we should establish clearly that we are still dealing with the same covenant. So let me give you these proofs.

The first is that *there is but one covenant of grace*, and it is the same covenant in the Old Testament as it is in the New Testament. We notice that the great promise made in the Old Testament ("I will be their God"—the promise made to Abraham in Genesis 17:8) is mentioned several times in the New Testament. It is one and the same promise. The greatest thing that can happen to anybody is to say, "My God." Nothing is to be compared with this, and it is the New Testament term as well as the Old Testament term.

The second proof is that *you find the same kind of blessing in the Old Testament and in the New Testament*. Take Psalm 51 and see what David prays there: "Create in me a clean heart, O God; and renew a right spirit within me" (verse 10); he wants to have the joy of his salvation restored to him (verse 12). Sometimes Christian people speak very wrongly of the kind of spiritual experience that was enjoyed by the Old Testament saints. There is a tendency to say that we have this experience but that they had nothing. You would be very surprised to hear that the psalmist is further on spiritually than you are!

⟶ A THOUGHT TO PONDER ⟵
There is but one covenant of grace, and it is the same covenant in the Old Testament as it is in the New Testament.

THE COVENANT OF GRACE IN THE BIBLE

And the scripture, foreseeing that God would justify the heathen through faith, preached before the gospel unto Abraham, saying, In thee shall all nations be blessed.

GALATIANS 3:8

The third proof of there being only one covenant is that *the Bible teaches very clearly that there is only one Gospel*; the Gospel is the same in the Old Testament as it is the New Testament. Again I am surprised when a preacher does not see it in the Old Testament, for if a man does not see it there, I doubt if he understands the Gospel in the New Testament. Take the Gospel that was preached by God in the Garden of Eden and also the promise made to Abraham; that is the essence of the Gospel. Look at all the types and shadows; look at the various offerings described in Leviticus and elsewhere. Look even at the very furniture of the Tabernacle. All these things preach the Gospel; they are types of the Gospel and its message.

It is most important that we should grasp that whenever we read the Bible. Listen to the teaching of the prophets; look at the great passages in Isaiah and in Jeremiah, and indeed in all the prophetic books. The statements of the Gospel are the same in both Testaments. Consider, too, the specific statements made by Paul in Galatians 3:8 where he speaks of God justifying the heathen through faith. He says, "And the scripture, foreseeing that God would justify the heathen through faith, preached before the gospel unto Abraham, saying, In thee shall all nations be blessed." Surely this statement in and of itself is enough to show that there is only one Gospel.

My fourth proof is that *there are a number of direct statements that tell us that the Old Testament saints are now in the kingdom of God in exactly the same way as we are and share all the blessings of God with us*. Take, for example, Luke 13:28.

❧ A THOUGHT TO PONDER ❧
The Old Testament saints are now in the kingdom of God in exactly the same way as we are.

THE TWO DISPENSATIONS UNITED

The just shall live by his faith.

HABAKKUK 2:4

My fifth proof of there being one covenant is that clearly, according to the Scriptures, *there is only one way of obtaining salvation and all those blessings, and that is the way of faith.* All the Old Testament saints believed explicitly in God, and they exercised faith. In Habakkuk 2:4 we read, "The just shall live by his faith." This is the theme and the message of the Old Testament from beginning to end; and—for example, in Hebrews 11—it is reiterated in the New Testament. Paul, quoting from Habakkuk, says in Romans 1:17, "The just shall live by faith," and this is the theme of all his epistles.

But Paul puts it still more clearly and specifically in Romans 4:23-25, where, referring to Abraham, he says, "Now it was not written for his sake alone, that it was imputed to him; but for us also, to whom it shall be imputed, if we believe on him that raised up Jesus our Lord from the dead; who was delivered for our offences, and was raised again for our justification." It is clear that we receive justification by faith, exactly as Abraham received it by faith. For one more example under this heading, read again from the end of Hebrews 10 through chapter 11 to the beginning of chapter 12. It is the same truth, elaborated at length.

The sixth proof is that *there is only one mediator under the two dispensations*—the same mediator, the Lord Jesus Christ—"the Lamb slain from the foundation of the world" (Revelation 13:8). Take the promise made to Adam about the seed of the woman. God says that salvation is going to happen in that way, and other Scriptures prove that the seed of the woman is no other than the Lord Jesus Christ. He is the mediator in the Old Testament types—they all point to Him; also the prophecies all point to Him. It is always the Lord Himself.

✖ A THOUGHT TO PONDER ✖

It is clear that we receive justification by faith, exactly as Abraham received it by faith.

September

LIFE IN CHRIST

FROM

God the Father, God the Son

AND

Fellowship with God

DOUBTFUL CHRISTIANS

But though we, or an angel from heaven, preach any other
gospel unto you than that which we have preached unto you,
let him be accursed.

GALATIANS 1:8

Christianity, as has often been pointed out, is Christ Himself. He is
not only central, He is absolutely vital, and therefore we have to
see that we are concerned primarily and always with Him. What
reveals at once that so many people who call themselves Christian
are not Christian is that Christ as a person is not at all essential to
them.

I am referring here to people who think that a Christian is just
a good man or woman. Obviously you can be a "good" man without even mentioning the Lord Jesus Christ; but in Christianity He
is vital, and if the truth concerning Him is not the truth, the whole
position vanishes. Now that is something that one cannot overem-
phasize. The Christian faith is entirely concerned about Him—who
He is, and what He has done, and what He has made available and
possible for us. And therefore you see the vital importance of our
being quite clear in our minds and absolutely right about all of
these things.

So I make no apology for putting it as dogmatically and as
bluntly as that. To me, those who apologize for saying such a thing
are very doubtful Christians, if indeed they are Christians at all.
There is an intolerance about the Christian faith, expressed like this
by the apostle Paul: "But though we, or an angel from heaven,
preach any other gospel unto you than that which we have preached
unto you, let him be accursed" (Galatians 1:8). And we must say
the same thing. The truth is clear, it is well defined, it is perfectly
definite; and we must be certain, therefore, with regard to what we
believe about Christ. It is not enough to say, "I believe in Christ."

✎ A THOUGHT TO PONDER ✎
Christianity, as has often been pointed out, is Christ Himself.

From *God the Father, God the Son*, p. 246.

BELIEF IN JESUS CHRIST

But these are written, that ye might believe that Jesus is the Christ,
the Son of God; and that believing ye might have life
through his name.

JOHN 20:31

What do we believe about Christ? What is the teaching about Him? Why do you think the four Gospels were ever written? Surely there can be no hesitation about answering this question. They were written—God caused men to write them and guided them through the Spirit as they did so—in order that the truth concerning the Lord Jesus Christ might be known exactly. All sorts of false stories were current in the first century. They were apocryphal gospels, and in them things were being ascribed to Him and He was reported to have done and said things that had never happened. So the Gospels were written in order to define the truth, in order to exclude certain falsehoods and give the facts plainly and clearly.

Luke, in the introduction to his Gospel, says: "Forasmuch as many have taken in hand to set forth in order a declaration of those things which are most surely believed among us, even as they delivered them unto us, which from the beginning were eyewitnesses, and ministers of the word; it seemed good to me also, having had perfect understanding of all things from the very first, to write unto thee in order, most excellent Theophilus, that thou mightest know the certainty of those things, wherein thou hast been instructed" (1:1-4). You will find that John, at the end of his Gospel, virtually says the same thing: "But these are written, that ye might believe that Jesus is the Christ, the Son of God . . ." (20:31).

But not only do the Gospels tell us that—there are also several sections in other parts of the New Testament that specifically make the same point. Take the first epistle of John, for example. Why was it written? To counteract the false teaching that was current, the teaching that denied that Jesus Christ had come in the flesh, that docetism, that false doctrine.

✎ A THOUGHT TO PONDER ✐

The Gospels were written in order that the truth concerning the Lord Jesus Christ might be known exactly.

From *God the Father, God the Son*, pp. 246-247.

OLD TESTAMENT PROPHECIES FULFILLED

For all the promises of God in him are yea, and in him Amen,
unto the glory of God by us.

2 CORINTHIANS 1:20

What does the Old Testament tell about Christ as it focuses attention upon Him and compels us to consider Him? First, it says that He is the fulfillment of all the Old Testament prophecies and promises. The great central statement of that is in 2 Corinthians 1:20: "For all the promises of God in him are yea, and in him Amen, unto the glory of God by us." They come to a focus, to a point, in Him.

He is the fulfillment of the promise that was given in the Garden of Eden when God said that the seed of the woman would bruise the serpent's head (Genesis 3:15). There is also the promise given to Abraham in Genesis 17 about the seed. Paul refers to this in Galatians 3:16: "He saith not, And to seeds, as of many; but as of one, And to thy seed, which is Christ."

Take, for instance, the promise given in Genesis 49:10: "The scepter shall not depart from Judah, nor a lawgiver from between his feet, until Shiloh come; and unto him shall the gathering of the people be." That is a tremendous promise and a most vital statement, and it was literally fulfilled in the coming of the Lord Jesus Christ. It is a fact of history that the scepter and lawgiver did remain with Judah until A.D. 70, and since then, with the destruction of Jerusalem and the casting out of the Jewish nation among the nations, that has no longer been the case. The scepter and the lawgiver remained there until Christ came, and then it departed, in that external sense. And likewise the statement "and unto him shall the gathering of the people be" obviously has been fulfilled and only fulfilled in the Lord Jesus Christ.

✒ A THOUGHT TO PONDER ✒

Christ is the fulfillment of all the Old Testament prophecies and promises.

From *God the Father, God the Son*, p. 248.

PROPHECIES ABOUT CHRIST'S BIRTH

But thou, Bethlehem Ephratah, though thou be little among
the thousands of Judah, yet out of thee shall he come forth
unto me that is to be ruler in Israel; whose goings forth have
been from of old, from everlasting.

MICAH 5:2

Take a number of prophecies with regard to Christ's birth. First of all we are told something with regard to the time of His appearance. In Malachi 3:1 the prophet says, "Behold, I will send my messenger, and he shall prepare the way before me: and the Lord, whom ye seek, shall suddenly come to his temple, even the messenger of the covenant, whom ye delight in: behold, he shall come, saith the LORD of hosts." That is very significant. Furthermore, you remember that in Micah 5:2 we are given an exact prophecy with regard to the place of His birth—that it was to be in Bethlehem. "But thou, Bethlehem Ephratah, though thou be little among the thousands of Judah, yet out of thee shall he come forth unto me that is to be ruler in Israel; whose goings forth have been from of old, from everlasting." We are told that He was to be of the tribe of Judah and of the house of David in Jeremiah 23:5-6: "Behold, the days come, saith the LORD, that I will raise unto David a righteous Branch, and a King shall reign and prosper, and shall execute judgment and justice in the earth. In his days Judah shall be saved, and Israel shall dwell safely: and this is his name whereby he shall be called, THE LORD OUR RIGHTEOUSNESS."

Then in Isaiah 7:14 we are told that He is to be born of a virgin. The prophet is promising a sign, and a sign is obviously something unusual. If a virgin has a child, it is unusual, and it is a sign. We are specifically told in Matthew 1:22-23 that this verse in Isaiah was indeed a prophecy that our Lord would be born of a virgin.

☙ A THOUGHT TO PONDER ☞

We are given an exact prophecy with regard to the place of His birth.

SPECIFIC PROMISES FULFILLED

. . . they shall look upon me whom they have pierced, and
they shall mourn . . .
ZECHARIAH 12:10

Prophecy tells us that Christ is to be "a light to lighten the Gentiles" (Luke 2:32), a most astounding thing to have said to the Jews. But it was said many times in the prophecy of Isaiah, in 42:6 and 60:3 and in other places. We are also told in Isaiah 53 that His death is to be vicarious. We are told that He will enter into the city of Jerusalem riding on a donkey (Zechariah 9:9), and you remember how that was fulfilled. We are told that He is to be sold for thirty pieces of silver, and that with His price a potter's field will be purchased (Zechariah 11:12-13). We are told that lots would be cast for His garments (Psalm 22:18). We are told that He will be given vinegar to drink in His sorrow (Psalm 69:21). We are even told that He would utter certain words on the cross: "My God, my God, why hast thou forsaken me?" (Psalm 22:1). Psalm 22:16 says that His hands and feet will be pierced, and Zechariah 12:10 adds, ". . . they shall look upon me whom they have pierced, and they shall mourn." And we are told in Isaiah 53:9 that He will make His grave with the wicked and with the rich in His death, and we know that He was buried in the tomb of Joseph of Arimathea.

The Bible also exhorts us to consider Him because He is the only one by whom we can be reconciled to God and by whom we can know God. We read in Hebrews 12:24 that He is "the mediator of the new covenant." He said Himself, "I am the way, the truth, and the life: no man cometh unto the Father, but by me" (John 14:6). Anyone who says a thing like that must be looked at and considered. If we value our salvation and want to know God, we must listen to such a person.

❧ A THOUGHT TO PONDER ❧
We are told in Isaiah 53 that Christ's death is to be vicarious.

From *God the Father, God the Son*, pp. 250-251.

THE INCARNATION

The word was made flesh, and dwelt among us.
JOHN 1:14

The doctrine of the Incarnation does not teach, neither does it involve the idea, that a change took place in the personality of the Son of God. There was a change in the form in which He appeared, there was a change in the state in which He manifested Himself, but there was no change in His personality. He is the same Person always. In the womb of the virgin Mary and lying as a helpless babe in the manger, He is still the second person in the holy Trinity.

We must never so state the doctrine of the Incarnation as to give the impression that we say that the Son of God was changed into a man. That is why that phrase about God becoming man is misleading. We see this in John 1:14: "The word was made flesh, and dwelt among us." That very phrase "was made" has often caused people to think that the Son of God was changed into a man. This is partly due to the fact that it is not really the best translation. Instead of saying, "The Word was made flesh," what we really mean is that He *became* flesh or that He *took on* flesh. The idea of making gives the impression of being changed into, but that is wrong.

In other words, the way in which the Scripture generally puts it is this: In Romans 8:3 we are told that He came "in the likeness of sinful flesh." That is better. Or take it as it is put in 1 John 4:2: "Hereby know ye the Spirit of God: Every spirit that confesseth that Jesus Christ is come in the flesh is of God." Jesus Christ has not been changed into a man; it is this eternal Person who has come in the flesh. That is the right way to put it.

❧ A THOUGHT TO PONDER ❧

We must never so state the doctrine of the Incarnation as to give the impression that we say that the Son of God was changed into a man.

CLAIMS OF DIVINITY

. . . the only begotten Son, which is in the bosom of the Father . . .

JOHN 1:18

The Bible makes many claims to the effect that Christ is divine; it asserts and teaches His divinity or, still more accurately, His deity. The first evidence is that certain names are ascribed to Him, each of which clearly implies His deity. Here are some of them. He is described as the "Son of God" forty times; He is referred to as "his Son" (God's Son); God refers to Him audibly as "my Son." So there, in various forms, is that title "Son," "Son of God."

Then five times He is also referred to as the "only begotten Son of God." You find it in John 1:18 (". . . the only begotten Son, which is in the bosom of the Father . . ."), and there are many others. A notable one is the Parable of the Wicked Husbandman, when God says, "They will reverence my son" (Matthew 21:37). The teaching there is perfectly clear—the words are uttered by our Lord Himself.

He is described in Revelation 1 as "the first and the last," and in the same chapter as "the Alpha and Omega," the beginning and the end. These are obviously terms of deity; there is nothing before the beginning and nothing after the end. Then Peter, preaching in Jerusalem—you will find it recorded in Acts 3:14—refers to Him as "the Holy One": "But ye denied the Holy One and the Just." Again, these are terms of deity.

Then He is actually referred to as "God." Thomas says, "My Lord and my God" (John 20:28). He is also described as "Emmanuel . . . God with us" in Matthew 1:23; and there is a most remarkable statement in Titus 2:13 where He is referred to as our "great God and our Saviour Jesus Christ." So there you have a number of names that are ascribed to Him, all of which are divine names.

∽ A THOUGHT TO PONDER ↫

Certain names are ascribed to Him, each of which clearly implies His deity.

DIVINE ATTRIBUTES OF CHRIST

*For he hath put all things under his feet. But when he saith
all things are put under him, it is manifest that he is excepted,
which did put all things under him.*

1 CORINTHIANS 15:27

The Bible ascribes to Christ certain divine attributes. For instance, *omnipotence*. Hebrews 1:3 says that He upholds "all things by the word of his power"—no stronger statement than that is possible. "All things are put under him" (1 Corinthians 15:27).

Then *omniscience* is attributed to Him. In John 2:24-25 you will find the claim, "he knew what was in man." It was not necessary for anybody to tell Him.

Then *omnipresence* is attributed to Him also. Matthew 18:20 says, "For where two or three are gathered together in my name, there am I." In Matthew 28:20 He says, "And, lo, I am with you alway, even unto the end." And in John 3:13 there is a very striking statement: "And no man hath ascended up to heaven, but he that came down from heaven, even the Son of man which is in heaven." He said those words while He was on earth—the Son of man who "is in heaven." And, indeed, the apostle Paul writes that He "filleth all in all" (Ephesians 1:23)—again a very comprehensive statement.

Another divine attribute is His *eternity*: "In the beginning was the Word" (John 1:1). We also have statements about His *immutability*: He cannot change. Hebrews 13:8 tells us, "Jesus Christ the same yesterday, and to day, and for ever." Then, of course, the Bible asserts His *preexistence*. Colossians 1:17 tells us, "And he is before all things." In John 17:5 He prays, "And now, O Father, glorify thou me with thine own self with the glory which I had with thee before the world was."

✑ A THOUGHT TO PONDER ✑

The Bible ascribes to Christ certain divine attributes.

From *God the Father, God the Son*, pp. 267-268.

DIVINE OFFICES OF CHRIST

*Who shall change our vile body, that it may be fashioned like unto
his glorious body, according to the working whereby he is able
even to subdue all things unto himself.*

PHILIPPIANS 3:21

Christ is said to hold and to fulfill certain divine offices. First of all,
creation: "All things were made by him; and without him was not
any thing made that was made" (John 1:3). You will find the same
thing repeated in Colossians 1:16, and again in Hebrews 1:10. But
we are also told that He preserves everything. Hebrews 1:3 refers
to His "upholding all things by the word of his power." And again
in Colossians 1:17 you find that "by him all things consist."

Notice also that He did not hesitate to claim *the power to forgive sins*. He said to the paralyzed man, "Son, thy sins be forgiven
thee" (Mark 2:5). He also claimed *power to raise the dead*; you
find that mentioned several times in John 6:39-44: "And this is the
Father's will which hath sent me, that of all which he hath given me
I should lose nothing, but should raise it up again at the last day. And
this is the will of him that sent me, that every one which seeth the
Son, and believeth on him, may have everlasting life: and I will raise
him up at the last day. The Jews then murmured at him, because he
said, I am the bread which came down from heaven. And they said,
Is not this Jesus, the son of Joseph, whose father and mother we
know? how is it then that he saith, I came down from heaven? Jesus
therefore answered and said unto them, Murmur not among yourselves. No man can come to me, except the Father which hath sent
me draw him: and I will raise him up at the last day."

The apostle Paul claims that Christ also has *power to transform our bodies*: "Who shall change our vile body [or this body of
our humiliation], that it may be fashioned like unto his glorious
body, according to the working whereby he is able even to subdue all
things unto himself" (Philippians 3:21).

ᔕ A THOUGHT TO PONDER ᔐ
Christ did not hesitate to claim the power to forgive sins.

From *God the Father, God the Son*, pp. 268-269.

NAMES AND WORSHIP

Go ye therefore, and teach all nations, baptizing them in the name of the Father, and of the Son, and of the Holy Ghost.

MATTHEW 28:19

Further evidence for the deity of Christ is the way in which the names of God the Father and Jesus Christ the Son are coupled together. There are several examples of this. Christ Himself said, "Go ye therefore, and teach all nations, baptizing them in the name of the Father, and of the Son, and of the Holy Ghost." Romans 1:7 speaks of "God our Father, and the Lord Jesus Christ." In 2 Corinthians 13:14, in the so-called apostolic benediction, we read, "The grace of the Lord Jesus Christ, and the love of God, and the communion of the Holy Ghost, be with you all." First Thessalonians 3:11 says, "Now God himself and our Father, and our Lord Jesus Christ, direct our way unto you." And, indeed, you will find it in James 1:1, "James, a servant of God and of the Lord Jesus Christ . . ."

A further piece of evidence supporting the divinity of Christ is that divine worship is ascribed to Him. He accepted such worship from men and women when He was on earth. You will find that in Matthew 28:9 and in Luke 24:52. But you get it also by way of exhortation in 1 Corinthians 1:2 where Paul refers to "all that in every place call upon the name of Jesus Christ our Lord." That is worship. In 2 Corinthians 12:8-9 Paul tells us, "For this thing I besought the Lord thrice . . ."—that this is the Lord Jesus Christ is quite clear from the context. In Acts 7:59 we read of Stephen, as he was being stoned, "And they stoned Stephen, calling upon God, and saying, Lord Jesus, receive my spirit." Indeed, our Lord Himself already prepared us for all this when He said, "That all men should honour the Son, even as they honour the Father" (John 5:23).

☙ A THOUGHT TO PONDER ❧

The names of God the Father and Jesus Christ the Son are coupled together.

From *God the Father, God the Son*, pp. 269-270.

THE HUMANITY OF CHRIST

And the child grew, and waxed strong in spirit, filled with wisdom:
and the grace of God was upon him.

LUKE 2:40

The Scriptures also teach about Christ's humanity. Take, for instance, what you read in 1 Timothy 2:5: "For there is one God, and one mediator between God and men, the man Christ Jesus." He is described as "the man." Notice—you cannot have read the Gospels without noticing—the frequency with which the term "the Son of man" is used about Him. It is used over eighty times! Now *the Son of man*, of course, is a very special term, and it has a very special significance.

Then the Scriptures make abundantly plain and clear that Christ had a typical human, physical nature. Take that statement in Hebrews 2:14, where we are told that because "the children are partakers of flesh and blood . . . he also himself likewise took part of the same."

Another very striking bit of evidence under this heading is that He obviously looked like a man. Not only that, we also have evidence to prove that He looked like a typical Jew. You remember what we are told of the incident of the woman of Samaria meeting our Lord at the well, and how she expressed her astonishment that He should speak to her: "How is it that thou, being a Jew, askest drink of me, which am a woman of Samaria?" (John 4:9). She had no idea who He was, but when He spoke to her, she at once recognized that He was a Jew.

Then, under this same heading of His physical frame, the Scriptures teach us that He still had this human body even after His resurrection. When He appeared to the disciples, when Thomas was present in the room and He was anxious to prove to Thomas that He was the same person, He said, "Reach hither thy finger, and behold my hands; and reach hither thy hand, and thrust it into my side: and be not faithless, but believing" (John 20:27).

❦ A THOUGHT TO PONDER ❧
Christ obviously looked like a man.

From *God the Father, God the Son*, pp. 271-272.

LIMITATIONS

But of that day and that hour knoweth no man, no, not the angels
which are in heaven, neither the Son, but the Father.

MARK 13:32

Another piece of evidence for the humanity of Christ is that here
on earth He was subject to certain [self-imposed] limitations in His
knowledge. There is an instance of this in Mark 11:13—the incident of the barren fig tree. We are told that our Lord came to it
expecting to find fruit. He did not know that it had none. Also, in
Mark 13:32 we read these most important and momentous words,
"But of that day and that hour knoweth no man, no, not the angels
which are in heaven, neither the Son, but the Father." He said specifically that He did not know the precise time of this day that is coming; not only the angels, but even He did not know it, but only the
Father.

That brings us to another proof of Christ's humanity, which is
that He was subject to physical limitation. In John 4, in the instance
of the woman of Samaria, we are told that He was weary. He sat
down by the side of the well and did not go with the disciples to
buy provisions because He was physically tired. We read that He
fell asleep in the boat on the sea, in the stern of the vessel (Mark
4:36-41). In the incident of the barren fig tree we are told that as
He was going to Jerusalem one morning He was hungry. He endured
physical agony in the Garden of Gethsemane, sweating great drops
of blood. And finally, of course, and conclusively and most important of all, He actually, literally died; and His death—this physical
limitation—is the ultimate proof of His humanity.

Further evidence of Christ's humanity was that He was tempted.
We find this in Hebrews 2:18, in addition to the Gospel accounts of
His temptation in the wilderness.

☙ A THOUGHT TO PONDER ☙
Christ was subject to physical limitation.

From *God the Father, God the Son*, p. 273.

CHRIST THE PROPHET

He that hath seen me hath seen the Father.

JOHN 14:9

How did Christ act as a prophet on earth? He did so in all His teaching: His teaching concerning God the Father; His exposition of the law in the Sermon on the Mount; in all He told us of God's love, of God's gracious purpose, of His nature and His person. All this was a part of the exercise of His prophetic function, and supremely He told us about Himself. All this is vital, and I emphasize it because we sometimes forget that a part of our salvation consists in our receiving this knowledge that our Lord has given. This is why we must realize that this Gospel applies to us. All He taught applies to us; the Gospel is vital for Christian people and for Christian living. Christ is our Prophet.

And then He taught us by His life and example. "He that hath seen me hath seen the Father" (John 14:9). "Look at me," He said in effect. "Have not my works shown you?" (See John 10:37-38.) "Hast thou not known me, Philip?" (John 14:9). "If you only look at Me, you will learn about God."

Then let me go on to show you how He has continued to exercise His prophetic function ever since His ascension, after He left earth and returned to heaven. He said that He would speak through the Holy Spirit. "I have yet many things to say unto you, but ye cannot bear them now. Howbeit when he, the Spirit of truth, is come, he will guide you into all truth: for he shall not speak of himself; but whatsoever he shall hear, that shall he speak: and he will show you things to come. He shall glorify me: for he shall receive of mine, and shall show it unto you" (John 16:12-14). The Holy Spirit would not speak of Himself or about Himself, but the Holy Spirit would be told what to say. Christ would send the Holy Spirit to instruct. As the Son did not speak of Himself but from the Father, so the Spirit speaks as our Lord instructs Him.

✎ A THOUGHT TO PONDER ✐
Christ exercised His prophetic function as He told us about Himself.

From *God the Father, God the Son*, pp. 294-295.

CHRIST THE PRIEST

*Wherefore, holy brethren, partakers of the heavenly calling,
consider the Apostle and High Priest of our profession,
Christ Jesus.*

HEBREWS 3:1

What are the evidences for saying that Christ is God's appointed High Priest? Well, it is interesting to observe that there is only one book in the Bible that describes Him directly and explicitly as Priest, and that is, of course, the Epistle to the Hebrews. Hebrews describes Him as such in a number of verses: "Wherefore, holy brethren, partakers of the heavenly calling, consider the Apostle and High Priest of our profession, Christ Jesus" (3:1). "Seeing then that we have a great high priest, that is passed into the heavens, Jesus the Son of God, let us hold fast our profession" (4:14). "So also Christ glorified not himself to be made an high priest; but he that said unto him, Thou art my Son, to day have I begotten thee" (5:5). "Whither the forerunner is for us entered, even Jesus, made an high priest for ever after the order of Melchisedec" (6:20). "For such an high priest became us, who is holy, harmless, undefiled, separate from sinners, and made higher than the heavens" (7:26). "We have such an high priest, who is set on the right hand of the throne of the Majesty in the heavens" (8:1).

But, of course, in many other places the teaching is implicit—by implication it is there. For instance, listen to our Lord Himself. He said, "For even the Son of man came not to be ministered unto, but to minister, and to give his life a ransom for many" (Mark 10:45). This is also something that is constantly taught by the apostle Paul. In Romans 3:24-25 he says, "Being justified freely by his grace through the redemption that is in Christ Jesus: Whom God hath set forth to be a propitiation through faith in his blood, to declare his righteousness for the remission of sins that are past, through the forbearance of God."

❧ A THOUGHT TO PONDER ☙

There is only one book in the Bible that describes Him directly and explicitly as Priest—the Epistle to the Hebrews.

From *God the Father, God the Son*, pp. 303-304.

THE CHRISTIAN AND THE WORLD

And we know that we are of God, and the whole world lieth in
wickedness [or, in the wicked one].

1 JOHN 5:19

The New Testament teaches that however much the world may change on the surface, it is always under the control of evil and of sin. This admits that the powers of evil can be mollified a great deal, and they have been mollified during the passing of the centuries. There have been periods when the world has been getting better, but these have been followed by a terrible declension, and the teaching of the New Testament is that the whole time the world has been lying "in the wicked one."

Now that is where, it seems to me, we have been so steadily fooled for the last hundred years; and when I say "we," I mean the Christian as well as the non-Christian. How confident people were toward the end of the nineteenth century that the world was being Christianized! But we must not be deluded by all these changes that are merely superficial. The world, says John to these people, is under the dominion of Satan and sin. It is in the grip of evil; it always has been, and it always will be.

According to the New Testament (and here we get the realism), the world will always be the world; it will never get better. I do not know the future. There may be another period of apparent reform and improvement, but the world will still be lying "in the wicked one," and indeed the New Testament tells us it may "wax worse and worse" (2 Timothy 3:13). Indeed the evil of the world is so essentially a part of it and its life that its final outlook will be judgment and destruction. You will find this teaching everywhere. The evil in the world cannot be taken out; it is to be destroyed. There is to be an ultimate climax, and there will be a terrible end.

∾ A THOUGHT TO PONDER ∾

The teaching of the New Testament is that the whole time the world has been lying "in the wicked one."

From *Fellowship with God*, pp. 17-18.

FULL AND LASTING JOY

And these things write we unto you, that your joy may be full.
1 JOHN 1:4

The apostle is anxious that these Christian people, to whom he is writing, should have fullness of joy, though they are in the world, which lies under the power of the evil one.

Now that is the amazing thing that is offered and promised to us in the New Testament. It is by no means a message confined to this epistle. We see it in Paul's epistle to the Philippians: "Rejoice in the Lord always: and again I say, Rejoice" (4:4). Our Lord promised in John 16:33, "In the world ye shall have tribulation." He described the world as an evil place, and He forewarned His followers what to expect from it. He said, "If the world hate you, ye know that it hated me before it hated you"; but His great promise was that He would give them the joy that He Himself possessed. There would be a period at the crucifixion and before the resurrection when they would be unhappy and miserable. "But," He said, "I will see you again, and your heart shall rejoice, and your joy no man taketh from you" (John 16:22). He also said, "These things have I spoken unto you . . . that your joy might be full" (John 15:11)—the very word that John repeats in his first epistle.

That is Christ's promise, and perhaps there is nothing that is more characteristic of the book of the Acts of the Apostles than this very note. If you are feeling tired and in need of a spiritual tonic, go to the book of Acts, and there you will find this irrepressible joy that these people had in confirmation of the Lord's promise!

❧ A THOUGHT TO PONDER ☙
Christ described the world as an evil place, but His great promise was that He would give them joy.

From *Fellowship with God*, pp. 23-24.

HOW TO KNOW THE JOY

And these things write we unto you, that your joy may be full.
1 JOHN 1:4

The first thing that is essential before we can ever have and hold this joy is the absolute centrality of the Lord Jesus Christ. John starts with Him in 1 John 1:1-3: "That which was from the beginning, which we have heard, which we have seen with our eyes, which we have looked upon, and our hands have handled, of the Word of life; (For the life was manifested, and we have seen it, and bear witness, and show unto you that eternal life, which was with the Father, and was manifested unto us;) That which we have seen and heard declare we unto you, that ye also may have fellowship with us: and truly our fellowship is with the Father, and with his Son Jesus Christ. And these things write we unto you, that your joy may be full."

You will never know any joy until you know Christ. He is the source of joy; He is the fount of all blessings; everything comes through Him. So before John begins to discuss anything else, he talks about Him.

Here we come to the great watershed that divides Christian preaching and teaching from every other teaching; it is based solely on the Lord Jesus Christ. The Christian Church has nothing to say to the world until it believes on Him. Indeed, the Church's message to the world is one of condemnation until it believes on Christ. Christ is central, He is essential, He is the beginning and the end, and John has nothing to say to these people by way of encouragement unless they are absolutely clear about Him. It is through Him that we have access to God; and it is through Him that we have fellowship with God.

❧ A THOUGHT TO PONDER ❧
You will never know any joy until you know Christ.

From *Fellowship with God*, pp. 32-33.

BARRIERS TO FELLOWSHIP WITH GOD

This then is the message which we have heard of him, and declare
unto you, that God is light, and in him is no darkness at all.

1 JOHN 1:5

There are certain things that tend to militate against fellowship with God and to rob us of it; there are certain things that will stand between us and the fellowship that in turn leads to joy.

First of all, there is *sin—unrighteousness*. John has told us about the possibility of great joy (verse 4); then comes a word that almost crushes us to the ground at once: "This then is the message which we have heard of him, and declare unto you, that God is light, and in him is no darkness at all"—and fellowship seems hopeless. But then, thank God, he tells us how this can be dealt with. If we recognize and confess sin, then there is the blood that cleanses, and God is faithful and just to forgive us our sins (1:7, 9).

The second hindrance that John talks about in 1 John 2:3 is *lack of love for the brethren*. If there is anything wrong in my relationship to God, I lose the fellowship, and I lose the joy. Yes, but if there is anything wrong in my relationship with my Christian brothers and sisters, I also lose the joy, and John works this out in a very subtle way. You lose contact with the brethren, and you lose contact with God; you lose your love to God in the same way.

The third hindrance is *a love of the world*, a desire or hankering after its pleasures and its whole sinful mentality. This again is an interruption to fellowship with God. You cannot mix light and darkness.

The last thing that interrupts fellowship with God, he tells us at the end of 1 John 2, is *false teaching about the person of Jesus Christ*. Obviously if the only way to God is through Christ, if I am in any way wrong about my teaching or doctrine concerning Him, then automatically I sever the communion, and again I lose my joy.

❧ A THOUGHT TO PONDER ❧

Certain things tend to militate against fellowship with God and to rob us of it.

PROCLAMATION

That which we have seen and heard declare we unto you.
1 JOHN 1:3

The lack of proclamation in the preaching of the Church accounts for so much of the present state of the Church and the present state of the world and of society. A man standing in a Christian pulpit has no business in saying, "I suggest to you" or "Shall I put it to you" or "On the whole I think" or "I am almost persuaded" or "The results of research and knowledge and speculation all seem to point in this direction." No! "These things *declare* we unto you."

The old charge that has so often been brought up against the Church and her preachers is that we are dogmatic; but the preacher who is not dogmatic is not a preacher in the New Testament sense. We should be modest about our own opinions and careful as to how we voice our own speculations. But here, thank God, we are not in such a realm; we are not concerned about such things. We do not put forward a theory that commends itself to us as a possible explanation of the world and what we can do about it; the whole basis of the New Testament is that here is an announcement, a proclamation—those are New Testament words.

The Gospel, according to the New Testament, is a herald; it is like a man with a trumpet who is calling people to listen. There is nothing tentative about what he has to say; something has been delivered to him, and his business is to repeat it. It is not the business of the messenger, first and foremost, to examine the credentials of the message—he is to deliver it. We are ambassadors, and the business of the ambassador is not to say to the foreign country what he thinks or believes; it is to deliver the message that has been delivered to him by his home government. That is the position of these New Testament preachers, and that is how John puts it here. "I have an amazing thing to reveal," he says in essence.

❧ A THOUGHT TO PONDER ❧
The Gospel is like a man with a trumpet who is calling people to listen.

From *Fellowship with God*, pp. 46-47.

THE AUTHORITY OF THE APOSTLES

That which was from the beginning, which we have heard,
which we have seen with our eyes, which we have looked upon,
and our hands have handled, of the Word of life.

1 JOHN 1:1

The declaration of the Church comes to us on the authority of the apostles. See 2 Peter 1:16. Our only authority is the apostolic witness, and our Gospel is based upon what they have said. In the opening verses of 1 John, John keeps on repeating it. Three times he talks about having "seen" it, twice he says, "we have heard" it, and he also says, we "have handled" it. He emphasizes and repeats that because it is the whole foundation of the preaching of the Church, and there is no message apart from it. The message is what the apostles have seen, what they have witnessed, and what they have experienced and shared together.

Now, one of the first things we must recapture is the essential difference between witness and experience. What is our fundamental authority as Christian people? There are large numbers today who would say that it is experience. A man once wrote that he had been listening to a radio discussion between a Christian and a modern scientific humanist. During this discussion the scientific humanist asked the Christian, "What is your final proof of the reality and the being of God?" "And," said the writer of this article, "the Christian failed badly in my opinion. He tried to produce certain arguments, but he should have turned to the scientific humanist and said, 'I am the proof of the being of God.'"

I would have been entirely on the side of the Christian in that argument, for I am not a proof of the being of God, nor is my experience. The only reality of the being of God is the Lord Jesus Christ. Experience is of value in confirming, in supporting, in helping me to believe these things, but I must never base my position upon it.

❧ A THOUGHT TO PONDER ❧

The declaration of the Church comes to us on the authority of the apostles.

CHRISTIAN EXPERIENCE

That which we have seen and heard declare we unto you,
that ye also may have fellowship with us: and truly our fellowship
is with the Father, and with his Son Jesus Christ.

1 JOHN 1:3

The Christian experience is a definite and a certain experience—
"that which we have seen and heard declare we unto you, that ye
also may have fellowship with us." Now if people do not know what
they have, how can they wish for others to share it with them? So
that is the starting point—that the Christian experience is not a
vague one; it is not indefinite or uncertain. Rather, it is a well-defined
experience, and true Christians know what they have; they are aware
of what they possess. They are in no uncertainty themselves as to
what has happened to them as to their personal position. "These
things write we unto you," says John, "that your joy may be full"—
that you may share what we have. You cannot invite someone to
share something with you unless you know exactly what you are
asking him to share.

We are dealing with what may be called the great New
Testament doctrine of the assurance of salvation, which has been
subjected to considerable criticism. People have regarded it as pre-
sumption. They have said this is something that is impossible, and
that no one should be able to claim such a thing.

But John is a man who tells us that he *knows*, and it is because
he knows and because of what he has experienced that he is writing.
Christians are not men and women who are hoping for salvation,
but those who have experienced it. They have it; there is no uncertainty. They "know whom [they] have believed" (2 Timothy 1:12);
and it is because John has possessed this that he writes about it.

✎ A THOUGHT TO PONDER ✎

Christians are not men and women who are hoping for salvation,
but those who have experienced it.

WHAT DOES FELLOWSHIP MEAN?

*. . . and truly our fellowship is with the Father, and
with his Son Jesus Christ.*

1 JOHN 1:3

What does *fellowship* mean? To be in a state of fellowship means that we share in things. We are partakers or, if you like, partners—that idea is there intrinsically in the word. That means something like this: The Christian is one who has become a sharer in the life of God. Now that is staggering and astounding language, but the Bible teaches us that; the New Testament offers us that, and nothing less than that.

Peter writes, "Whereby are given unto us exceeding great and precious promises: that by these ye might be partakers of the divine nature, having escaped the corruption that is in the world through lust" (2 Peter 1:4). That is it, and there are many other similar statements. Indeed, the whole doctrine of regeneration and rebirth leads to this; born again, born from above, born of the Spirit—all carry exactly the same idea. This, then, is what John is so anxious to impress upon the minds of his readers—that Christians are not merely people who are a little bit better than they once were and who have just added certain things to their lives. Rather, they are men and women who have received the divine life.

In some amazing and astounding manner we know that we are partakers of the divine nature, that the being of God has somehow entered into us. I cannot tell you how—I cannot find it in the dissecting room. It is no use dissecting the body—you will not find it, any more than you will find the soul by dissecting the body; but it is in us, and we are aware of it. There is a being in us—"I live; yet not I, but Christ liveth in me" (Galatians 2:20); how, I do not know. We will understand in glory, but somehow we know now that we are sharers in the life of God.

❧ A THOUGHT TO PONDER ☙

The Christian is one who has become a sharer in the life of God.

FELLOWSHIP WITH THE FATHER— FROM OUR SIDE

*. . . and truly our fellowship is with the Father, and
with his Son Jesus Christ.*

1 JOHN 1:3

"Our fellowship is with the Father." We have communion with God.
This can be looked at from our side. What does this wondrous thing
that has been made possible for us in Christ mean from our side? It
means, obviously and of necessity, that we have come to know God.
God is no longer a stranger somewhere away in the heavens; He is
no longer some stray force or power somewhere, some supreme
energy. God is no longer some potentate or lawgiver far removed and
faraway from us; God now is someone we know.

Consider the apostle Paul especially as he deals with this. You
will find that in writing to the Galatians he talks about their knowing God; "but now, after that ye have known God, or rather are
known of God . . ." (Galatians 4:9). That is the idea. God is now a
reality—we know Him; that is the very essence of this matter. You
cannot have communion, you cannot have conversation with a person without knowing that person; there is nothing distant—there is
an intimacy and a knowledge.

The Christian, says John, is one who has come to know God, but
it is not only that. God not only is a great person—I speak with
reverence—the Christian is one who has come to know God as
Father. That is why John uses his terms so carefully—"our fellowship is with the Father." The Christian is one who turns to God and
addresses Him as "Abba, Father." That is how Paul puts it in
Romans 8:15—we have the spirit of adoption, the result of which
is that we know God in an intimate way so that we address Him as
"Abba, Father" because we are His children. This also means that
we delight in God and that we have joy in His presence. We know
God in that way.

⮾ A THOUGHT TO PONDER ⮾

It means, obviously and of necessity, that we have come to know
God.

FELLOWSHIP WITH THE FATHER— FROM GOD'S SIDE

. . . and truly our fellowship is with the Father, and with his Son Jesus Christ.

1 JOHN 1:3

There are always two sides to fellowship. We will now look at fellowship from God's side. Paul said in writing to the Philippians, "For it is God which worketh in you both to will and to do of his good pleasure" (2:13). That is the way to have fellowship with God. You are aware of the surging of those holy desires, and you say to yourself, "It is God speaking to me; it is God saying something and calling forth a response in me." "We love him, because he first loved us," says John later on in 1 John [4:19], and God has fellowship with us in that way.

Not only that, He reveals His will to us. He shows us what He would have us to do. He leads us. He opens doors and shuts them; sometimes He puts up barriers and obstacles. You know what I am speaking about. It means that you are aware of the fact that you are in the hands of God, and that He is dealing with you, and that as you go forward in this journey called life, God is there. Sometimes the door is shut, and you cannot understand it. You say, "I wanted to go there, but I cannot," and then you say, "But God is with me, and He has shut the door." Then suddenly you find the door opened, and you know it is the One who is walking with you who has suddenly opened it. That is having fellowship with God—knowing that He is there in these various ways in which He manipulates our lives and speaks to us and gives us wisdom and understanding. Every one of these things contains a danger; they all need to be carefully qualified, and yet they are essential to fellowship and communion.

Then He supplies us with strength according to our need and according to our situation.

✎ A THOUGHT TO PONDER ✐

Having fellowship with God means knowing that He is there.

THE HOLINESS OF GOD

This then is the message which we have heard of him, and declare
unto you, that God is light, and in him is no darkness at all.

1 JOHN 1:5

John has just said, "These things write we unto you, that your joy may be full." So how is it to be full? Well, "This then is the message which we have heard of him, and declare unto you, that God is . . ." What would you have expected there? I suggest that most of us would have expected, "God is love" or "God is mercy" or "God is compassion"; but the startling and astonishing thing is that he says, "God is light, and in him is no darkness at all." And we may say to John, "You have been saying that we are to be given an amazing joy, and then you confront us with that?"

But that is precisely what he does say. We must not start with the knowledge of God, though that is absolutely essential. Nor must we start with God as a source of philosophy. We must not even start with God as love.

Now we can see at once how by putting it like this we give an utter contradiction to what has been so popular especially since 1860. The great message that has been preached for a hundred years is, "God is love." That is the thing that has been emphasized, and we have been told that our fathers, and especially the Puritans with their preaching about justice and righteousness and repentance and sin and punishment and death, had been entirely contradicting and denying the Gospel of Jesus Christ. We have been told that God is love—that is what we needed, and there He was to meet us. Yet what an utter travesty of the Gospel that is! This is the message: "God is light, and in him is no darkness at all."

❧ A THOUGHT TO PONDER ☙

We must not start with God as a source of philosophy. We must not even start with God as love.

From *Fellowship with God*, pp. 106-107.

SIN

If we say that we have not sinned, we make him a liar, and his word is not in us.

1 JOHN 1:10

This is the failure to realize that we as sinners need forgiveness. It is the failure to realize the nature of sin, to grasp that our own natures are sinful, and to understand that we have all actually sinned and need forgiveness.

There are certain people who seem to say, "Yes, I believe in God, and I like to have fellowship with Him. And yet, you know, I have never been conscious of my sin. I do not understand that doctrine of yours. If you were to preach it to people gathered from the streets, I could understand that. But I have been brought up as a Christian; I have always tried to do good. I have never been conscious of the fact that I am a sinner, that I need repentance, and that I must be converted."

Well, says John, if that is your position, "[you] make him a liar, and his word is not in [you]." If we do not realize that we are sinners and need the forgiveness of God, if we do not realize that we have always needed it and that we still need it, if we think that we have always been perfect or that now we are perfect as Christians, if we do not realize that we must repent, then, says John, we are making God a liar, for the "him" referred to is none other than God Himself. John here is just stating the whole teaching of the Bible from beginning to end.

What, then, is he teaching? Paul has summarized it perfectly for us in Romans 3; this is his verdict: "There is none righteous, no, not one" (verse 10). That is the doctrine of the Bible; so if we say we have not sinned, we are denying the doctrine of the Bible.

✎ A THOUGHT TO PONDER ✐

If we say we have not sinned, we are denying the doctrine of the Bible.

ANALYZING FELLOWSHIP

*If we say that we have fellowship with him, and walk in darkness,
we lie, and do not the truth: But if we walk in the light, as he is in
the light, we have fellowship one with another, and the blood of
Jesus Christ his Son cleanseth us from all sin.*

1 JOHN 1:6-7

In order to make this fellowship active, we have certain things to
do, and God must do certain things to us. "If we walk in the light,
as he is in the light, we have fellowship one with another"—that is
what we do. "And the blood of Jesus Christ his Son cleanseth us
from all sin"—that is what He does. "If we confess our sins" (verse
9)—that again is our part, then "he is faithful and just to forgive us
our sins, and to cleanse us from all unrighteousness." So it is quite
inevitable in the matter of fellowship like this that though in a logical sense we persist in dividing up the aspect of fellowship into the
two sides—Godward and manward, they are constantly intermin-
gled, because it is a sharing together, it is an interaction of the one
upon the other.

In other words, fellowship is never mechanical but always something organic and vital. Of course, if we would understand it truly,
for the sake of clarity of thought we are allowed to analyze it in the
way we are doing, but we must remember that organic nature. To
use an illustration, what we are doing is what the musicians do when
they analyze a piece of music such as a sonata or a symphony. It is
right to say that it is composed of various parts, and you can make
an analysis of it; but if you are truly to appreciate it, you must always
remember it is a whole, and you must take it as such. You cannot
stop at an analysis, nor can you leave it at those various bits and portions; they are there, but they are parts of the whole.

∽ A THOUGHT TO PONDER ∾

Fellowship is never mechanical, but always something organic and
vital.

WALKING IN THE LIGHT

If we say that we have fellowship with him, and walk in darkness,
we lie, and do not the truth: But if we walk in the light, as he is in
the light, we have fellowship one with another, and the blood of
Jesus Christ his Son cleanseth us from all sin.

1 JOHN 1:6-7

John is fond of the phrase, "walking in the light"; how often this idea occurs in his Gospel, and here it is again. It is not obvious on the very surface that if you take this in an absolute literal sense it can mean only one thing, and that is absolute perfection. If to walk in the light as God is in the light is taken strictly literally, as it is expressed here, there is only one deduction to draw: As Christians our only hope of forgiveness and therefore of being Christians at all is that we should be absolutely perfect as God Himself is perfect.

But clearly that is impossible! Which of us is perfect? Which of us is without sin? "If we say that we have no sin, we deceive ourselves, and the truth is not in us" (verse 8); we cannot, therefore, be absolutely perfect. So immediately we find that this phrase of walking in the light as God is in the light must be interpreted in terms of the way in which John customarily employs this picture. And the key to that is to be found in the phrase in 1 John 1:6 where we read about walking in darkness: "If we say we have fellowship with him, and walk in darkness, we lie, and do not the truth."

We interpret this verse about "walking in the light" as the antithesis and the exact opposite of "walking in darkness." Therefore it does not mean that I claim absolute perfection; but it does mean that I claim that I now belong to a different realm, to the kingdom of light and to the kingdom of God.

❧ A THOUGHT TO PONDER ☙
I now belong to a different realm, to the kingdom of light.

From *Fellowship with God*, pp. 126-127.

JUSTIFICATION AND SANCTIFICATION

*If we confess our sins, he is faithful and just to forgive us our sins,
and to cleanse us from all unrighteousness.*

1 JOHN 1:9

John does not use the terms *justification* and *sanctification*; they are
Paul's great words. But, of course, John teaches exactly the same doctrine. Furthermore, I think that much of the trouble with regard to
these matters has arisen because people will not see that fact. John,
in his own pictorial way, is teaching precisely the same truth as the
apostle Paul teaches in his more logical and legal manner by means
of his terms *justification* and *sanctification*, *righteousness* and
redemption, and so on.

What is meant by *justification*? Justification is the New
Testament term that represents our standing in the presence of God.
Justification means not only the forgiveness of our sins, but also
that our sins have been dealt with and have been removed from us.
Justification states that God regards us as righteous, as if we had
not sinned. In other words, it is a stronger term than forgiveness;
we may be forgiven, and yet our sins remain upon us. But what
God does for us in justification is to remove the guilt altogether, to
remove the sin. He does not punish us for it; He looks upon us as
righteous, as if we had not sinned; our sin has been removed.

Sanctification, on the other hand, is that condition in which the
sin principle is dealt with. Justification does not deal with the sin
principle within us; it deals with the sins that we have committed.
But after our sins have been forgiven, and sin and guilt have been
removed from us, the sin principle will remain within us, and what
the New Testament means by this doctrine of sanctification is the
process whereby the very principle and the activity of sin within us
is being taken out of us and removed.

❧ A THOUGHT TO PONDER ❧

Justification means not only the forgiveness of our sins, but also
that our sins have been removed from us.

From *Fellowship with God*, pp. 137-138.

September 30

JESUS, HIS SON

... the blood of Jesus Christ his Son ...
1 JOHN 1:7

I would not say there is no value at all in good, uplifting, and moral teaching or that there is no benefit to be derived by society from the consideration of noble ideas and exalted conceptions with regard to life. That is all right, but it is just not Christianity. It has nothing to do with it, in a sense, and we can do no greater violence to the New Testament doctrine than to represent the message of Christ's birth as but some vague general message of goodwill and of good cheer and happiness. That is not its message at all.

If we do not start with the person of the Lord Jesus Christ, if we are not absolutely clear about Him, then there is nothing. There is no good news, there is no evangel, there is no gospel; there is nothing to cheer us up, there is no hope. We are just living in the darkness of the world, and we are unutterably foolish in trying to persuade ourselves that things are better than they really are. There is no such thing, in a sense, as "the Christmas spirit." That is *not* the Christian message, which is not a vague spirit; it is a message of news concerning Christ. So, therefore, we must of necessity start at this point and be absolutely clear about this matter.

As has often been pointed out, Christianity is Christ. It all centers around Him, and every doctrine that we have and every idea that we possess is something that comes from Him. Therefore, of necessity we must start with Him, and of course John in this letter has already done so. The whole message that John has to deliver to us is that there is only one way of fellowship and communion with God, and that is because of the Lord Jesus Christ. It is He alone who can enable us to know this fellowship, for there is "one mediator between God and men, the man Christ Jesus" (1 Timothy 2:5).

❧ A THOUGHT TO PONDER ❧
Christianity is Christ.

From *Fellowship with God*, pp. 148-149.

October

WALKING WITH GOD

FROM

Walking with God

AND

Children of God

OUR FELLOWSHIP WITH GOD

. . . if any man sin . . .

1 JOHN 2:1

John is concerned fundamentally about our walk with God and our fellowship with Him, and therefore he says, "My little children, these things write I unto you . . ." because sin always ultimately breaks fellowship with God and therefore immediately casts us off from the source of all our blessedness. It is no use saying you want to walk with God and then deliberately sinning. The moment you sin, fellowship is broken; the moment you fall into transgression, you interrupt the fellowship. The one thing that matters is fellowship with God. I do not know what may await you. You may be tried, you may be persecuted; there may be war and calamity; there may be terrible things awaiting you. The one thing that matters is that you are right with God. That being so, do not sin because sin breaks the fellowship.

Not only that—sin is utterly inconsistent with our profession. It is totally inconsistent with our professed hatred of sin and with our professed desire to be delivered from it. Christians are people who realize and know that sin is the central problem in life, and they therefore say that they want to be delivered and emancipated from it. So if they continue to sin, they deny what they profess to believe. Such a position is completely inconsistent and self-contradictory.

And sin also leads always to an evil conscience. When men and women sin, they are under a sense of condemnation, they are unhappy. I am speaking true to experience, am I not? "Little children, these things write I unto you, that ye sin not." Sin will rob you of happiness and joy and will give you a sense of condemnation.

❧ A THOUGHT TO PONDER ❧
The one thing that matters is fellowship with God.

From *Walking with God*, pp. 17-18.

THE ADVOCATE, PART 1

We have an advocate with the Father, Jesus Christ the righteous.
1 JOHN 2:1

How does Christ accomplish our restoration to fellowship with God? John puts it here in these verses in a very beautiful way. Christ does it, says John, by being our *advocate*. "If any man sin"—if any of you should happen to fall into sin—then you, we, all of us together—"have an advocate with the Father, Jesus Christ the righteous." John uses the same [Greek] word in his Gospel, in chapter 16 verse 7, where our Lord said that He would send us another *comforter*. So what is an advocate? An advocate is one who represents another. He stands before a court, and he presents the case of someone else; he represents this person and puts forward the pleas. And John tells us that the Lord Jesus Christ is, for all who believe on Him and trust Him, "an advocate with the Father."

However, this word merits our closer attention. We must never think of it as if the Lord Jesus Christ were there pleading for us before an unwilling God. You will find that certain hymns suggest that, and statements have often been made that sound as if God were opposed to us and as if God, who is utter righteousness and absolute perfection, is insisting on His pound of flesh and insisting upon His right to punish us for our sins. They picture the Lord Jesus Christ as pleading desperately and urgently, trying to persuade the Father and at last succeeding in getting Him to change His opinion.

But that is an impossible suggestion, and we must be very careful not to view this idea of advocacy in that way. It is impossible because we are told so plainly and clearly in the Word of God that "God so loved the world, that he gave his only begotten Son" (John 3:16). So as we consider the advocacy, let us get rid of the idea that God is unwilling and that He is one who is not prepared to forgive.

✑ A THOUGHT TO PONDER ✐
We must never think of it as if the Lord Jesus Christ were there pleading for us before an unwilling God.

From *Walking with God*, pp. 36–37.

THE ADVOCATE, PART 2

He ever liveth to make intercession for us.

HEBREWS 7:25

Christ is not our advocate before an unwilling God. But at the same time we must be very careful not to go to the other extreme and think that what John means by "advocate" is just that the work of Christ on the cross prevails and continues throughout eternity and is there always in the mind of God, and that therefore in that sense Christ and His work are advocates for us. We must not think that, because that makes it something quite passive, and that is an idea we must reject, not only because of 1 John 2:1, but also because of those magnificent words in Hebrews 7 where the whole argument is that "he ever liveth to make intercession for us." Christ is unlike the Levitical priests who came and lived and died and then a new person had to be appointed. The whole point about Him, says the author of Hebrews, is that He *lives*. He is without beginning and without end—it is an eternal priesthood—and it is because "he ever liveth" that He is able to "save . . . to the uttermost"—and must forever and ever irrespective of what may happen—those "that come unto God by him."

In other words, it does seem to me that once more we are confronted by a conception that baffles our understanding. But of this we can be quite certain: As the Lord Jesus Christ looked after His disciples and followers while here on earth, as He looked after their interests and did certain things for them, so He is now equally active for us there in heaven. He is representing His people; He is there looking after us and our interests. This is not a conflict between Father and Son; but it seems to me that in the economy of the blessed Trinity, the Father has handed this particular work to the Son.

❧ A THOUGHT TO PONDER ❧

As the Lord Jesus Christ looked after His disciples while here on earth, so He is now equally active for us there in heaven.

WALKING WITH GOD

And hereby we do know that we know him,
if we keep his commandments.

1 JOHN 2:3

Are you keeping God's commandments? Keeping His commandments does not mean I just put on the wall a list of specific injunctions and do my best to keep them. Rather, it means that I am always
concerned to be living the Christian life as fully as I can, that my
great object is to be well-pleasing in His sight. I know what He wants
me to do; I find it in the Old and New Testaments. I have the Ten
Commandments and the Sermon on the Mount that apply to me,
and I have the whole moral, ethical teaching of the New Testament.
Those are His commandments, and I have to keep them. "And if you
can say quite honestly," says John in essemce, "that you are very concerned about doing that; if you can say you are striving to do that
and that is your ambition in life, you can know that you are in Him,
for to know Him is to walk as He walked." "He that saith he abideth
in him ought himself also so to walk, even as he walked" (verse 6).
That puts it perfectly once and forever.

The Bible often describes our life as a walk. "Enoch *walked* with
God" (Genesis 5:24); "Noah *walked* with God" (Genesis 6:9). Then
read what God said to Abraham in Genesis 17:1—"*Walk* before
me, and be thou perfect." "I," said Jesus Christ, "am the light of
the world: he that followeth me shall not *walk* in darkness, but
shall have the light of life" (John 8:12). Then listen to Paul saying the
same kind of thing: "For ye were sometimes darkness, but now are
ye light in the Lord: *walk* as children of light" (Ephesians 5:8).

This is a wonderful picture of the Christian life. It is a journey;
we walk along, and what John says here quite simply and without
any explanation is this: "If you say you are in Him, then you ought
to walk as He walked."

❧ A THOUGHT TO PONDER ❧
The Bible often describes our life as a walk.

October 5

LOVING THE BRETHREN

He that loveth his brother abideth in the light.
1 JOHN 2:10

As Christians look at their fellow men and women, they see people exactly like themselves before their eyes were opened, and now they are sorry for them. They begin to love hateful persons instead of hating them. They say, "We are all in the same position," and they begin to have an eye of compassion for them. Their knowledge of the love of God in Christ makes them love other people even as they have been loved themselves. They are new men and women with a new outlook; they are in a new realm. They feel the love of God in their heart, and they want to love Him and glorify Him, and they know they can glorify God most of all by being new men and women, by living as Christ lived and thereby showing and proving that they are indeed true disciples.

Christ our Lord put this perfectly once in the parable of the man who was a servant and was in trouble. He went to his lord and pleaded for forgiveness, and that lord forgave him. But there was another man who was a servant under the first servant who came to him and made exactly the same plea, but the forgiven servant took the other by the throat and said, "No, I won't let you off—you have to pay to the last farthing." Well, said our Lord (Matthew 18:23-35), that man must not think he has been forgiven, for the man who does not forgive will not be forgiven.

What this means is that you and I can only be happy about the fact that we are Christians if we find this loving, forgiving spirit within ourselves. It is idle for us to say that we know God has forgiven us if we ourselves are not loving and forgiving. People who say they are in the light but who hate and do not forgive their brother are in darkness even now.

❧ A THOUGHT TO PONDER ❧
It is idle for us to say that we know that God has forgiven us if we ourselves are not loving and forgiving.

THE LOVE OF THE WORLD

Love not the world.

1 JOHN 2:15

What is "the world" is this case? Now I think it is important that we should agree that he is not referring here to creation as such; he is not thinking of the mountains and the valleys and rivers, the streams and the sun and the moon and the stars. He does not mean the physical world. There are people who have even thought that to "love not the world, neither the things that are in the world" means to shut one's eyes to the glory and beauty of nature.

But it does not mean that; neither does it mean the life of the world in general. It does not mean family relationships, though there are people who have misinterpreted it like that; they have often regarded marriage as sinful. Not once but very often in my ministerial life have I had to deal with nice, sincere Christian people who have solemnly believed, through misinterpreting a text like this, that Christian people should not marry. Their reason is that marriage involves certain relationships that they regard as sinful; they would regard the very gift of sex as being sinful in and of itself.

So "the world" does not mean creation; it does not mean family relationships; it is not the state; it does not mean engaging in business or a profession or all these things that are essential to life; it does not mean governments and authorities and powers, for all these have been ordained by God Himself. There is nothing so grievous as to misinterpret "the world" in some such terms as that.

What, then, does it mean? Clearly the very text and the whole teaching of the Bible shows that it must mean the organization and the mind and the outlook of mankind as it ignores God and does not recognize Him and as it lives a life independent of Him, a life that is based upon this world and this life only. It is the whole outlook upon life that is exclusive of God.

✐ A THOUGHT TO PONDER ✐

"The world" ignores God and lives a life independent of Him, a life that is based upon this world and this life only.

From *Walking with God*, pp. 84-85.

THE ANTICHRIST

He is antichrist.
1 JOHN 2:22

The antichrist is the one who, in one sense, stands instead of Christ, taking the Christian name and yet opposing the very kingdom of truth that the name implies. John says, "As ye have heard that antichrist shall come, even now are there many antichrists. . . . They went out from us, but they were not of us; for if they had been of us, they would no doubt have continued with us: but they went out, that they might be made manifest that they were not all of us" (verses 18-19). So when we think of the antichrist, we have to bear that in mind. "These antichrists who have arisen," says John, "belonged to us, but they were not of us." In other words, they took up the Christian position, they claimed they were Christians, they professed to be teachers of the Christian Church, and yet they have been separated from the Christians in order that it would be clear to all that they were not of them. In other words, they claimed to delight in the true religion and yet they destroyed it.

The antichrist was already at work in the days of Paul and of John. Further, it is abundantly clear that although there have been many imitations of him, he will reach his maximum power just before the end of this age. I think it is equally clear that Daniel pictures the political aspect of this power, whereas Paul emphasizes the ecclesiastical aspect, and in Revelation 13 you get both—the beast from the sea (the political) and the beast from the earth (the ecclesiastical). And the last point, I think, of which we can be certain is that this power will ultimately be concentrated in one particular person. John says there were many antichrists, and yet the teaching is clear that there is going to be an ultimate antichrist, one person, a person having terrible power, able to work miracles and do such wonders that he almost deceives the elect themselves.

◆ A THOUGHT TO PONDER ◆
There is going to be an ultimate antichrist, one person, able to do such wonders that he almost deceives the elect themselves.

From *Walking with God*, pp. 100-101.

THE ANOINTING OF THE HOLY SPIRIT

But ye have an unction from the Holy One.
1 JOHN 2:20

What is it that enables us to stand and to remain and to avoid the seduction of false teaching that would separate us from God and Christ and eventually lead to our condemnation? Well, John says here that it is all due to the work of the Holy Spirit. Christians are who they are because of the Holy Spirit. Christians, he says, are those who have received an unction or anointing—that is his way of describing the Holy Spirit. It is because of Him that they are able to discern and understand and avoid the subtle dangers that threaten them within the realm even of the Christian Church itself. John says in verses 20-21, "But ye have an unction from the Holy One, and ye know all things. I have not written unto you because ye know not the truth, but because ye know it, and that no lie is of the truth." Then he adds in verse 27, "But the anointing which ye have received of him abideth in you."

John's words "unction" or "anointing" are just a very graphic way of describing the influence and the effect of the Holy Spirit upon the believer. It is the wording of the Old Testament where we are frequently told that prophets, priests, and kings, when they were inducted as it were, were anointed with oil; that was the mechanism, the ceremonial, that was used to set them apart for their office. Samuel anointed first Saul and then David as king. The same anointing was given to the priests and prophets, and the results of that pouring of the oil upon them was that in that way they were regarded as consecrated; they had become anointed ones who were now enabled to do their duty.

✎ A THOUGHT TO PONDER ✎

John's words "unction" or "anointing" are just a very graphic way of describing the influence and the effect of the Holy Spirit upon the believer.

From *Walking with God*, pp. 118-119.

ANOINTED

Wherefore he saith, When he ascended up on high, he led captivity captive, and gave gifts unto men.

EPHESIANS 4:8

We are told that our Lord was, as it were, anointed and set apart for His Messianic and saving work when the Holy Spirit came upon Him in Jordan when He was baptized by John the Baptist; and in a sense, the same thing is true of the individual Christian. "Ye have an unction from the Holy One," says John (1 John 2:20). Who is that? The context makes it quite plain—He is none other than our Lord Himself; and in verse 27 the reference is still to the Lord Jesus Christ.

This is an interesting point that can be looked at in two ways. We are told by the apostle Paul in Ephesians 4:8 that "when he ascended up on high, he . . . gave gifts unto men" (Ephesians 4:8). It was the Lord Jesus Christ who sent the Holy Spirit upon the infant Christian Church. The Holy Spirit did not come until Christ had ascended into heaven; then the Spirit came. He comes from the Father and the Son, or from the Father through the Son; it is as a result of the perfect work of the Son that the Father gives the Holy Spirit to all who belong to Him. That is one way of looking at it.

But there is another way of looking at it. Because we are incorporated into Christ and into the life of Christ, we partake of what is true of Him. Therefore, as He has been anointed and has received the Holy Spirit without measure, all of us who are in Him receive the gift of the Holy Spirit because we are in Him. That is why any kind of teaching that would ever suggest that you can be a Christian without receiving the Holy Spirit is unscriptural. It is impossible for one to be a Christian and then later on receive the Holy Spirit. To be in Christ means that you are receiving the Spirit.

❧ A THOUGHT TO PONDER ❧

Any kind of teaching that would ever suggest that you can be a Christian without receiving the Holy Spirit is unscriptural.

ALL THINGS

. . . the same anointing teacheth you of all things . . .

1 JOHN 2:27

John does not teach here that a Christian knows everything. "But surely," says someone, "when it says 'ye know all things' (verse 20), doesn't 'all things' mean just that?" But if you think that, then you must mean that every Christian knows everything—astronomy, geometry, the classics, and everything else that is in the realm of knowledge—which is patently and obviously ridiculous! No; we must take these statements within their context. John obviously does not mean secular knowledge.

Does he then mean spiritual knowledge? No, he does not mean spiritual knowledge in every sense either, for this good reason: If John is here saying that every man or woman who receives the Holy Spirit automatically knows the whole of spiritual truth, how can you apply the New Testament teaching about growing in grace and in knowledge? How can there then be any development in our knowledge and understanding? Not only that, I think we can say that if that were true, then there would be no need for the New Testament epistles. Clearly that is not the case. John's reference to "all things" here is a reference to the particular subject with which he is dealing. It is not an all-inclusive, all-comprehensive statement.

John does not teach here that because of this knowledge every Christian is infallible. For if the unction of the Holy Spirit means that every Christian knows everything, it would follow that every Christian would have to agree with every other Christian about every aspect of Christian doctrine. But that is not the case. There are divergences and differences among Christians who manifest the Holy Spirit in their lives—about the question of baptism, about the prophetic teaching, about church order, and many other subjects. Added to that, Christians—good Christians—have from time to time fallen into error.

☙ A THOUGHT TO PONDER ☙

John does not teach here that because of this knowledge every Christian is infallible.

Is Instruction Needed?

But grow in grace, and in the knowledge of our Lord and Savior Jesus Christ. To him be glory both now and for ever. Amen.
2 PETER 3:18

The Bible does not teach that Christians do not need instruction. "But surely," says someone, "that must be wrong. Look at this verse from 1 John: 'the anointing which ye have received of him abideth in you, and ye need not that any man teach you' (2:27). John says we do not need any man to teach us, and yet you say that the Christian Church still needs instruction. How do you reconcile this?"

It seems to me that the answer is as simple as this: The very fact that John is writing to them proves that they need instruction. If they do not, then John need have no concern about them at all. If the Christian needs no instruction, then the apostles' claim to be divinely inspired when they wrote their epistles was a sheer waste of time. These epistles are full of instruction. We are told that the Christian is to "grow in grace, and in the knowledge of our Lord and Savior Jesus Christ." There is milk provided for him, and there is strong meat. That is impossible if you take this statement literally and maintain that John is saying the Christian never needs teaching. Clearly that is not what he means.

So let us put it in this positive form: Surely the context here determines the interpretation. What John is really saying is what the apostle Paul says in 1 Corinthians 2:13-14. He is saying that the Christian has spiritual understanding that the natural man does not have. These things are only understood in a spiritual manner, and what John is here saying is that the Christian, having received the Holy Spirit, has a spiritual understanding. "You," says John, "are holding fast to this truth because the Holy Spirit has given you this enlightenment and understanding."

❧ A Thought to Ponder ❧

The Christian, having received the Holy Spirit, has a spiritual understanding.

UNDERSTANDING TRUTH

But we have the mind of Christ.
1 CORINTHIANS 2:16

In 1 John 2:21-22 John is dealing with the particular truth of the birth of our Lord: "I have not written unto you because ye know not the truth, but because ye know it, and that no lie is of the truth. Who is a liar but he that denieth that Jesus is the Christ? He is antichrist, that denieth the Father and the Son." These people, because they had the Holy Spirit and His enlightenment, understood the doctrine concerning the person of the Lord Jesus Christ and the work that He had come to perform. If they had not received the Spirit, they could not have done that; but they did understand these things. They understood the doctrine of the two natures in one person. They had an unction that enabled them to explain these things—"we have the mind of Christ" (1 Corinthians 2:16).

This is the wonderful thing that is true of Christians. They may not have much natural ability, but if they have the Holy Spirit they can understand this truth, and that is why the Christian faith is not only a faith for philosophers—it is a faith for anybody. It is not something that depends upon the natural man's ability; it is an enlightenment, an unction. The Holy Spirit enables men and women to see and to understand something of the glorious nature of salvation. Though they may be simple, though they may be ignorant, though the world may dub them as being unintelligent, if they have this enlightenment they understand things that the greatest natural philosopher cannot understand.

That is what John says: "You understand these things; the other man does not." Or we can put it like this: Because they have this anointing, Christians understand error and are able to save themselves from deviations from the truth. Simple people have heard and recognized the centralities of the faith when the more learned have become confused and have tended to go astray.

❧ A THOUGHT TO PONDER ☙

The Holy Spirit enables men and women to understand something of the glorious nature of salvation.

LIARS

*Who is a liar but he that denieth that Jesus is the Christ? He is
antichrist, that denieth the Father and the Son.*

1 JOHN 2:22

The language used in this verse is very strong; John does hesitate to
refer to these antichrists as *liars*. Some say, "Here is the man who
appears as the great apostle of love and who talks so much about
love in this particular epistle. So how is it that he should thus
describe these people who had gone out, and those who had seduced
them, as liars?"

What we have here is in many ways very characteristic of the
New Testament. John is not the exception; John did not use language
like this because he was Boanerges, one of "the sons of thunder"
(Mark 3:17); you find others doing the same thing. Listen to the
apostle Paul using language like that to the Galatians: "But though
we, or an angel from heaven, preach any other gospel unto you
than that which we have preached unto you, let him be accursed"
(Galatians 1:8). You cannot imagine anything stronger than that. Or
listen to him as he writes to the Corinthians: "If any man love not the
Lord Jesus Christ, let him be Anathema" (1 Corinthians 16:22).

Remember, too, the preaching of John the Baptist when he looked
at his congregation, which consisted of Pharisees and others, and said,
"O generation of vipers, who hath warned you to flee from the wrath
to come?" (Luke 3:7). Think also of the words of our blessed Lord
Himself as He addressed the Pharisees toward the end of His life;
He referred to them as "whited sepulchres" (Matthew 23:27).

Now I emphasize all this merely because we must be careful
lest we put ourselves into a position in which we claim that we are
more Christian than the Lord Jesus Christ Himself and His blessed
apostles. The New Testament uses strong language. Here it is in its
essence—*liars*.

✎ A THOUGHT TO PONDER ✐

We must be careful lest we put ourselves into a position in which
we claim that we are more Christian than the Lord Jesus Christ
Himself.

From *Walking with God*, pp. 131-133.

October 14

NOT ASHAMED

And now, little children, abide in him; that, when he shall appear,
we may have confidence, and not be ashamed
before him at his coming.

1 JOHN 2:28

John has been teaching, in effect, "Beloved people, don't believe the lie. It not only robs you of doctrine, it robs you of life; it is that which robs you of God's greatest gift that has been made possible by the incarnation of His Son. If the eternal son had not come from God and been made flesh, if there is no union between human nature and the Son of God, how can we have a new nature?"

In 1 John 2:28 John emphasizes one final thing: "And now, little children, abide in him; that, when he shall appear, we may have confidence, and not be ashamed before him at his coming." "Don't believe that lie," says John in effect, "because if you do, you will find yourself face to face with it as a fact. These people have denied the truth," says John; "don't believe in a kind of phantom body and that the eternal God came upon a man and then left him. It is unreal," says John, "don't believe it. The day is coming when you will face the fact—the God-Man is coming into this world. He will come again, and then you will see Him; and if you believe that lie, you will be ashamed when you see Him."

Writing in the Apocalypse, John says, "Every eye shall see him, and they also which pierced him" (Revelation 1:7). And when they see Him they will cry out "to the mountains and rocks, Fall on us, and hide us . . . from the wrath of the Lamb" (Revelation 6:16). That is a fact; this is not fancy. The God-Man will come again, and if you want to rejoice in that day, if you want to have confidence when you look at Him, and if you want to say, "Even so come, Lord Jesus," then avoid this lie, beware of these liars who deny that Jesus is the Christ.

✎ A THOUGHT TO PONDER ✐

The God-Man will come again, and if you want to rejoice in that day, beware of these liars.

From *Walking with God*, p. 140.

RIGHTEOUSNESS

If ye know that he is righteous, ye know that every one that doeth righteousness is born of him.

1 JOHN 2:29

Now righteousness obviously does not just mean morality, nor does it just mean living a good life. There are plenty of people who are outside the Christian church today who deny the elements of the Christian faith, but who are quite moral and decent. They are quite good people, using the term *good* in its moral or philosophical connotation; but they do not conform to what the New Testament means by *righteous*. *Righteousness* means the quality of life that was lived by the Lord Jesus Christ Himself.

So John puts it like this: "Every one that doeth righteousness . . ." If you see people who are living the quality of life that was lived by the Lord Jesus Christ, you can know for certain, says John, that they are born of God—they could not do it otherwise. No one can really live the Sermon on the Mount until he or she is born again; the Sermon on the Mount is impossible to the natural man or woman. Indeed, the Christian life as a whole is impossible to such persons. It does not matter how good people are—they cannot live the Christian life. They can live a moral, ethical life up to a point, but they cannot live the Christian life, and the New Testament does not even ask them to. The New Testament standard of living for the Christian condemns the natural man and woman, and it should drive them to see the absolute necessity of the rebirth.

John reasons as follows: "If, then, we are born of God, does it not follow of necessity that we must be living a certain quality of life? If you are breaking the commandments and are living in sin, you cannot claim you are a child of God. The child of God must be living a different type of life."

❧ A THOUGHT TO PONDER ❧

Righteousness means the quality of life that was lived by the Lord Jesus Christ Himself.

From *Children of God*, p. 12.

CHILDREN OF GOD

*Behold, what manner of love the Father hath bestowed upon us,
that we should be called the sons of God: therefore the world
knoweth us not, because it knew him not.*

1 JOHN 3:1

How have we become children of God? John answers in this way:
"Behold, what manner of love the Father hath bestowed upon us."
This is a very interesting way of putting it. John does not merely
say that God has shown His love to us, nor that He has revealed it
or manifested it or indicated it. He does not merely say that God
loves us, though He does love us and He has shown and displayed
His love to us. "Yes," says John, "but He has gone further—He
has *bestowed* His love upon us." Now that means there is a sense
in which God has put His love into us, implanted Himself if you like,
infused or injected His love within us, and we must emphasize that
because what really matters is the word *that*, which should be translated "in order that." "Behold, what manner of love the Father
hath bestowed upon us, in order that we may become, be made,
the children of God"; that is what John actually says.

In other words, what really makes us children of God is that God
has put His own life into us. God's nature is love, and He has put His
nature into us so that we have the love of God. We cannot be children of God if we are not like God; the child is like the parent, the
offspring proclaims the parentage, and God in that way makes us
His children. He puts His own nature into us, and we become His
children, and that nature that is in God is in us, and it is acting and
manifesting and expressing itself. Paul says that "the love of God
. . . is shed abroad in our hearts by the Holy Ghost" (Romans 5:5).

✎ A THOUGHT TO PONDER ✐
What really makes us children of God is that God has put His own
life into us.

From *Children of God*, pp. 16-17.

DESTINED FOR GLORY

We shall be like him.

1 JOHN 3:2

"We shall see him as he is." "Now we see through a glass, darkly; but then face to face: now I know in part; but then shall I know even as also I am known" (1 Corinthians 13:12). Do you know that you are destined for that? We shall see Him as He is—what a blessed, glorious vision to see the Son of God in all His glory, as He is, face to face—standing and looking at Him and enjoying Him for all eternity. It is only then that we will begin to understand what He did for us, the price He paid, the cost of our salvation. You and I are destined for that glorious vision; we shall see Him as He is, face to face.

But consider something still more amazing and incredible. We shall be like Him. "We know that, when he shall appear, we shall be like him; for we shall see him as he is." This is John's way of addressing the whole doctrine of the resurrection of our bodies, the ultimate final resurrection, the ultimate glorification of God's people. What John is telling us, in other words, is that when that great day comes, we shall not only see Him—we shall be made like Him. Paul says that God's purpose is that we shall be "conformed to the image of his Son" (Romans 8:29). That is the argument, and that is the doctrine.

In other words, while we are here on earth, the Holy Spirit is working in us, doing His work of holiness in us and ridding us of sin, so that eventually we shall be faultless, blameless, without spot, and without rebuke. We shall have been delivered from every sin and vestige and appearance of sin within us; and in addition to that, our very bodies shall be changed and shall be glorified.

◈ A THOUGHT TO PONDER ◈

We shall see Him as He is—standing and looking at Him and enjoying Him for all eternity.

October 18

HOLINESS

And every man that hath this hope in him purifieth himself, even as he is pure.

1 JOHN 3:3

Holiness is not something we are called upon to do in order that we may become something; it is something we are to do because of what we already are. There is a great deal of teaching on this subject that really amounts to this: We are to be holy and live the holy life in order that we may become truly Christians; every phase or aspect of the doctrine of justification by works really teaches that. But any suggestion we may have in ourselves that we are to deny ourselves certain things, that we are not to do certain things, and that we are to discipline ourselves in order that we may become Christian is a denial of the doctrine of justification by faith. I am not to live a good and holy life in order that I may become a Christian; I am to live the holy life *because* I am a Christian. I am not to live this holy life in order that I may enter heaven; it is because I know I am going to enter heaven that I must live this holy life.

That is the emphasis here: "Every man that hath this hope in him purifieth himself, even as he is pure." I am not to strive and sweat and pray in order that at the end I may enter into heaven. No; I start rather from the standpoint that I have been made a child of God by the grace of God in the Lord Jesus Christ. I am destined for heaven; I have an assurance that I have been called to go there and that God is going to take me there, and it is because I know this that I am preparing now.

✎ A THOUGHT TO PONDER ✐

Holiness is not something we are called upon to do in order that we may become something; it is something we are to do because of what we already are.

TO TAKE AWAY OUR SINS

And ye know that he was manifested to take away our sins;
and in him is no sin.

1 JOHN 3:5

Why did the Son of God ever come into this world? When we think about the Lord Jesus Christ and especially about His death on that cross on Calvary's hill, what is its purpose? Is it just something about which we sentimentalize? What does it represent to us? What is the explanation of it all?

That is the question that John answers here, and let me put the answer in a negative form. Our Lord did not only come to give us a revelation of God, though that is a part of the purpose. He said, "He that hath seen me hath seen the Father" (John 14:9), and we also read, "No man hath seen God at any time; the only begotten Son, which is in the bosom of the Father, he hath declared him" (John 1:18). But that is not all, though He indeed revealed the Father and has come to do that. In the same way, He has not only come to teach us about God. There is incomparable teaching there, such as the world had never known before and has not known since, but He did not come only to do that. There is also, of course, the example of His life, a matchless one, but He has not come only to give us an example of how we should live in this world. He is not just a teacher or a moral exemplar; He has not come merely to give us some kind of picture as to the nature and being of God. All that is there, but that is not the real reason, says John.

He has really come, he says, because of our sins, because of the predicament and the position of men and women, because of this whole question of law. He has not come only to instruct us and to give us encouragement in our endeavor and a great example. No; there is a fundamental problem at the back of it all, and that is our relationship to God in the light of God's holy law.

❧ A THOUGHT TO PONDER ☙

He has not come only to instruct us and to give us encouragement in our endeavor and a great example.

No Sin

In him is no sin.
1 JOHN 3:5

There can be no true view of salvation and of the redemption that is possible for us in the Lord Jesus Christ unless we are right about the person. That is why John used such strong and striking language in 1 John 2 when he talked about those people who were leading them astray by denying the person of our Lord. "Those antichrists," he said in essence, "are liars, and they must be called such because they are robbing us of the whole of our salvation." If we are wrong about the person, we shall be wrong everywhere.

So as we look at this person we are reminded again in this verse that here is one who has been in this world of ours with all its sin and its shame, but who was without sin. He "was in all points tempted like as we are, yet without sin" (Hebrews 4:15). He remains unique and separate. He alone is the Son of God. He is not just a great moral teacher, nor just a great religious genius. He is not one who has gone a little bit further than all others in this quest for God and for truth. No; He is the Son of God incarnate—"in him is no sin."

But not only was there no sin in Him and in His birth—He committed no act of sin. He always honored God's holy law; He obeyed it fully and carried it out perfectly. God gave His law to man. He intended that the law should be carried out, that it should be honored and obeyed. Let me go further and say this: No one can ever be with God and spend eternity with Him unless they have honored the law. God's law must be kept, and without fulfilling it there is no fellowship with Him and no hope of spending eternity with Him. What God has demanded from man, man has failed to do; but here is One who does it.

❧ A Thought to Ponder ❧
If we are wrong about the person, we shall be wrong everywhere.

From *Children of God*, pp. 53-54.

DELIVERED

And ye know that he was manifested to take away our sins;
and in him is no sin.

1 JOHN 3:5

When John says that "he was manifested to take away our sins," he is not stopping at the guilt of our sins, for salvation goes beyond that. We are delivered from the guilt—this first thing is essential; but thank God, the process does not stop there. He delivers us also from the power and from the pollution of sin. His work is such that He takes away our sin in a more vital sense. We are growing in grace and in the knowledge of the Lord; we are increasingly being made to conform to the image of His Son. We are being delivered—we have been, we are, and we shall be ultimately. The glorification is coming when He will take away our sin altogether, so that we shall be blameless and faultless and spotless and perfect in His holy presence.

The hymn that tells us, "There was no other good enough to pay the price of sin" also tells us this: "He died that we might be forgiven"; yes, but "He died to make us good" is equally true. The apostle Paul, writing to Titus, says: "[He] gave himself for us, that he might redeem us from all iniquity, and purify unto himself a peculiar [special] people, zealous of good works" (Titus 2:14).

So we must never separate sanctification from justification; we must never talk about a kind of series of separate blessings. It is all one—it all belongs together. And it is all a matter of this law that condemns us and from which Christ delivers us through the cross and by the gift of new life. He went to that cruel death on the cross not only so that you and I might have pardon. Thank God, that does come out of it, that is the first thing. But He did it really to separate, to put aside, a people for Himself as a special treasure and possession who, as Paul puts it, should be "zealous of good works," who should live a holy life.

❧ A THOUGHT TO PONDER ❧
He delivers us from the power and from the pollution of sin.

From *Children of God*, pp. 56-57.

A MIGHTY BATTLE

He that committeth sin is of the devil; for the devil sinneth from the beginning. For this purpose the Son of God was manifested, that he might destroy the works of the devil.

1 JOHN 3:8

We see that our Lord did not come into the world only to teach. He did do that, and He gave incomparable teaching. We must realize what he came primarily to do. "For this purpose the Son of God was manifested," not that He might teach us, not that He might give us a glorious example to follow, not that He might give us some transcendent idea that would illuminate our minds and thrill us. Not at all! He came, He was manifested, He appeared that He might "destroy the works of the devil."

We see that sin is unrighteous, that it is a transgression of the law, and that *sin* means we are violating God's holy will for us and God's holy purpose with respect to us. But this is the other part: "To continue in a life of sin and evil," says John in essence, "is just to identify yourself at once with the devil and his ways and with everything that belongs to him." And it is this that is emphasized in this verse.

Our Lord came into this world to wage a great fight; He entered into a mighty battle. The way in which He was victorious in this fight is celebrated especially on Easter Day. This is the day that reminds us of the fact of Christ's victory. It is not a day that reminds us of certain principles in life. You often hear people thank God for this whole "principle of resurrection," how the flowers begin to appear, and how the trees and life come into being in the Spring. Now, that has nothing to do with this blessed message of the resurrection. We are concerned about a fact, not a principle of nature; and the fact is that in the resurrection our Lord ultimately established His conquest over the devil.

❧ A THOUGHT TO PONDER ❧

Our Lord came into this world to wage a great fight.

OUR ADVERSARY

He that committeth sin is of the devil; for the devil sinneth from the beginning. For this purpose the Son of God was manifested, that he might destroy the works of the devil.

1 JOHN 3:8

We begin by considering this "adversary," as he is described (1 Peter 5:8), the devil. The Son of God came because there was a certain state and condition in this world that had been produced by the devil. Now whether we like it or not, the fact is that the whole drama of redemption, as it is outlined in the Bible, simply cannot be understood at all unless you accept the biblical doctrine with regard to the devil. It is an essential part of this message; it is there from the very beginning and right through to the end.

And this is the biblical teaching. The explanation of the problem of mankind and the whole state of our world is to be traced back to this fact about the devil. According to the Bible, God made the world perfect; so what has gone wrong with it? And here is the answer. Someone who is described in various terms and to whom various names are given in the Bible came and spoke to the man and the woman whom God had placed in that perfect world. He is called "Lucifer," "the son of the morning," and "the god of this world." He is called "the serpent," "the prince of the power of the air," and "the strong man armed."

There are various names given in the Scriptures, but they all describe the same person. And according to this teaching, this is the explanation of evil and of sin and of all our miseries in this world. The devil came and spoke to man, and he enticed him to sin. So man went against God; and the result of all this is the state of the world as it has been from the moment that man fell.

❧ A THOUGHT TO PONDER ❧

The whole state of our world is to be traced back to this fact about the devil.

From *Children of God*, pp. 61-62.

LOOK FORWARD IN ANTICIPATION

For this purpose the Son of God was manifested, that he might destroy the works of the devil.

1 JOHN 3:8

As we believe the message of the Gospel, we are translated from the kingdom of darkness into the kingdom of light—the kingdom of God's dear Son. He is building up His own kingdom; he is drawing men and women unto Himself out of the world; He is going on with the work. He is in glory seated at the right hand of God, and He must reign until His enemies shall be made His footstool. He is going on until the number of the elect shall have been gathered in. And when that has happened, He will come again. He will return into this world as King and Lord, and He will finally finish the work. He will come with a mighty sword, and not only evil and sin but Satan himself and all his cohorts shall be cast into the lake of fire and will finally be banished from the sight of God for all eternity. And our guarantee of all this is the glorious fact of the resurrection: He "was manifested, that he might destroy the works of the devil."

Remember then what He has already destroyed, and look forward in anticipation; the blessed hope that faces us as Christian people is that He will destroy these works of the devil utterly, completely, and finally. Evil and sin will be finally destroyed out of existence, burnt, destroyed forever. God shall be all and in all, and if we are in the army of the mighty Victor who has already risen from the grave and thereby conquered death, if we belong to Him, we shall behold that final judgment of Satan, and we shall dwell for all eternity in a perfect state with no sin and no sorrow, with no sighing and no tears.

❧ A THOUGHT TO PONDER ☙

We shall dwell for all eternity in a perfect state with no sin and no sorrow, with no sighing and no tears.

SINLESS PERFECTION?

He that committeth sin is of the devil; for the devil sinneth from the beginning. . . . Whosoever is born of God doth not commit sin.
1 JOHN 3:8-9

The man or woman who is righteous will show that by living a righteous life; the one who is not righteous shows it by not living a righteous life. That is why this reference to the devil is so significant: "He that committeth sin is of the devil; for the devil sinneth from the beginning." That is his characteristic, his nature, his habit; that is his way of living. That is the thing that is so true of the devil: He sins from the beginning; he *goes on sinning.* "And that man," John says in essence, "who goes on sinning is therefore the man who is proclaiming that he has the kind of nature that the devil has. He does not have the new nature that the Christian has."

We must remember that the apostle here is speaking about *all* Christians. Now some of the people who believe in sinless perfection tell us that the apostle here is only talking about *some* Christians. But at this point they become inconsistent, because they forget the message of verse 6; they say he is only speaking about some, but John is speaking about all Christians: "Whosoever abideth in him sinneth not." If a man does not abide in Christ, he is not a Christian at all; to be a Christian means to be abiding in Christ. Now there are some who would have us believe that you can be a Christian without abiding in Christ, but surely that denies the whole doctrine of rebirth. We are in Christ or we are not, and if we are not in Christ we are not Christians at all. "If any man hath not the Spirit of Christ, he is none of his" (Romans 8:9); if we have not been born of the Spirit, we are not Christians. You cannot be in Christ one day and out the next; every Christian is in Christ and abides in Him. John is not only speaking to certain Christians—he is speaking to all Christians.

⟡ A THOUGHT TO PONDER ⟡
We must remember that the apostle here is speaking about *all* Christians.

From *Children of God,* pp. 76-77.

THE DIVINE SEED

Whosoever is born of God doth not commit sin;
for his seed remaineth in him.

1 JOHN 3:9

The power of sin is not immediately destroyed in us. God has chosen to do this work gradually. This word "seed" is rather significant. Does that not simply mean God's method and plan in every realm? In the realm of nature you sow the seed, but it may be weeks and months and perhaps years before you get the full bloom. Why does God do it like that? My answer is, I do not know, but that is God's method; it is His way, and it seems to me that is what we are taught in the Scriptures. We are taught about being "babes in Christ," we are taught about growing and developing, we are taught about "growing in grace." John has already dealt with that when he said, "Every man that hath this hope in him purifieth himself, even as he is pure" (1 John 3:3).

It is a process, a development, and surely if we do not interpret a section like this in that way, then it means that we are denying what he has already told us in the first chapter: "If we say we have no sin, we deceive ourselves, and the truth is not in us" (verse 8).

John's object in writing is "that ye sin not. And if any man sin, we have an advocate with the Father" (2:1). But why is that if the Christian is immediately delivered and made perfect? This is a great mystery. It is not for us to understand, but we must face the facts. We must realize that experience, the experience of the greatest saints, denies the teaching of sinless perfection, and we see that it is not in accordance with the teaching of Scripture.

John exhorts us to strive to purify and cleanse ourselves and to interpret Scripture in our daily lives. We do not just have to submit and resign ourselves in order to be made perfect; we are to understand the Scriptures and their doctrine. We are to see their implication and to implement them in our daily lives.

❧ A THOUGHT TO PONDER ❧
Sinless perfection is not in accordance with the teaching of Scripture.

From *Children of God*, pp. 79-80.

HATED BY THE WORLD

Marvel not, my brethren, if the world hate you.
1 JOHN 3:13

Let me put this as a historical fact. This is one of the great principles that we find in the Bible from the beginning. There are many people who have difficulty with this verse. If this is true of you, you have somehow failed to understand the first great essential divisions of the Bible. The difference between Cain and Abel was in Cain, not in Abel. Cain (the world) hates Abel (the Christian). Look at Joseph and his brethren. Look at David and Saul; read the story of how King Saul treated David and tried to get rid of him—the jealousy, envy, and malice. Look at the treatment that was meted out to the prophets, those men of God who were trying to save the nation. It is there everywhere.

Look at the supreme example of our Lord Himself. Here is the Son of God incarnate; here is the eternal life in the flesh. Look at the world sneering at Him, how they picked up stones to cast at Him, how they shouted, "Crucify Him, away with Him!" The world crucified the very Son of God who had come to save it! "Marvel not, my friends, if the world hate you." The world does not hate you because you are hateful people; the case of Cain and Abel proves that. Cain did not hate his brother because there was something hateful about him. There was nothing hateful in Abel, but Cain hated him in spite of that.

Neither does the world hate us because we are good. Let us be quite clear about that. The world does not hate *good* people; the world only hates *Christian* people. That is the subtle, vital distinction. If you are just a good person, the world, far from hating you, will admire you; it will cheer you. And what is true of the individual is true of the whole Church. The world, we are told, hates Christians, not because they are hateful, not because they are good, not because they do good, but specifically because they are Christians, because they are of God, because they have Christ within them.

❧ A THOUGHT TO PONDER ❧
The world does not hate *good* people; the world only hates *Christian* people.

From *Children of God*, pp. 101-102.

WHAT IS PRAYER?

*And hereby we know that we are of the truth, and
shall assure our hearts before him.*

1 JOHN 3:19

What is prayer? Well, I cannot think of a better way of describing it
than these two words that we have at the end of 1 John 3:19:
"Hereby we know that we are of the truth, and shall assure our
hearts *before him*." That is prayer; prayer is coming before Him.
Now we are always in the presence of God—"in him we live, and
move, and have our being" (Acts 17:28)—and we are always under
His eye. But prayer is something still more special. Prayer is having
a special audience and going immediately and directly to Him—
"before him." Prayer is something in which we turn our back upon
everything else, excluding everything else, while, for the time being,
we find ourselves face to face with God alone. There is a sense in
which one cannot expound it further; it is just that.

We have to realize that is exactly and precisely what we do
when we pray. Obviously, therefore, in a sense the most vital thing in
prayer is the realization that we are before Him. And you will find
that the saints have always talked a great deal about this. That is
the difficulty; thoughts will keep on obtruding themselves, and our
imaginations will wander all over the world, and certain ideas and
proposals and wants and needs will intrude. But all that must be
dismissed, and we must just start by realizing that we are actually
and literally in the presence of the living God. "Before him."

Now, says John, this whole question of brotherly love is of
importance because of that. It is when you come there, when you are
before Him, that you begin to realize the importance of what you are
doing with the rest of your life and with the rest of your time. It is
when you come there that you begin to see the relevance of this.

❧ A THOUGHT TO PONDER ❧

We must just start by realizing that we are actually and literally in the
presence of the living God.

October 29

CONFIDENCE IN PRAYER

*Beloved, if our heart condemn us not, then
have we confidence toward God.*

1 JOHN 3:21

This matter of "confidence" is absolutely vital to true prevailing prayer. Let me remind you how the Scripture puts it. Have you noticed that the word *boldness* is used in connection with prayer in the Scriptures? You often find it in the epistle to the Hebrews: "Let us therefore come boldly unto the throne of grace, that we may obtain mercy, and find grace to help in time of need" (4:16); or again, "Having therefore, brethren, boldness to enter into the holiest by the blood of Jesus" (Hebrews 10:19); or, "let us draw near with a true heart in full assurance of faith" (Hebrews 10:22). Or consider what Paul says in Ephesians 3: ". . . in whom we have boldness and access with confidence by . . . faith" (verse 12). That is the way to pray; if our petitions are to be of any value, we must have boldness and assurance and confidence in our access.

How is this to be obtained? Well, it seems to me that we are here dealing with the answer, and it is a question of sonship. The consciousness of our sonship and the assurance of our sonship is to be determined by our love of the brethren. It works like this: If I am truly loving the brethren, then I remember that I am a child of God. Therefore, when I am before God in prayer I argue like this: "I must think of God now not as my Judge but as my Father." John goes on to remind us of that in 1 John chapter 4. I do not come to God, therefore, in a spirit of fear, because "fear hath torment" (1 John 4:18). So, assured of my sonship, I know that God delights in me, that God indeed is much more ready to bless me than I am to ask to be blessed.

☙ A THOUGHT TO PONDER ☙
I must think of God now not as my Judge but as my Father.

From *Children of God*, pp. 128–129.

October 30

ASSURANCE IN PRAYER

Beloved, if our heart condemn us not, then have we confidence toward God. And whatsoever we ask, we receive of him, because we keep his commandments, and do those things that are pleasing in his sight.

1 JOHN 3:21-22

Over and above my confidence is my right of access; I must have assurance with regard to my petitions.

James puts it like this: "If any of you lack wisdom, let him ask of God . . ." But notice this: "But let him ask in faith, nothing wavering. For he that wavereth is like a wave of the sea driven with the wind and tossed. For let not that man think that he shall receive any thing of the Lord" (James 1:5-7). If you are uncertain, doubtful, or hesitant and lacking assurance in your petition, you will not get your request, says James. Listen to the psalmist in Psalm 66:18: "If I regard iniquity in my heart, the Lord will not hear me." If I go to God with a double mind, holding on to my sin and knowing that I am living a wrong life, I will not have confidence in my prayer. "God is greater than our heart, and knoweth all things" (1 John 3:20); if I am condemning myself and know I am wrong, how much more so must God.

Now I think that our Lord Himself has answered this question in John's Gospel. He put it like this: "If ye abide in me, and my words abide in you, ye shall ask what ye will, and it shall be done unto you" (John 15:7). Or again: "I have chosen you, and ordained you, that ye should go and bring forth fruit, and that your fruit should remain; that whatsoever ye shall ask of the Father in my name, he may give it you" (John 15:16).

If I am keeping God's commandments, then I can be certain that my life is being controlled by the Holy Spirit, and therefore I know that any petitions and desires I may have were created in me by the Holy Spirit.

✎ A THOUGHT TO PONDER ✍

If I go to God holding on to my sin and knowing that I am living a wrong life, I will not have confidence in my prayer.

From *Children of God*, pp. 129-130.

A Christian Is a Spiritual Person

*Now we have received, not the spirit of the world,
but the spirit which is of God.*
1 CORINTHIANS 2:12

What is a Christian? I am never tired of putting forward that question, because I think that of all things that are misunderstood in the world today, this is the one that is most misunderstood. What is a Christian—a good person, a moral person, a formal member of a church, one who pays an occasional visit to God's house? Is that a Christian? Shame upon us if ever we have given that impression! No; a Christian is a spiritual person. Is that not the statement of the New Testament everywhere—a *spiritual* man or woman?

A spiritual person is one who has received the Holy Spirit—that is New Testament terminology. Christians are people who are altogether different from those who are not Christians. They are not just a little bit better or people who do certain things. No; they themselves are different; they are spiritual. "We have received," says Paul, "not the spirit of the world, but the Spirit which is of God; that we might know the things that are freely given to us of God. . . . He that is spiritual judgeth all things" (1 Corinthians 2:12, 15). Not so with the natural man. That is the difference.

Now there are some people who say that you become a Christian and then later you receive the gift of the Holy Spirit. But you cannot be a Christian unless you have received the gift of the Holy Spirit. It is that, in a sense, that makes you a Christian. It means new birth; it means being born again; it means, to use the language of Peter, to be "partakers of the divine nature" (2 Peter 1:4). It means, to use the language of our Lord Himself, that God is *abiding* in us. "He that keepeth his commandments," says John, "dwelleth in him, and he in him" (1 John 3:24). And if you want the best commentary on that, read John 14, those great words of our Lord: "I will not leave you comfortless: I will come to you" (verse 18); or as some would translate it, "I will not leave you orphans, I will come again."

❧ A Thought to Ponder ❧

A Christian is a *spiritual* man or woman.

From *Children of God*, p. 140.

November

TESTS OF TRUTH AND LOVE

FROM

The Love of God

TEST THE SPIRITS

Beloved, believe not every spirit, but try the spirits whether they are of God: because many false prophets are gone out into the world.

1 JOHN 4:1

The position of the Scripture is one that faces two extremes: The Spirit is essential, and experience is vital; however, truth and definition and doctrine and dogma are equally vital and essential. And our whole position is one that proclaims that experience that is not based solidly upon truth and doctrine is dangerous.

There is the necessity for testing and trying the spirits. "Beloved, believe not every spirit, but try the spirits whether they are of God." Now some people object root and branch to this process of testing. There are many reasons for that, of course. In the case of some people it is nothing but slackness, indolence, and laziness—a desire for ease.

But there are those who feel that this whole process of testing and trying the spirits is unscriptural. According to such people, the moment you begin to discuss and consider and define, you cease to be a spiritual person. But my reply to this is that we must test and try the spirits because Scripture commands and exhorts us to do so, and for me that is enough. "Beloved, believe not every spirit, but try the spirits."

Not only that, but Scripture tells us why we ought to do so: "because many false prophets are gone out into the world." Alas, there are false prophets; there are evil spirits; there is a devil who is so clever and subtle that he can transform himself into an angel of light. If we were confronted with the Holy Spirit only, there would be no need to test the spirits, but the very name "*Holy* Spirit" suggests other spirits, devilish spirits—and there are such powers.

❧ A THOUGHT TO PONDER ❧

We must test and try the spirits because Scripture commands and exhorts us to do so.

From *The Love of God*, pp. 18-20.

TRUTH AND ERROR

*Now we have received, not the spirit of the world, but the
Spirit which is of God; that we might know the things
that are freely given to us of God.*

1 CORINTHIANS 2:12

An important reason for testing and trying the spirits is the evidence provided by the long history of the Church of the havoc that has often been wrought in the Church because people would not try and test the spirits, because they said, "I have received such a wonderful experience, and therefore I must be right." What we are concerned about is not a matter of sincerity and honesty—we are concerned about truth and error, and truth and error have to be defined.

Is this something only for theologians and professors of theology or for ministers and leaders? Is it only for certain people? The answer is that it is for *all*. "Beloved"—he is writing to the average church member—"believe not every spirit, but try the spirits" (1 John 4:1). Later on he says, "Ye are of God, little children" (verse 4), and I think he used the expression "little children" deliberately—"you, the ordinary church members, little children—you hear us because you are of the truth."

It is the duty and the business of everyone examining the name *Christian* to be in a position to try and examine and test the spirits. Indeed, we are given the power to do so—"greater is he that is in you, than he that is in the world" (1 John 4:4). We have been given this capacity by God through the Holy Spirit; the Spirit dwells in us, and therefore we have this power of discrimination and understanding. The apostle Paul tells us that at great length in 1 Corinthians. For example, "Now we have received, not the spirit of the world, but the Spirit which is of God; that we might know the things that are freely given to us of God" (1 Corinthians 2:12). That is it!

❧ A THOUGHT TO PONDER ❧

We are concerned about truth and error, and truth and error have to be defined.

HOW TO TEST THE SPIRITS

. . . try the spirits . . .
1 JOHN 4:1

How is this testing to be done? How are we to know whether certain spirits are true or false?

There are those who claim that the gifts of the Spirit are absolutely essential, and that unless men and women are able to manifest certain gifts of the Spirit, they have not received the Spirit. They say, for example, "You have not received the Holy Spirit unless you are able to speak in tongues or have done this or that." They refer to a particular gift, and they say that if you have not experienced that, you have not received the Spirit, in spite of the fact that the apostle Paul asks the question, "Do all speak with tongues?" (1 Corinthians 12:30). The whole of chapter 12 of 1 Corinthians is designed to show that the gifts are distributed by the Spirit. He may or may not give these gifts, and the manifestation of gifts is not an essential proof of the possession of the Spirit.

But let me go on to particular matters. A very dangerous way of testing or examining the claim to having the Spirit is to judge in terms of phenomena, as in the gift of healing or the particular result of a ministry. These are the tests that are put up. People say, "Surely this man must be right. Haven't you heard what he has been doing? Haven't you heard of the cures he is able to bring about? Look at the results he has had." The test of phenomena, taken alone, is an extremely dangerous one because evil spirits can work miracles; our Lord warned His followers that these spirits would be able to do such marvelous works.

The fact that people are full of fervor does not imply that they have the Holy Spirit. Evil spirits are often very fervent. Great excitement is not a proof of the Spirit; great energy is not a proof of the Spirit; much assurance or confidence is not a proof of the Spirit.

✎ A THOUGHT TO PONDER ✐

The test of phenomena, taken alone, is an extremely dangerous one because evil spirits can work miracles.

From *The Love of God*, pp. 21-22.

November 4

THE ULTIMATE TEST

Hereby know ye the Spirit of God: Every spirit that confesseth that Jesus Christ is come in the flesh is of God.

1 JOHN 4:2

The most important test is conformity to scriptural teaching. "Hereby know ye the Spirit of God: Every spirit that confesseth that Jesus Christ is come in the flesh is of God." How do I know that this is a spiritual test? All I know about Him, I put up to the test of Scripture. Indeed, you get exactly the same thing in the sixth verse of 1 John 4 where John says, speaking of himself and the other apostles, "We are of God: he that knoweth God heareth us; he that is not of God heareth not us. Hereby know we the spirit of truth, and the spirit of error." The first thing to ask about a man who claims to be filled with the Spirit and to be an unusual teacher is, does his teaching conform to Scripture? Is it in conformity with the apostolic message? Does he base it all upon this Word? Is he willing to submit to it? That is the great test.

Another test is the readiness to listen to scriptural teaching; to abide by it is always a characteristic of the true prophet. You will find that the other man rather tends to dismiss it. "Ah yes," he says, "but you are legalistic, you are just a theologian. I have experience, I have felt, and I have produced this and that." The tendency is not to abide by the teaching of Scripture but to be almost contemptuous of it; that has always been the characteristic of those who have tended to go astray. Read the history of the Quakers, and you will find that such an attitude became a prominent feature—the inner light rather than the objective teaching of Scripture itself.

✎ A THOUGHT TO PONDER ✎
The most important test is conformity to scriptural teaching.

MARKS OF A PERSON OF THE SPIRIT

*For God hath not given us the spirit of fear; but of power,
and of love, and of a sound mind.*

2 TIMOTHY 1:7

The greatest test is that the true Spirit always glorifies Christ. Christ is always in the center; He is always given the preeminence. And the true prophet is not the man who talks about experiences and visions and what he has done and seen, but about Christ. And when you have heard Him you do not say, "What a wonderful man"; you say, "What a wonderful Savior!" You do not say, "What a wonderful experience this man has had"; you say, "Who is the Man of whom the Spirit is speaking?" The attraction is to Christ; the Spirit glorifies Christ.

I now mention what I believe to be the perfect balance in this matter. "God," said Paul to Timothy "hath not given us the spirit of fear; but of power, and of love, and of a sound mind" (2 Timothy 1:7). This is discipline, balance. The man who has the Holy Spirit is the man who always manifests balance and proportion. "Be not drunk with wine, wherein is excess; but be filled with the Spirit" (Ephesians 5:18); there is power and balance, but no excess. Speak one at a time, says Paul to the people of Corinth. "But," they say, "we cannot. Isn't that quenching the Spirit?" "No," says Paul; "let all things be done . . . in order" (see 1 Corinthians 14:40). The Holy Spirit is the Spirit of order, not of disorder. Doctrine and love are required; experience and power, intellect and mind—the whole person is involved and functions as this perfectly balanced body with no schism, with no rivalry and competition, but with the whole manifesting and ministering unto the glory of the Lord and Savior, Jesus Christ. Make sure the Spirit of God is in you, and then make sure that it is the Spirit of God and not some false, evil spirit to whom you are listening.

✑ A THOUGHT TO PONDER ✎

The greatest test is that the true Spirit always glorifies Christ.

THE TEACHING OF THE ANTICHRIST

*Hereby know ye the Spirit of God: Every spirit that confesseth
that Jesus Christ is come in the flesh is of God: And every spirit
that confesseth not that Jesus Christ is come in the flesh is not of
God: and this is that spirit of antichrist, whereof ye have heard
that it should come; and even now already is it in the world.*

1 JOHN 4:2-3

What is the teaching of the antichrist? It is not a denial of Christ—
it is a misrepresentation of Christ; it is a teaching that either does
something to Him or detracts something from Him. You remember
how John put it; he said these people "went out from us, but they
were not of us; for if they had been of us, they would no doubt
have continued with us: but they went out, that they might be manifest that they were not all of us" (1 John 2:19). They were in the
church. The antichrists had arisen *within* the Christian church; they
said they believed in Christ. And yet, says John, their teaching is such
that we can prove that they do not truly believe in Him.

Now this is a very important principle to grasp. Merely for people to say, "Yes, I believe in the Lord Jesus Christ; I always have
believed in Him" is not enough, until we have tested them further.
The apostle Paul says that these people preached "another Jesus."
Ah, yes, they were preaching Jesus, but it was *another* Jesus; it was
not the Jesus that Paul preached (2 Corinthians 11:4). They preached
Christ, yes, but what sort of Christ, what kind of Jesus? That is the
question.

Therefore we ask this question: How can we decide whether
the teaching concerning Jesus Christ is true or false? And here the
one answer is given perfectly clearly. Our ultimate authority, our
only authority, is the apostolic teaching. That is the whole point of
the first epistle of John.

∾ A THOUGHT TO PONDER ∾

The teaching of the antichrist is not a denial of Christ—it is a misrepresentation of Christ.

From *The Love of God*, pp. 29-30.

THE TEACHING OF THE APOSTLES

. . . built upon the foundation of the apostles and prophets.
EPHESIANS 2:20

John's whole purpose in writing his first epistle was to say to the early Christians, "Hold on to what I and the other apostles have told you." You remember how he began. "That which was from the beginning, which we have heard, which we have seen with our eyes, which we have looked upon, and our hands have handled, of the Word of life" (1 John 1:1-2). He is referring to the apostles, and he says that he writes these things so that these Christians "may have fellowship with *us*" (1 John 1:3). Who are they? They are still the apostles.

Now this is something that is absolutely primary and fundamental. The claim of the New Testament is that it alone is authoritative in these matters. It teaches us that the apostles and prophets were the people to whom God, through the Holy Spirit, had revealed spiritual truth, and He meant them to teach it and to write it. The apostle Paul tells us in Ephesians 2:20 that the Christian Church is "built upon the foundation of the apostles and prophets." All teaching must derive from them, and so you have this extraordinary claim in the New Testament. These men claimed a unique authority.

Listen to the apostle Paul putting it again in writing to the Galatians; he uses strong language like this: "But though we, or an angel from heaven, preach any other gospel unto you than that which we have preached unto you, let him be accursed" (1:8). "What egotism!" says someone. No, it is not egotism; it is the claim of a man who has been commissioned by God. God has set him apart; God has given him the revelation. And he goes on to argue in so many of his letters that what he preached was also the message that was preached by the other apostles. This apostle and all the apostles did not hesitate to say that they exhorted these people to test every teaching by their teaching. And you and I are still committed to the same position.

❧ A THOUGHT TO PONDER ❧
The apostles and prophets were the people to whom God revealed spiritual truth.

From *The Love of God*, pp. 30-31.

THE APOSTOLIC TEACHING ABOUT JESUS

. . . Jesus Christ is come in the flesh . . .

1 JOHN 4:2

What is the apostolic teaching concerning Christ? Now in a phrase in our text John gives us the perfect answer. John does not use words like this haphazardly. Listen to the way in which he puts it: "Hereby know ye the Spirit of God: Every spirit that confesseth that Jesus Christ is come in the flesh is of God: And every spirit that confesseth not that Jesus Christ is come in the flesh is not of God" (1 John 4:2). Now here is the statement: "*Jesus Christ is come in the flesh.*" Jesus Christ arrived in the world "in the flesh." What does this mean? Let me try to show you how John in putting it like this was countering and answering some of those grievous heresies that had already arisen even in his day in the church, before the end of the first century.

Take the expression "Jesus Christ." Why does John say, "*Jesus Christ* is come in the flesh"? Why did he not say that Jesus or Christ has come in the flesh? Ah, that is most important; that is his way of emphasizing the unity of the blessed person. The Lord Jesus Christ has two natures—the divine and the human—and yet there is only one person. The earlier chapters of 1 John make it plain that there were false prophets, antichrists, in the early church, and some of them said something like this: "Jesus of Nazareth was just a man like every other man; but when He was baptized by John in the Jordan, the eternal Christ came upon Him and began to use Him; and the eternal Christ continued with the man Jesus until He came to the cross. But on the cross the eternal Christ went away, back to heaven, and it was only the man Jesus who died. There were two persons— the man Jesus and the eternal Christ." No! says John; "*Jesus Christ,*" one person but two natures—the two natures in one person.

❧ A THOUGHT TO PONDER ❧

The Lord Jesus Christ has two natures—the divine and the human— and yet there is only one person.

From *The Love of God*, pp. 31-32.

LOVING ONE ANOTHER

. . . let us love one another . . .

1 JOHN 4:7

I do not hesitate to say that the ultimate test of our profession of the Christian faith is this whole question of our loving one another. Indeed, I do not hesitate to aver that it is a more vital test than our orthodoxy. I am the last man in the world to say anything against orthodoxy, but I am here to say that it is not the final test. Orthodoxy is absolutely essential; this epistle [1 John] has shown us that repeatedly, and it will show it to us again. We must believe the right things, for apart from that we have nothing at all and we have no standing whatsoever; so the correctness of belief is absolutely essential. And yet I say that when we come to the realm of experience and self-examination, the test of orthodoxy is not the ultimate test.

Alas, let us admit it—it is possible for a person to be absolutely correct and yet not to be a Christian. It is possible for men and women to give perfect intellectual assent to the propositions that are to be found in the Bible; it is possible for them to be interested in theology and to say that one theology is superior to another and to accept and defend and argue about it, and yet to be utterly devoid of the grace of the Lord Jesus Christ and of the love of God in their hearts. This is a terrible thought, it is a terrible possibility, but it is a fact. There have been men also who have clearly been perfectly orthodox—champions of the faith—and yet they have denied that very faith in the bitterness with which they have sometimes defended it. I repeat, the test of orthodoxy, while it is so vital and essential, is not enough. There is a more thoroughgoing test, and it is this test of brotherly love—love for one another.

✎ A THOUGHT TO PONDER ✍

The ultimate test of our profession of the Christian faith is our loving one another.

From *The Love of God*, pp. 39-40.

GOD IS LOVE

Beloved, let us love one another: for love is of God; and
every one that loveth is born of God, and knoweth God.
He that loveth not knoweth not God; for God is love.

1 JOHN 4:7-8

"God is love." No one can answer against that; one trembles even to handle it; it cannot be analyzed. I simply want to point out that John does not say merely that God loves us or that God is loving. He goes beyond that. He says, "God is love." God essentially is love; God's nature is love; you cannot think of God without love.

Of course he has already told us that God is light in exactly the same way—that was the first pronouncement. "This then is the message . . . God is light" (1 John 1:5); and in exactly the same way "God is love" and God is spirit. This battles the imagination; it is something that is altogether beyond our comprehension, and yet we start with it.

Augustine and others deduce from this the doctrine of the Trinity. I think there may be a great deal in that; the very fact that God is love declares the Trinity—God the Father loves the Son, and the link is the person of the Holy Spirit. Ah! this high doctrine; it is beyond us. All I know is that God, in the very essence of His nature and being, is love, and you cannot think of God and must not think of Him except in terms of love. Everything that God is and does is colored by this; all God's actions have this aspect of love in them and the aspect of light in the same way. That is how God always manifests Himself—light and love.

"Therefore, because that is the fundamental postulate, because that is so true of God," John is saying, "that works itself out for us like this: Because God is love, we ought to love one another. For 'love is of God.'" In other words, love is from God, love flows from God. It is as if John were turning to these people and saying, "God loves, and this love I am talking about is something that only comes from God—it is derived from Him."

✎ A THOUGHT TO PONDER ✐
God, in the very essence of His nature and being, is love.

From *The Love of God*, p. 43.

THE MANIFEST LOVE OF GOD

In this was manifested the love of God toward us, because that
God sent his only begotten Son into the world, that we might live
through him. Herein is love, not that we loved God, but that he
loved us, and sent his Son to be the propitiation for our sins.

1 JOHN 4:9-10

The apostle is anxious to remind us that God is actually manifesting that essential nature of His. He is love, but mercifully for us He has "manifested" that love, He has made it unmistakably plain and clear. So we can put John's immediate argument like this: "If only you really understood this love, if only you knew something about it, then most of your problems and difficulties would immediately vanish." So he proceeds to tell us something further about this great and wondrous and glorious love of God.

Surely we all must agree that this is something that is equally true of us. The more I study the New Testament and live the Christian life, the more convinced I am that our fundamental difficulty, our fundamental lack, is the lack of seeing the love of God. It is not so much our knowledge that is defective but our vision of the love of God. Thus our greatest object and endeavor should be to know Him better, and thus we will love Him more truly. Now John's object is to help these first Christians to whom he writes in just this way, because he is quite sure that once they love God, they will love one another.

This is something we find running right through the Bible; the second commandment follows the first. The first commandment is, "Thou shalt love the Lord thy God with all thy heart, and with all thy soul, and with all thy mind. . . . And the second is like unto it, Thou shalt love thy neighbor as thyself" (Matthew 22:37, 39). But you will never do the second until you have done the first; so we must start with the love of God.

∾ A THOUGHT TO PONDER ∾

It is not so much our knowledge that is defective but our vision of the love of God.

From *The Love of God*, pp. 49-50.

"WE OUGHT ALSO . . ."

Beloved, if God so loved us, we ought also to love one another.
1 JOHN 4:11

The question is, what do you do about those people who seem to irritate you and are a problem to you and who really make things rather difficult? Here is John's answer: "If God so loved us, we ought also to love one another." This means something like this: Instead of giving way to that instinctive feeling that I have, instead of speaking or acting or reacting at once, I stop and I talk to myself. I remind myself of the Christian truth that I believe, and I apply it to the whole situation. Now that is something that you and I have to do. This life of which the New Testament speaks is full of the intellectual aspect. It is not a feeling. You do not wait until you feel like loving other people—you make yourself love other people ("we ought"). According to the New Testament, Christians can make themselves love other Christians, and they are failing sadly if they do not do so.

How do they do it? They remind themselves of this truth: "If God so loved us." In other words, this is the procedure. The first thing I do when I feel irritated and disturbed and bewildered and perhaps antagonistic is to look at myself. Now that is half the battle. We all know perfectly well from experience that in this kind of problem the whole difficulty is that we are always looking at the other person and never at ourselves. But if I start with myself—if God so loved *me*—what do I find?

But usually I instinctively feel that I am being wronged, that I am not being dealt with fairly. I feel it is the other person who is difficult. "One minute!" says the Gospel; "stop for a moment and look at yourself and remind yourself of exactly what you are." The Gospel brings us immediately face to face with this self that is in us that is the cause of all these troubles.

❧ A THOUGHT TO PONDER ❧

Christians can make themselves love other Christians.

From *The Love of God*, pp. 68-69.

PRIDE

O wretched man that I am!
ROMANS 7:24

Self-sufficiency, self-consciousness—oh, to get away from the self!

"O wretched man that I am! who shall deliver me from the body of this death?" (Romans 7:24). How can I get away from this wretched, ugly self I am always thinking about? Isn't that the cry of every man and woman convicted of sin by the Holy Ghost? Now the effect of 1 John 4:9-10 is to expose all that, and I really am not prepared to listen to people who tell me that they glory in the revelation of God's love unless they have dealt with themselves. There is no value in any striving to keep the tenets of the Christian faith unless those tenets have made you see yourself in the world, unless they have flashed upon you in such a way as to make you see the manifestation of self; that is what the love of God always does. "Herein is love, not that we loved God, but that he loved us." It is incredible that God could love such a person as I have been describing. That is the amazing thing! That is love, says John.

Therefore, if you believe and know all that, it makes you see yourself as you are, and do you see what happens at once? The moment you see yourself like that, you cry with John Bunyan:

He that is down need fear no fall,
He that is low in pride.

John Bunyan meant that when I see myself as I really am, nobody can insult me. It is impossible, because they can never say anything that is bad enough about me. Whatever the world may say about me, I am much worse than they think. When we see ourselves in the light of this glorious Gospel, no one can hurt us, no one can offend us.

☙ A THOUGHT TO PONDER ☚
Self-sufficiency, self-consciousness—oh, to get away from the self!

From *The Love of God*, p. 70.

THE INVISIBILITY OF GOD

No man hath seen God at any time. If we love one another,
God dwelleth in us, and his love is perfected in us.

1 JOHN 4:12

Why does God say, "No man hath seen God at any time"? Why does John suddenly introduce this idea of the invisibility of God?

John does not say that we cannot love God except through loving our brethren; that is not his argument. Nor does he say that we can only love God by means of loving our brethren. Rather, he tells us that we are to love God—that we *can* love God and that we *should* love Him.

It seems to me that John is here introducing a new theme, a new idea, into his great discussion of the question of loving the brethren. And this new theme I would describe as the theme of assurance of salvation; it is the whole question of our knowledge of God and of the way in which we can know God. In other words, I am suggesting that John here is linking up with that with which he left off at the end of verse 8. Let me reconstruct it to you in this way: "Beloved," he says, "let us love one another: for love is of God; and every one that loveth is born of God, and knoweth God. He that loveth not knoweth not God; for God is love. . . . No man hath seen God at any time. If we love one another, God dwelleth in us, and his love is perfected in us" (verses 7-8, 12).

"So," says John in effect, "it is important that you love the brethren from the standpoint of your own assurance of salvation and from the standpoint of your fellowship with God." John is more like a poet than a logician. Although he tends to arrive at his position in circles instead of straight lines, though there is something of the mystic in his thinking, nevertheless there is firm logic at the back of it; there is a definite line of reason.

✒ A THOUGHT TO PONDER ✑

It is important that you love the brethren from the standpoint of your own assurance of salvation.

GOD DWELLS IN US

No man hath seen God at any time. If we love one another,
God dwelleth in us, and his love is perfected in us.

1 JOHN 4:12

God dwells in us. That is one of the grounds of my assurance, my
certainty. "No man hath seen God at any time." Very well, then,
do we go on in doubt and almost in despair wondering whether there
is a God? No! says John; "if we love one another, God dwelleth in
us, and his love is perfected in us."

Now, I confess very readily that I approach a theme like this with
fear and with a sense of awe. Consider the great statement in John
14 of this intimate union between the believer and God the Father
and God the Son, of Their abiding in us and dwelling in us. We are
familiar with chapters 14, 15, 16, and 17 of John's Gospel, and
here we have the same thing again. "God dwelleth in us, and his love
is perfected in us." And John goes on to say in 1 John 4:13, "Hereby
know we that we dwell in him, and he in us, because he hath given
us of his Spirit," and in verse 15, "Whosoever shall confess that Jesus
is the Son of God, God dwelleth in him, and he in God."

At this point, like Moses, we take off our shoes! We are concerned with something that is glorious and magnificent, and so we
have to be very careful as we handle it. The statement is that if we
love one another, God—God who is love, God the Almighty, God the
eternal—*dwells in us.* I think that the great thing at this point is to
realize that we must not materialize that conception. We must not
think of God in material terms; God is spirit. It is God, who is spirit,
who dwells in us.

✎ A THOUGHT TO PONDER ✎

It is God, who is spirit, who dwells in us.

MORALITY AND CONFORMITY

Hereby know we that we dwell in him, and he in us,
because he hath given us of his Spirit.

1 JOHN 4:13

We are reminded here of the nature of the Christian life. I am increasingly convinced that most of our troubles arise from the fact that our whole conception of the Christian life tends to be inadequate. I am not referring to people outside the church at the moment, but to Christian people. I speak for myself when I say that there is nothing of which I have to remind myself more constantly than the very nature of the Christian life. We are all the same; the first Christians were the same as well, and that is why the epistles were written. It was because of this constant tendency to think and conceive of the Christian life in an inadequate manner that the apostles were led and moved by God to write their letters with their wonderful instruction.

What is the Christian life? Living as a Christian does not just mean moral living, nor just being good and decent. Of course it includes those things, but that is not the whole of the Christian life. Is it not obvious that there are large numbers of people who think seriously that constitutes the Christian life? There are many people attending morning services in church who say that just because they are not guilty of certain things, they are true Christians. To which I reply, "Hereby we know we that we dwell in him, and he in us, because he hath given us of his Spirit"; then our little morality shrivels into nothing. Morality is essential, but God forbid that we should reduce this glorious life to just a little decency and morality!

Then there are those who think of Christianity just as a matter of religious conformity. But to regard that as the whole of Christianity is to miss the splendor of this great thing that is expounded in the New Testament.

❧ A THOUGHT TO PONDER ❧

Living as a Christian does not just mean moral living, nor just being good and decent.

From *The Love of God*, pp. 92-93.

KNOWING GOD

Hereby know we that we dwell in him, and he in us,
because he hath given us of his Spirit.

1 JOHN 4:13

We may know, and should know, that we are in a relationship to God and that we possess His life. That is the nature of the Christian life. "Hereby," says John, "know we"—we know it, and we are certain of it. John's whole business in writing this letter is that we may have this knowledge: "These things have I written unto you that believe on the name of the Son of God; that ye may know that ye have eternal life, and that ye may believe on the name of the Son of God" (1 John 5:13).

Now we all possess this knowledge, and we must never be satisfied with anything less than that. This knowledge is to me the very essence of the New Testament teaching. What the Bible offers us is nothing less than this knowledge that God is in us and we in Him, and we should not rest for a moment until we have it. We have no right to be uncertain—"that ye may *know*." Christians who are uncertain of these things are doing dishonor to the Gospel of Jesus Christ, to the work of Christ upon the cross, and to His glorious resurrection. We must not rest until we have full and certain assurance, confidence, and jubilation. The whole of the New Testament has been written in order that we may have it, and I argue that this is something that really must be inevitable. I cannot understand anyone who not only lacks this certainty, but who would even be prepared to argue against such a certainty.

As unbelievers we were dead; we had no spiritual life. A Christian must be born again, by faith, in order to have the life of God in his soul. So is it possible that we can have such life in us and not know it? I say that is impossible!

✎ A THOUGHT TO PONDER ✎
We must not rest until we have full and certain assurance, confidence, and jubilation.

From *The Love of God*, pp. 95-96.

HOW WE KNOW GOD

Hereby know we that we dwell in him, and he in us,
because he hath given us of his Spirit.

1 JOHN 4:13

How do we have knowledge about God? "Hereby know we that we dwell in him, and he in us." How? The answer is, "because he hath given us of his Spirit." So it all comes down to that in the last analysis. How do I know I have received God's Spirit? How may I know for certain that I have been given and received something of the Holy Spirit of God?

Are you concerned about these things, and have you a desire to have them? Are you concerned about the life of your soul? Are you concerned about knowing God? I assure you that if you are, the Holy Spirit is in you, for people apart from God "mind earthly things" (Philippians 3:19)—carnal, fleshly things. Are you concerned about immortality and the things invisible and eternal? If you are minding these things, that is a proof that the Holy Spirit is in you.

Do you have a sense of sin? Are you aware that there is an evil principle within you? Not simply that you do certain things you should not do and feel annoyed with yourself because of it. No; rather, I mean that you are aware that you have an evil nature, that there is a principle of sin and wrong in your heart, that there is a fountain emitting unworthy, ugly, and foul things, and in a sense you hate yourself. Our Lord said that the man who loves himself is in a very dangerous condition. The apostle Paul was a man who could say about himself, "In me (that is, in my flesh,) dwelleth no good thing. . . . O wretched man that I am!" (Romans 7:18, 24). If you have ever felt yourself a sinner, and if you have hated this thing that gets you down, that is proof that you have received the gift of the Holy Spirit.

❧ A THOUGHT TO PONDER ❧

If you have ever felt yourself a sinner, that is proof that you have received the gift of the Holy Spirit.

From *The Love of God*, pp. 96-98.

GOD WORKING IN YOU

Work out your own salvation with fear and trembling.
For it is God which worketh in you both to will and
to do of his good pleasure.
PHILIPPIANS 2:12-13

Are you aware of the fact that God is working in you? "Work out your own salvation with fear and trembling," says Paul, "for it is God which worketh in you." This is a marvelous, wonderful thing. It is one of the great tests of the possession of the Holy Spirit. It means something like this: We are aware of the fact that we are being dealt with; it is not that we decide to do things. You see, moralists and religious conformists are doing it all themselves, and that is why they are so proud of themselves. They get up on Sunday morning instead of spending the morning in bed, and they go to church. They do it because *they* have decided to do it, not because they have been moved. They are in control the whole time; and having done it, they preen themselves with their wonderful, ennobling ideals. How marvelous they are!

But that is not what the Bible talks about. "It is God which worketh in you both to will and to do." In other words, you are aware of the power of God dealing with you, surging and rising within you, and you are amazed and astonished. Far from being proud you say, "It is not I. This is not the sort of person I am. It is God doing something; it is Christ dwelling within me; it is the Holy Spirit who is in me. I am taken up beyond myself, and I thank God for it." Is God working in you? Are you aware of a wonder-working power active in you, moving, disturbing, leading, persuading, drawing you ever onward? If you are, it is because you have received from God the gift of the Holy Spirit.

❧ A THOUGHT TO PONDER ❧

You are aware of the power of God dealing with you, surging and rising within you, and you are amazed and astonished.

From *The Love of God*, p. 99.

THE FULLNESS OF BLESSING

Hereby know we that we dwell in him, and he in us,
because he hath given us of his Spirit.

1 JOHN 4:13

How does this blessing come? Well, I do not see any evidence in the New Testament to support what used to be called a "tarrying meeting." Some people had that idea. God had certain blessings to give, and they thought they had to wait until they received them. But the gift is given by God in His own way and time; this gift does not come of necessity at once. It is God's gift, and He knows when to give it and when to withhold it.

Do you remember the case of Moody? This was his story. He became conscious of his lack and need, and he began to pray to God about it. He gave obedience to the Word of God as well as he could, and he went on praying for months. Nothing happened to him, but still he went on praying. Yes, he waited for it, but it did not come, and the story is that one day, walking down a street in New York, not in a tarrying meeting, not even in a prayer meeting, suddenly God overwhelmed him with this mighty blessing. It was so mighty that Moody felt he would be killed by it, and he held up his hand and said, "Stop, God!"

God has His own time. God knows when to give the gift, and we must never imagine that by going to a meeting or following a certain procedure it is bound to come. No; the Holy Spirit is sovereign, and He gives in His own way. It may be dramatically or suddenly or quietly; that is irrelevant, because what really matters is that we receive the gift. The essence of it all, I think, can be put very simply: "Trust and obey."

❧ A THOUGHT TO PONDER ❧
God has His own time. God knows when to give the gift.

From *The Love of God*, pp. 114-115.

CONFESSING CHRIST

Whosoever shall confess that Jesus is the Son of God,
God dwelleth in him, and he in God.

1 JOHN 4:15

John's whole case is that you cannot believe that Jesus is the Son of God unless God dwells in you and you in God; that is his argument. "Whosoever shall confess that Jesus is the Son of God, God dwelleth in him, and he in God." And the way in which God dwells in us is by the Holy Spirit. So we can say that the people who do confess that Jesus is the Son of God have the Holy Spirit already within them. Or to put it another way, they cannot believe that Jesus is the Son of God without possessing the Holy Spirit.

Now this is a doctrine that is common to the whole of the New Testament. The apostle Paul puts it like this: "But we speak the wisdom of God in a mystery, even the hidden wisdom, which God ordained before the world unto our glory: which none of the princes of this world knew: for had they known it, they would not have crucified the Lord of glory. . . . But God hath revealed them unto us by his Spirit: for the Spirit searcheth all things, yea, the deep things of God" (1 Corinthians 2:7-8, 10).

You see, the whole case can be put like this: Even the princes of this world, the great men of the world, looked at Jesus of Nazareth and saw nothing but a man, a carpenter. They may have regarded Him as a kind of unusual religious genius, but they did not know He was the Lord of glory. Why not? Well, says Paul, because they had not received the Holy Spirit. But you and I, he says to the Corinthians, we understand these things, we believe them. Why? Because God has revealed them to us by His Spirit, the Spirit who searches all things, "yea, the deep things of God."

✎ A THOUGHT TO PONDER ✎
God has revealed "the deep things of God" to us by His Spirit.

THE APOSTOLIC WITNESS

And we have seen and do testify that the Father sent the Son to be the Saviour of the world. Whosoever shall confess that Jesus is the Son of God, God dwelleth in him, and he in God. And we have known and believed the love that God hath to us. God is love; and he that dwelleth in love dwelleth in God, and God in him.

1 JOHN 4:14-16

The apostolic witness is most important. What is it? John, in effect is putting it like this: "The important thing is to know God. But how can I know God? 'No man hath seen God at any time.' But we have seen and do testify that Jesus is the Son of God." That is the statement.

Notice how he puts it. He had not had a vision. What then? Thank God, "we have seen." He said it all in his introduction: "That which . . . we have seen with our eyes, which we have looked upon, and our hands have handled, of the Word of life . . . That which we have seen and heard declare we unto you," said John. No man has seen God, but we have seen Jesus, and Jesus said, "He that hath seen me hath seen the Father" (See John 14:9).

In other words, the apostolic vision on which my faith is grounded is this: It is a belief in that which the apostles tell us they saw, and the explanation of their understanding of what they saw is found in the four Gospels. The statements in the Gospels are not simply objective statements; they are statements plus interpretation, and at long last modern man has come back to see that. They used to contrast John with Matthew, Mark, and Luke. They said that John preached, but that Matthew, Mark, and Luke just gave the facts. But they now have to admit that what all four wrote was facts plus interpretation. Like John, the men who wrote the first three Gospels believed and understood that Jesus is the Son of God and the Savior of the world. They saw and testified; in other words, they saw, and they expounded.

❧ A THOUGHT TO PONDER ❧

The explanation of the apostles' understanding of what they saw is found in the four Gospels.

THE SAVIOR

*And we have seen and do testify that the Father sent the Son to be
the Saviour of the world.*

1 JOHN 4:14

"And we have seen and do testify that the Father sent the Son to be
the Saviour of the world." The whole Gospel in a phrase! This is
the only time in which John uses the expression "Saviour" in the
entire epistle. He gives the same teaching, of course, in other places.
He says that our Lord is "the propitiation for our sins: and not for
ours only, but also for the sins of the whole world" (1 John 2:2).
There is a sense in which he repeats the thought here, but he does not
use this precise phrase but describes Him as "the Saviour of the
world."

The word "Saviour" does not merely mean helper. We are not
told that the Father sent the Son to help mankind; it does not mean
that He is just someone who assists. Nor does it mean that He is
just one who teaches or indicates to us what we ought to do; He is
not merely an instructor. Indeed, I would go further and say that
the term "Saviour" and its connotation must not be thought of in
terms of an example or pattern or encourager. I use these terms
because so often people speak about our Lord as Savior, and yet if
you ask them to define what they mean by that, they say that Christ
as Savior is One who is marching ahead of us and is leading the
way.

Now the element that is seen in such ideas is that ultimately
you and I have to save ourselves, and what the Lord does is to aid
and assist us—to give us encouragement and make it somewhat
easier for us to do so. Now that, of course, is clearly a complete
denial not only of the biblical teaching, but also of the historic faith
and creeds of the Christian Church.

✎ A THOUGHT TO PONDER ✐
The word "Saviour" does not merely mean helper.

From *The Love of God*, pp. 132-134.

THE SAVIOR OF THE WORLD

And we have seen and do testify that the Father sent the Son to be the Saviour of the world.

1 JOHN 4:14

The whole biblical meaning of this particular term should be put like this: Christ is the Savior as the result of something that He has done. We must get rid once and forever of the idea that we are the actors or doers and merely receive encouragement from Him. Not at all! The biblical representation is that God sent Him into the world to do something, and that we are saved as the result of something He has done quite apart from ourselves and our own action. He has acted, and it is His action that produces salvation and the way of escape for us.

Now here is something that is utterly fundamental and primary, and unless we are agreed with this statement there is really no point or purpose in proceeding any further. Salvation, according to the New Testament—take, for instance, Colossians 1 where you have a perfect illustration of salvation—is something that is entirely worked out by the Lord Jesus Christ. It is something that has come to men and women as a free gift to them, and they have nothing to do but to receive this gift. It is something provided; it is the righteousness of God that is given.

That is something that is surely basic, and of course there is no phrase, perhaps, that puts all this more perfectly than that great and glorious phrase that was uttered by our Lord Himself upon the cross when He cried out, "It is finished" (John 19:30). With His last breath, as it were, He cried out, "I have done it! I have completed the work that You gave Me to do." It is He who saves, and our salvation comes from Him and is derived from something He has done once and forever on our behalf.

✎ A THOUGHT TO PONDER ✐

Salvation, according to the New Testament, is something that is entirely worked out by the Lord Jesus Christ.

From *The Love of God*, pp. 135-136.

THE POWER AND GUILT OF SIN

And we have seen and do testify that the Father sent the Son to be the Saviour of the world.

1 JOHN 4:14

Our Lord and Savior Jesus Christ clearly saves us, in the first instance, from the guilt and the penalty of sin. We are all guilty before God and before His holy law. We are guilty in His presence; so the first thing I need is to be saved from the guilt of my sin. I need a Savior in that respect apart from anything else. I have broken the law of God, and I am under the condemnation of that holy law; so before I can talk about salvation or about being saved, I must be perfectly clear that I am delivered from the guilt of my sin. That is the glorious message that the New Testament Gospel brings to me.

In Christ my guilt is removed. It is no use my facing the future and proposing to live a better life. I am confronted by my own past—I cannot avoid it, I cannot escape it. I have broken the law—I must deal with the problem of my guilt—and I cannot do so. I cannot undo my past; I cannot make atonement for my misdeeds and for everything I have done against God. I must be delivered from the guilt of my sin, and Christ—and Christ alone—can so deliver me.

But having thus had the assurance that the guilt of my sin has been dealt with, I am still confronted by the power of sin. I battle the world and the flesh and the devil; forces and factors outside me are trying to drag me down, and I am aware of their terrible power. The man or woman who has not realized the power of sin all around him or her is a novice in these matters. There is only One who has conquered Satan, there is only One who has defeated the world, and that is this Son whom the Father sent into the world to be our Savior. Jesus Christ can deliver me from the *power* of sin as well as from the *guilt* of sin.

✎ A THOUGHT TO PONDER ✎

Jesus Christ can deliver me from the *power* of sin as well as from the *guilt* of sin.

From *The Love of God*, pp. 140–141.

MYSTICISM

And we have known and believed the love that God hath to us.
God is love; and he that dwelleth in love dwelleth in God,
and God in him.

1 JOHN 4:16

John has gone on repeatedly writing about the love of God, and you notice how he never tires of doing so. "In this was manifested the love of God toward us, because that God sent his only begotten Son into the world, that we might live through him" (1 John 4:9). "And we have seen and do testify that the Father sent the Son to be the Saviour of the world" (1 John 4:14). Now [verse 16] he repeats it again. This is because he knew that in his own day and age there were all those so-called mystery religions or curious cults that talked about the love of God; and they all tried to teach that you can know the love of God directly. That is always the characteristic of mysticism; what finally condemns mysticism is that it bypasses the Lord Jesus Christ. Anything that bypasses Christ is not Christian. I do not care what it is, however good, however uplifting or noble; it is Christ who is the manifestation of the love of God, says John.

I do not hesitate, therefore, to aver and to add strongly as follows: I must distrust any emotion that I may have within me with respect to God unless it is based solidly upon the Lord Jesus Christ. In Him God manifested His love. "God commendeth his love toward us, in that, while we were yet sinners, Christ died for us" (Romans 5:8). Therefore, I say that I must never attempt by any means or method to get to know God or to try to make myself love God except in and through my Lord and Savior Jesus Christ. I must avoid every other direct approach to God, every direct dealing with God.

❧ A THOUGHT TO PONDER ☙
Anything that bypasses Christ is not Christian.

From *The Love of God*, pp. 145–146.

KNOWING THE LOVE OF GOD

And we have known and believed the love that God hath to us.
God is love; and he that dwelleth in love dwelleth in God,
and God in him.

1 JOHN 4:16

How can my joy abound? How can I walk through this world with my head erect? How can I come through triumphantly? Well, here is the main thing: I should know the love that God has toward me. If I have that, I can say that "neither death, nor life . . . nor height, nor depth, nor any other creature, shall be able to separate us from the love of God, which is in Christ Jesus our Lord" (Romans 8:38-39).

Therefore, the questions come to us one by one: Do I know this love? Can I make this statement? It is made everywhere in the New Testament. Paul is particularly fond of stating it: ". . . the Son of God, who loved me, and gave himself for me" (Galatians 2:20). No man could state the doctrine of the atonement in all its plenitude and glory like the apostle Paul, and yet here he says in essence, "He died for me; He loved me." This is personal knowledge, personal appropriation. You find this everywhere in the New Testament. For example, "Whom having not seen," says Peter, "ye love; in whom, though now ye see him not, yet believing, ye rejoice with joy unspeakable and full of glory" (1 Peter 1:8).

Do we know that? These people did not see Him, and so we cannot argue and say, "It is all very well for those first Christians; they saw Him. If only I could see Christ, then I would love Him." But they did not see Him any more than we see Him. They had the apostolic witness and teaching and accepted this witness and testimony. They loved Him and rejoiced in Him "with joy unspeakable and full of glory."

✒ A THOUGHT TO PONDER ✒

They loved Him and rejoiced in Him "with joy unspeakable and full of glory."

Ten Tests: Tests 1–3

And we have known and believed the love that God hath to us.
God is love; and he that dwelleth in love dwelleth in God,
and God in him.

1 JOHN 4:16

I shall suggest to you ten tests that you can apply to yourself to know for certain that you know the love of God to you.

Here is the first. It is *a loss and absence of the sense that God is against us.* The natural man always feels that God is against him. He would be very glad if he could wake up and read that some bishop or other had proved that God never existed; he would be ready to believe that. The newspapers give publicity to anything that denies the faith; they know the public palate. That is why the natural man is at enmity against God; he feels God is against him. That is why when anything goes wrong he says, "Why does God allow this?" And when men and women are in a state of being antagonistic toward God, then, of course, they cannot love God. So one of the first tests, and I am starting with the lowest, is that we have lost that feeling that God is against us.

Second, there is *a loss of the fear of God, while a sense of awe remains.* Let us approach Him "with reverence and godly fear," writes the author of the Epistle to the Hebrews (12:28). John is going to elaborate on that; that is the rest of the fourth chapter of 1 John. We lose that craven fear of God, but oh, what a reverence remains.

Third, there is *a feeling and a sense that God is for us and that God loves us.* Now I put it like that quite deliberately because it is so very true to experience. I have lost the sense that God is against me, and I begin to have a feeling and sense that God is for me, that God is kind to me, that He is concerned about me, and that He truly loves me.

❧ A Thought to Ponder ❧
I have lost the sense that God is against me, and I begin to have a feeling and sense that God is for me.

From *The Love of God*, pp. 150-151.

TEN TESTS: TESTS 4–6

And we have known and believed the love that God hath to us.
God is love; and he that dwelleth in love dwelleth in God,
and God in him.

1 JOHN 4:16

Fourth, I have *a sense of sins forgiven*. I do not understand it, but I am aware of it. I know that I have sinned; "my sin is ever before me" (Psalm 51:3), as David says. I remember my sins, and yet the moment I pray, I know my sins are forgiven. I cannot understand it, I do not know how God does it, but I know He does it, and that my sins are forgiven.

A sense of sins forgiven leads me to the fifth test: *a sense of gratitude and thanksgiving to God*. No one can believe that God sent His only begotten Son into the world to die on the cross without feeling a sense of praise and thanksgiving. Think of Saul of Tarsus there on the road to Damascus. The moment he saw and understood something of what had happened to him, he said, "Lord, what wilt thou have me to do?" (Acts 9:6). That is, what can I do to repay You—how can I show my gratitude? Do you feel a sense of gratitude? Do you want to praise God? A sense of gratitude and a desire to praise is further proof of the knowledge of God.

Then sixth, there is *an increasing hatred of sin*. I sometimes think there is no better proof of a knowledge of God and knowledge of the love of God than that. You know, if you hate sin, you are like God, for God hates it and abominates it. We are told that He cannot look upon iniquity (Habakkuk 1:13); therefore, whatever your feelings may or may not be, if you have an increasing hatred of sin, it is because the love of God is in you—God is in you. No man hates sin apart from God.

✐ A THOUGHT TO PONDER ✐
No man hates sin apart from God.

TEN TESTS: TESTS 7–10

And we have known and believed the love that God hath to us.
God is love; and he that dwelleth in love dwelleth in God,
and God in him.

1 JOHN 4:16

Seventh, there is *a desire to please God and to live a good life because of what He has done for us*. The realization of His love should make us not only hate sin, but also desire to live a holy, godly life. If you do desire this, you love God, because our Lord said, "He that hath my commandments, and keepeth them, he it is that loveth me" (John 14:21).

Eighth, we have *a desire to know Him better and to draw closer to Him*. Do you want to know God better? Is it one of the greatest ambitions of your life to draw closer to Him, that your relationship to Him may be more intimate? If you have within you the faintest desire to know God better and are doing something about it, I say you love God.

I will put the ninth point negatively, and yet it may be the most important of all. I am referring to *a conscious regret that our love to Him is so poor, along with a desire to love Him more*. If you are unhappy at the thought that you do not love God as you ought to, that is a wonderful proof that you love Him.

My last test is that we have *a delight in hearing these things and in hearing about Him*. That is one of the best tests. There are certain people in the world—alas, there are many—who find all that we have been saying utterly boring; all that we have been saying would be strange to them. Such people are spiritually dead; they know nothing about this. So whatever the state of your emotions may be, if you can tell me quite honestly that you enjoy listening to these things and hearing about them, if you can say that there is something about them that makes things different, then I say that you know the love that God has for you.

❧ A THOUGHT TO PONDER ❧

Is it one of the greatest ambitions of your life to draw closer to Him?

From *The Love of God*, pp. 152-153.

December

THE VICTORY
OF FAITH

FROM

Life in God

AND

Out of the Depths

WHAT MAKES US CHRISTIAN?

Whosoever believeth that Jesus is the Christ is born of God:
and every one that loveth him that begat loveth him also
that is begotten of him.

1 JOHN 5:1

The New Testament at once shows us the total inadequacy of the common, current version of what constitutes a Christian. The New Testament terms are *regeneration, a new creation*, being *born again*. What makes men and women Christians is something that is done to them by God, not something they do themselves: "Whosoever believeth that Jesus is the Christ is born of God." And then, "Every one that loveth him that begat . . ." God, according to John, is the one who begets us; it is God's action, not ours.

Now we need to take time in emphasizing the obvious contrast in each of these subdivisions. How ready we are to think of being a Christian as the result of something we do! I live a good life—therefore I am a Christian; I go to a place of worship—therefore I am a Christian; I do not do certain things—therefore I am a Christian; I believe—therefore I am a Christian. The whole emphasis is upon myself, upon what I do. Whereas here, at the very beginning of the New Testament definition of a Christian, the entire emphasis is not upon man and his activity, but upon God. *He* who begat, *He* who produced, *He* who generates, *He* who gives life and being. Thus we see we cannot be a Christian at all unless God has done something to us.

But I go beyond that and say that what makes us a Christian is something that makes us like God. "Whosoever believeth that Jesus is the Christ is born of God." That "of" is an important word; it means "out of God"; this is one who has received something of God Himself.

✎ A THOUGHT TO PONDER ✎
We cannot be a Christian at all unless God has done something to us.

From *Life in God*, pp. 12-13.

THREE FRUITS OF REBIRTH

Whosoever believeth that Jesus is the Christ is born of God:
and every one that loveth him that begat loveth him also
that is begotten of him.

1 JOHN 5:1

The first fruit of the rebirth is that *I believe that "Jesus is the Christ."* And obviously, believing that is not something intellectual or something I only do with my mind. If I believe, I commit my whole life to Him. If I believe, I know I am delivered because Christ has done that for me. I see that apart from Him I am lost and undone and doomed. This is a profound action; it is a commitment; it is a banking of one's everything upon that fact.

The second fruit of rebirth is *love for God.* John's way of putting it is: "every one that loveth him that begat . . ." Christians see that they are hell-deserving sinners and that they would have arrived in hell were it not for His great love in sending His Son. They realize the love of God for them, and therefore they love God; they realize they owe everything to Him. It seems to me that this again is one of those fundamental things about Christian men and women. However good a life they may be living now as saints, they still feel that they are hell-deserving sinners in and of themselves, and that they owe everything to the grace of God; it is God's love alone that has made them what they are. They lose their sense of fear and a sense of enmity against God and are filled with a sense of profound gratitude to Him.

And the final thing is, of course, that we *love our brethren*— "Every one that loveth him that begat loveth him also that is begotten of him." We look at other believers, and we see in them the same disposition as in ourselves. We realize that they owe everything to the grace of God, just as we do. We realize that in spite of their sinfulness God sent His Son to die for them, exactly as He did for us; and we are aware of this bond. Though there are many things about them we do not like, we say, "That is my brother, my sister."

❧ A THOUGHT TO PONDER ❧
We realize that in spite of their sinfulness God sent His Son to die for them, exactly as He did for us.

From *Life in God*, pp. 19-20.

KEEPING GOD'S COMMANDMENTS

For this is the love of God, that we keep his commandments:
and his commandments are not grievous.

1 JOHN 5:3

There is nothing about which we can so deceive ourselves as the fact that we love God. A man may come to me and say he loves God. He says with Browning, "God's in His heaven, / All's right with the world"; but when something goes against him, he finds he does not love God. He says, "Why does God . . . ?" Feelings are very deceptive. How do we know we love God? There is the next step—when "we keep his commandments."

Our Lord emphasizes that in John 14:21: "He that hath my commandments, and keepeth them, he it is that loveth me." You cannot separate these things. Love is not a sentiment; it is the most active, vital thing in the world. If I love God, I want to please Him—I keep the commandments. And what I may regard as the love of God in my soul is a pure delusion unless it leads me to keep God's commandments and to live life as He wants me to live it.

"Again," says someone, "you have just shifted the problem. This keeping of the commandments—what is this?" "Well," says John in essence in a kind of footnote on which he is going to elaborate in the next verse, "what matters in this whole question of keeping the commandments is my attitude toward them. When I face the commandments of God, do I resent them? Do I feel that God is imposing an impossible load upon me? Do I groan and grumble and say, 'Oh, this hard taskmaster who asks of me the impossible'?"

"If that is your attitude toward the commandments of God," says John in effect, "you are not keeping them, and neither are you loving God, and you are not loving your brethren—you are outside the life altogether." For someone who is truly Christian does not find the commandments of God to go against the grain.

✎ A THOUGHT TO PONDER ✎

Someone who is truly Christian does not find the commandments of God to go against the grain.

From *Life in God*, pp. 30-31.

THE WORLD

Love not the world, neither the things that are in the world.
If any man love the world, the love of the Father is not in him.
For all that is in the world, the lust of the flesh, and the lust of the
eyes, and the pride of life, is not of the Father, but is of the world.
And the world passeth away, and the lust thereof: but he
that doeth the will of God abideth for ever.

1 JOHN 2:15-17

That is, perhaps, one of the fullest statements in Scripture of what the New Testament means by this term *the world*; here John once more comes back to it. He is always very anxious about it, as is every writer in the New Testament. You cannot read the New Testament truly without seeing the whole of the Christian life as a life of conflict; we are in an atmosphere and in a world where there is a great fight going on. There are two kingdoms, the kingdom of light and the kingdom of darkness, and you get these constant comparisons and contrasts. Paul says to the Ephesians, "For we wrestle not against flesh and blood, but against principalities, against powers, against the rulers of the darkness of this world, against spiritual wickedness in high places" (or "in the heavenlies") (Ephesians 6:12). "The world," says John, "is there the whole time, and the Christian is fighting against it." So it is of vital importance that we should know what he means by this.

Perhaps the best way of defining what the New Testament means by "the world" is that it is everything that is opposed to God and His Spirit. God calls upon men and women to worship Him and to glorify Him; He calls upon them to live for His glory. There is a famous quotation in the Shorter Catechism of the Westminster Confession that says, "The chief end of man is to glorify God and enjoy Him for ever." That is the chief object for which God created us; we are meant to glorify God in every way conceivable.

❧ A THOUGHT TO PONDER ❧
We are in a world where there is a great fight going on.

OVERCOMING THE WORLD

For whatsoever is born of God overcometh the world: and this is the victory that overcometh the world, even our faith.

1 JOHN 5:4

John means by this that the Christian is one who conquers the world, who masters it. He actually says a most extraordinary thing here, and for once I have to grant that the Revised Version is superior to the Authorized! The Authorized reads like this: "And this is the victory that overcometh the world, even our faith." But the Revised has, "This is the victory that has overcome . . . "; it has already happened.

Now John is saying two things here that at first sight, as so often with John, appear to be contradictory. He says that the Christian is one who has overcome the world and also that the Christian is one who overcomes the world. Christian people, John tells us, are men and women who are in an entirely new position with regard to this matter. They are not like the non-Christian. Christians are in this new position because of their faith. They have come to see the real meaning of the world; they have come to see what it is, and they hate it. They know that the world has already been conquered by the Lord Jesus Christ, and they know that they themselves are in Christ; therefore there is a sense in which the Christian has overcome the world. Christ has overcome it, and I am in Christ, and therefore I have overcome it.

And yet there is a sense in which I am still overcoming it. I am already victorious, but I still have to fight. The New Testament is fond of saying that. "But of him are ye in Christ Jesus," says Paul, "who of God is made unto us wisdom, and righteousness, and sanctification, and redemption" (1 Corinthians 1:30-31). He is already that to us; so there is a sense in which I am already sanctified, already glorified. Read the eighth chapter of Romans, and you will find that Paul tells us that explicitly (verses 29-30); in Christ Jesus we are already complete, it has all happened. And yet I am also still being sanctified, and I am still on the way to glorification.

✎ A THOUGHT TO PONDER ✎

Christ has overcome the world, and I am in Christ, and therefore I have overcome it.

From *Life in God*, pp. 41-42.

WE HAVE OVERCOME, AND WE ARE OVERCOMING

For whatsoever is born of God overcometh the world: and
this is the victory that overcometh the world, even our faith.

1 JOHN 5:4

I am trying to say how at one and the same time it can be said that as Christians we have overcome and we are overcoming. Think of it in terms of the Battle of Quebec. General Wolfe conquered the French general Montcalm on the Heights of Abraham, and as the result of that battle Canada was conquered. And yet we read in our history books that the fight for possessing Canada went on for some seventy or eighty more years. That is it; the country was captured, and then captured in detail. The position of Christian men and women is something like that in this world. They are no longer under the dominion of Satan; they have been taken out of his kingdom, but that does not mean that they have finished with Satan.

Or look at it like this—think of it in terms of two big estates with a road going down between. On one side of the road there is one estate, and on the other side there is another; one of them is the kingdom of Satan, and the other is the kingdom of God. Now this is what has happened to Christian men and women: They were in the estate under the dominion of Satan, but they have crossed over the road and are now in the kingdom of God. But though they are in this life and world, working in that new estate, the kingdom of God, Satan, their old enemy, is still there in that other kingdom, and he thinks that Christians will be foolish enough to listen to him. He forgets that they have been once and forever taken out of his dominion; he forgets that they are free. So Christians do not come under his dominion, but they are still subject to his attacks and onslaughts and his suggestions and insinuations. They have overcome, but they are still fighting; they still have to overcome as they go on in this life walking with God and with Christ.

☙ A THOUGHT TO PONDER ☙

Christians have overcome, but they are still fighting.

OVERCOMING BY FAITH

*Who is he that overcometh the world, but he that believeth that
Jesus is the Son of God?*

1 JOHN 5:5

As a Christian, because of what has happened to me, I am able to exercise faith and to live by faith. Here is the second step. First you see "Whatsoever is born of God overcometh the world," and then "This is the victory that overcometh the world, even our faith" (verse 4). In other words, my rebirth gives me this faculty of faith and enables me to exercise faith and to live by it.

Let me put it in this practical form: The world that I am fighting is very powerful; it is much more powerful than any one of us. The world conquers and masters everyone who is born into it, for indeed we have been born in sin and "shapen in iniquity" (Psalm 51:5); the world is in us the moment we begin to live. Read your Old Testament; look at those great heroes of the faith, the patriarchs, the godly kings, and the prophets—they all were conquered by the world, they all failed. "There is none righteous, no, not one" (Romans 3:10); the whole world is guilty before God (Romans 3:19); and therefore if I am to conquer and overcome that world, I need something that will enable me to do so. It is no use trying to fight the world immediately—that cannot be done. Monasticism recognizes that and says, "Run away from it."

So what do I need? I need emancipation; I need to be lifted to another realm; I need a force and a strength and a power that I do not have myself. That is my need, and here is the answer: I am given faith—I am given an outlook and understanding—I am introduced to a source of power—I see something that another person has never seen. I see a might and a power that is even greater than all that is opposed to me. Christians are men and women who have been introduced to another realm.

❧ A THOUGHT TO PONDER ❧

Christians are men and women who have been introduced to another realm.

From *Life in God*, pp. 51-52.

December 8

VICTORY OVER THE WORLD

*Who is he that overcometh the world, but he that believeth that
Jesus is the Son of God?*

1 JOHN 5:5

Faith enables us to have victory over the world and to overcome it directly—passively—by the resting of a naked faith upon the Lord Jesus Christ. I am increasingly convinced that this is the greatest lesson that we as Christian people can ever learn in this world. It is the possibility of directly and immediately and passively resting upon the power and the ability of our risen Lord. "This is the victory that overcometh the world, even our faith" (verse 4)—my faith in Him, my belief in Him, that He is the Son of God. The result of that is that I go to Him and rest upon Him.

This is something of the meaning that you will find enunciated everywhere in the Bible. Let me give you just one quotation that will illustrate it perfectly and represent all others: "The name of the LORD is a strong tower; the righteous runneth into it and is safe" (Proverbs 18:10). That is it! Read the various Psalms too, and see how those godly men of old were struggling against the world and its temptations and insinuations, and they will all tell you that was the only thing they could do. They say that the forces were too great for them. They might have failed, but they said, "There is only one thing to do—I will run into the tower, and there in the tower I am safe."

Or if you like it in New Testament form, it is the doctrine of the vine and the branches, as seen in the statement of our Lord: "Without me ye can do nothing" (John 15:5). It is put positively by the apostle Paul: "I can do all things through Christ which strengtheneth me" (Philippians 4:13); and "nevertheless I live; yet not I, but Christ liveth in me" (Galatians 2:20).

❧ A THOUGHT TO PONDER ❧
I will run into the tower, and there in the tower I am safe.

THE SIMPLICITY OF FAITH

*Who is he that overcometh the world, but he that believeth that
Jesus is the Son of God?*

1 JOHN 5:5

Simplicity of faith is one of the most difficult lessons to learn. Most of our defeats, I think, are due to the fact that we parley with sin, we attempt to fight it on our own. The rest of faith, in a sense, means that there are times when we do not even attempt to fight this battle against sin but simply look to Christ.

Perhaps an illustration will make my point clear. I once read a little pamphlet that was very simple but that, it seemed to me, shared the whole essence of this particular aspect of the doctrine. It was the story of a Christian in South Africa, traveling out in the country, and he came to an agricultural community. Owing to certain floods in the country, he had to stay where there was a kind of saloon or public house. He was amazed and saddened at the sight of the farmers, many of whom, he noticed, came there and spent in a few days all the money they had been able to earn and save as the result of their hard work through the year. They had a powerful craving for drink that they could not conquer.

He was especially attracted to one poor man who seemed to be a particular victim to this terrible affliction, and he began to talk to him. First of all he began to reason with him, pointing out the suffering that his wife and children had to endure. The poor man admitted it all and told the story of how he had been almost unconsciously led into it and found himself a helpless slave to drink before realizing that anything had happened—how he would give the whole world if he could stop it, but he was now a victim of it. Then this Christian went on to tell him about faith, the possibility of overcoming, and told him about the Lord Jesus Christ who had come into this world to save us. I will finish the story in tomorrow's meditation.

✎ A THOUGHT TO PONDER ✐
Simplicity of faith is one of the most difficult lessons to learn.

From *Life in God*, pp. 57-58.

RESTING ON CHRIST

*The name of the LORD is a strong tower; the righteous
runneth into it and is safe.*

PROVERBS 18:10

To continue yesterday's story, the Christian told the man that if only he looked to Christ and relied upon Him, he would be enabled to overcome his being captive to drinking. The man was a simple, illiterate man, and all he was anxious to do was to find the name of this person about whom this Christian was speaking, and he was told the name was Jesus.

The story went on to say how that poor man went away and, having worked again, came back to this same place to sell his grain. There again the tempters came, but he did not go with them, and his own wife and children were amazed. This Christian visitor came back in a year or so to find the man entirely changed. He began talking to him and asked him how it had happened. And the man's simple testimony was this: "I went back the first time, and my friends came and tempted me, and I felt weak. But suddenly I remembered the name Jesus. I could do nothing but keep on saying to myself, 'Jesus.' I cried to Jesus to do what you told me He would do." His faith was as simple as that, but it was enough, and he overcame. He did not go back; he was emancipated.

That is what I mean when I talk about this direct faith; it is simply resting upon Christ, and we have to do that. That is becoming as a little child, realizing our utter weakness and helplessness and hopelessness. When the fight is yet strong and the enemy is there and we feel we are on the point of falling, we must simply cry, "Jesus" and believe and know that He is looking upon us and that He is there and is ready to deliver us and protect us. "The name of the LORD is a strong tower; the righteous runneth into it and is safe" (Proverbs 18:10).

❧ A THOUGHT TO PONDER ❧
Direct faith is simply resting upon Christ.

LOOK AT THE LORD JESUS CHRIST

. . . but he that believeth that Jesus is the Son of God?

1 JOHN 5:5

As I look at the Lord Jesus Christ in terms of this fight against the world, I ask this question: Why did He ever come into this world? You see, I am now working out my faith in Christ. I believe that the person, Jesus of Nazareth, about whom I read in the Gospels, is the Son of God. Very well, I ask immediately, why did the Son of God ever take upon Himself the likeness of sinful flesh and live as man, as He indeed did? What is the meaning of it all? And there is only one answer to that question. It was because of the power of sin, the power of Satan, the power of evil. There is no other explanation. The Son of God came because He was the only way in which we could be delivered from the world.

In other words, it is the doctrine of sin again, the power of Satan and sin and evil. He came into this world because the world was dominated by sin, and it is only as I believe that "Jesus is the Son of God" that I begin to understand the nature of the fight in which I am engaged. People are optimistic about this world, and they are so because they have never understood the nature of sin. But if you believe that Jesus is the Son of God, you have to believe that the power of sin and evil and Satan is so tremendous that man had failed and the Son of God had to come.

Do you seen, then, how this enables us to overcome the world? How can I overcome the world unless I have seen the nature of the problem? The moment I have faith in Christ, I begin to understand the problem, for it is only the Christian who can see through this world. Everybody else is dominated by the world—governed by it. But the moment I become a Christian I see through the world.

✎ A THOUGHT TO PONDER ✐

The Son of God came because He was the only way in which we could be delivered from the world.

JESUS THE GOD-MAN

This is he that came by water and blood, even Jesus Christ;
not by water only, but by water and blood. And it is the Spirit
that beareth witness, because the Spirit is truth. For there are
three that bear record in heaven, the Father, the Word, and the
Holy Ghost: and these three are one. And there are three
that bear witness in earth, the Spirit, and the water, and the blood:
and these three agree in one.

1 JOHN 5:6-8

John is concerned to establish the reality of the Incarnation, to prove that Jesus Christ is really the Son of God incarnate, in the flesh. I believe that he was anxious to do so in order to correct a heresy that was very prevalent at that time. It taught something like this: Jesus of Nazareth was a man, but when He was baptized by John in the Jordan, the eternal Christ came upon Him and entered into Him, so that from the moment of the baptism the eternal Christ was dwelling in the human Jesus, and He continued to do so until just before the crucifixion took place; then the eternal Christ went back to heaven, and it was only the man Jesus who was crucified.

Now that was a very common heresy in the first centuries, and it is a heresy that has also been prevalent during these past centuries. The whole trouble during the last hundred years or so about the person of Christ has been nothing, in a sense, but a recapitulation of that ancient heresy; it puts a wedge between the man Jesus and the eternal Christ. And here John is concerned to assert the mighty fact that the baby in the manger is the God-Man. "Jesus Christ," and not Jesus only. The Incarnation is a reality, and the One who died upon the cross was not only the man Jesus—it was the God-Man who died. And I believe that John mentions this testimony and witness of water and the blood in order to establish the unity and the oneness of the person; not two persons, but one person with two natures.

❧ A THOUGHT TO PONDER ❧
The baby in the manger is the God-Man.

From *Life in God*, pp. 74-75.

DELIVERANCE

This is he that came by water and blood, even Jesus Christ;
not by water only, but by water and blood.

1 JOHN 5:6

The great business of the Messiah who was to come was to deliver the people from the thralldom and bondage of sin and its consequences. Men and women, as a result of their sin, were under the wrath of God. They needed to be delivered from the power of the world, the flesh, and the devil—the power of sin both inside and outside. So the Messiah, the Savior, had to make expiation for our sin and set us free from its power. This was His great task. And John tells us that Jesus Christ came as the Messiah and has done that, and we see Him doing it as we look at His baptism and as we see His death on the cross. His baptism, in a sense, is the beginning of His power as the Messiah—He came as the Messiah by "water." Through that He identifies Himself with our sin, and it is upon the cross that He deals with it, expiates it, and delivers us from the wrath of God and therefore from the power of sin and the power of the world, the flesh, and the devil.

Now I think we see why John does not refer to Christ's birth in his Gospel. He has been pointing to Christ as the Messiah, fixing his attention upon that, that Jesus is the Son of God. So he does not refer to the birth; but he does refer to the baptism. And so I think we see very clearly why it is that we have this phrase "not by water only, but by water and blood." The Lord Jesus Christ did not merely identify Himself with us and our sins—He went further. He dealt with it not in water only, but also in blood. His death is an absolute essential in addition to the baptism.

☙ A THOUGHT TO PONDER ❧

Through His baptism Christ identifies Himself with our sin, and it is upon the cross that He deals with it.

December 14

SPIRITUS EXTERNUS AND
SPIRITUS INTERNUS

*He that believeth on the Son of God hath the witness in himself:
he that believeth not God hath made him a liar; because he
believeth not the record that God gave of his Son.*

1 JOHN 5:10

Here is a matter of accepting testimony and witness. God has said,
"This is my beloved Son, in whom I am well pleased; hear ye him"
(Matthew 17:5). Am I to refuse Him? Well, the terrifying thing is that
if I do, I am saying that God's pronouncement is not true.

In addition to the external evidence, there is also the subjective or
internal evidence. John puts it in this way: "He that believeth on the Son
of God hath the witness in himself." So we are dealing here with these
two different stands—the external and the internal. I am not at all
sure but that this is not the most vital of all parts of the subject. It was
a great matter to the minds of the Reformers. They clearly defined this
matter. The believer is confronted by two great sources of certainty, one
outside and one inside—*spiritus externus* and *spiritus internus.*

But perhaps the best way to understand this is to ask ourselves,
"How may I know that the Bible is the Word of God?" There are
two main ways. There is the Word itself—the testimony of the Holy
Spirit, and the agreement of the books written within it. This general
consensus, the internal unity of the Bible, and various other arguments—this is the *spiritus externus*—the outside testimony. But
according to the Reformers, that is not enough to give people certainty. They need something inside as well, and the Holy Spirit also
gives them that internal certitude—the *spiritus internus.*

Let me put this personally. There was a time when I read the
Bible and thought it was a wonderful book; I felt it was a unique
book. Later I was confronted with the great evidence given to me
in the Gospels and the Old and New Testaments, and I had a feeling within me that this was the Word of God. That is what it
means—this internal evidence.

✺ A THOUGHT TO PONDER ✺
The believer is confronted by two great sources of certainty, one outside and one inside.

From *Life in God*, pp. 86-87.

THE WITNESS

He that believeth on the Son of God hath the witness in himself.
1 JOHN 5:10

First I am to receive the witness of God, and only after that am I likely to have the evidence and the witness within myself. The Lord Himself said, "If any man will do his [God's] will, he shall know of the doctrine" (John 7:17). So if you want to be certain, believe first, and then you will be certain.

So this question of order is a vitally important one. Believe God, and then have the belief within yourself. To reverse the order would be insulting to God. Someone may say, "Well, I will only believe if I have proof." But God says, "I ask you to believe because I am speaking"; so not to believe is dishonoring to Him. To try to insist that you must have proof is to detract from His glory. So first I must believe because God is the witness; and if I do, then I shall have the witness of the Spirit within myself.

The other practical thing, of course, is just to learn exactly what believing His evidence means, and here John puts it in a very few words: "He that believeth on the Son of God hath the witness in himself." Oh, what important words these are; what an important word is that little word "on"! John does not mean us to say, "Well, on the whole I am satisfied with the evidence, and I am prepared to believe that Jesus of Nazareth is the Son of God."

That is not it! "He that believeth on the Son of God . . ." Such a person has abandoned himself to Him. He has surrendered to Him. You may not realize the full implications of the statement, but you hand over your whole life into the strong arms of the Son of God. And you will very soon have the witness. You will know who He is, and all your uncertainties will have gone. Jesus is not only the Christ—He is the Son of God, the Messiah, the deliverer of the world.

✣ A THOUGHT TO PONDER ✣
First I must believe because God is the witness; then I shall have the witness of the Spirit within myself.

From *Life in God*, pp. 88-89.

THE CERTAINTY OF EVERLASTING LIFE

These things have I written unto you that believe on the name of the Son of God; that ye may know that ye have eternal life, and that ye may believe on the name of the Son of God.

1 JOHN 5:13

The knowledge that we have eternal life is something that is possible to us. That is something that needs to be emphasized. There are those who would tell us that eternal life is something to which we attain only when we come to die and leave this world and go into the next. They suggest that it is wrong for anyone to claim that he *has* eternal life. Such people dislike the doctrine of assurance. "We do not know," they say, "and we must not seek to know. Faith means that you are always grasping at it, but it is something you cannot actually have while you are in this world."

But that is a philosophical concept of faith that is not in accordance with what we have here. John says in essence, "My whole object in writing to you now is that you may know that you have eternal life and know it certainly. I want you to *know* that you possess it."

You find the other apostles saying the same thing. What was more characteristic of the apostle Paul than this assurance? In Romans 8 he says, "For I am persuaded, that neither death, nor life, nor angels, nor principalities, nor powers, nor things present, nor things to come, nor height, nor depth, nor any other creature, shall be able to separate us from the love of God, which is in Christ Jesus our Lord" (verses 38-39). "I know whom I have believed," he writes to Timothy (2 Timothy 1:12). "I *know*," he says. There is no uncertainty about it.

So it seems to me that to interpret faith as a kind of constant uncertainty is to deny the teaching of the Word of God that we are His children.

❧ A THOUGHT TO PONDER ❧

The knowledge that we have eternal life is something that is possible to us.

MY VIEW OF THE WORLD

These things have I written unto you that believe on the name of the Son of God; that ye may know that ye have eternal life, and that ye may believe on the name of the Son of God.

1 JOHN 5:13

What is my view of the world when I know for certain that I have eternal life? What is my attitude to the world in which we are all living, the world as we see it in the newspapers? Is that what interests me? What am I anxious to obtain? Or am I more interested in other things—spiritual things? According to John, Christians are men and women who have come to view the world in an entirely new manner. They see that it is governed by sin. They have come to regard it as a place in which evil forces are at work and whose whole mind is but the working of the spirit of the world. They know that it is something they have to fight, something to withstand, and they realize that unless they do so, they will be defeated by it.

Do I hate the world? A good way of answering is this: The apostle Paul, looking at his surroundings, said, "For which cause we faint not; but though our outward man perish, yet the inward man is renewed day by day. For our light affliction, which is but for a moment, worketh for us a far more exceeding and eternal weight of glory . . . for the things which are seen are temporal; but the things which are not seen are eternal" (2 Corinthians 4:16-18). In looking at "the things which are seen," how much time do I spend in thinking about the Lord God? How much do I think about the glory that is with Him? Which do I meditate upon most—the eternal or the worldly?

❧ A THOUGHT TO PONDER ❧

How much do I think about the glory that is with God? Which do I meditate upon most—the eternal or the worldly?

From *Life in God*, pp. 97-98.

THE UNUSUAL AND THE SPECTACULAR

These things have I written unto you that believe on the name of
the Son of God; that ye may know that ye have eternal life, and
that ye may believe on the name of the Son of God.
1 JOHN 5:13

There is a tendency in mankind to pay great attention to and to concentrate upon the unusual and the spectacular. We seem to do that instinctively; I suppose it is one of the results of the Fall. Anything unusual or exceptional always attracts attention much more than the usual and the ordinary; that is why some sort of calamity or extraordinary thing in nature always attracts and interests us much more than the perpetual and wonderful things of nature from day to day. Wordsworth said about himself at the end of his great ode *Intimations of Immortality*:

> To me the meanest flower that blows can give
> Thoughts that do often lie too deep for tears.

That is right, and we ought all to put it like that. But the trouble with most of us is that because it is always there we do not marvel at it; that little flower in the hedgerow does not give rise in us thoughts that "lie too deep for tears." But if we see a tree struck by lightning we are interested because it is unusual, because it is exceptional.

Now, we tend to do that self-same thing in the whole matter of Christian experience. I attribute this to the Fall, and, of course, one must point out in passing that this is something that tends to be organized and often becomes a business. Those who produce books know that the spectacular always appeals to the mind; so they pick out exceptional cases and give them great publicity. But this contradicts essential New Testament teaching. The New Testament never lays stress upon the way in which certainty comes to us; what it is interested in is the fact that it *has* come.

❧ A THOUGHT TO PONDER ❧

There is a tendency in mankind to pay great attention to the spectacular. I suppose it is one of the results of the Fall.

GOD'S WORK IN US

These things have I written unto you that believe on the name of the Son of God; that ye may know that ye have eternal life, and that ye may believe on the name of the Son of God.

1 JOHN 5:13

I have the assurance that if God's work in me has begun, the work will end. I "know" that if I have eternal life, I shall stand one day faultless and blameless, without spot and blemish, in the presence of God's glory. So as I meet temptation and sin in this world, I realize that I am not left to myself. I cease to feel helpless and frustrated. I say, "If God is in me, if God has destined me for that, then He will come and hold me though all hell and the devils be opposed to me." That was the mighty argument of a man like Martin Luther. It was because he knew he had eternal life that he could defy all those enemies the way he did, and all those who have this hope in them can say the same thing.

> *And were this world all devils o'er*
> *And watching to devour us,*
> *We lay it not to heart so sore;*
> *Nor they can overpower us.*

If we have eternal life and know that we have it, we know that God's work in our souls will be carried on until it ends in ultimate perfection and glory. As Paul puts it in that mighty bit of logic in the middle of the eighth chapter of Romans, "Whom he called, them he also justified; and whom"—you see the jump—"he justified, them he also glorified." If He starts, He will finish; so if the life is in me, I can be certain of the glory. Far from presuming on that in order to sin, while I am in this life and world I rather say with John, "Every man that hath this hope in him purifieth himself, even as he is pure" (1 John 3:3).

☙ A THOUGHT TO PONDER ☙

God's work in our souls will be carried on until it ends in ultimate perfection and glory.

From *Life in God*, pp. 111-112.

WE ARE EXHORTED TO PRAY

*And this is the confidence that we have in him, that, if we ask
any thing according to his will, he heareth us.*

1 JOHN 5:14

We must be exceptionally careful in the matter of comparing
Scripture with Scripture. The Bible never contradicts itself. We must
never base our doctrine upon one statement only; or to put it in
another way, our doctrine must never be so formulated as to be in
conflict with any other statement of Scripture or to contradict any
other clear and obvious scriptural teaching.

Then, having done that, we come to certain conclusions. One
conclusion is that there is an element of mystery about this question of prayer; it is one of those aspects of God's gracious dealings
with us that is beyond our understanding. Now I feel like saying,
"Thank God for that!" I mean that in an ultimate and absolute sense
you and I simply cannot reconcile God's omniscience and foreknowledge and sovereignty with this fact of prayer that we find so
clearly taught in Scripture.

But there are so many other things one cannot understand. I cannot understand how a holy God would ever forgive or can ever forgive a single soul. I cannot understand it, but thank God, I believe
it! I cannot understand the eternal mind and heart, but I thank God
for a revelation that assures me that God can be just and a justifier
of the ungodly. And there are many other instances and illustrations that I could give of exactly the same thing, and this question
of prayer is one of them. In an ultimate philosophical sense there is
an element of mystery about it, but praise God, we are not left with
philosophy. We have a Gospel that comes to us in its simplicity and
tells us what to do. So though our little minds cannot understand it
philosophically, there is nothing that is so plain and clear in Scripture
as that we are taught and exhorted to pray. Go through the
Scriptures, and notice the frequency of the exhortations to pray.

✑ A THOUGHT TO PONDER ✒

Prayer is one of those aspects of God's gracious dealings with us
that is beyond our understanding.

FOLLOWING THE EXAMPLE OF JESUS IN PRAYER

And if we know that he hear us, whatsoever we ask, we know that we have the petitions that we desired of him.

1 JOHN 5:15

One sees the very Son of God Himself at prayer. So if you are interested in the philosophical aspect of prayer, go immediately to the case of our Lord Jesus Christ. There is the only begotten, the eternal Son of God; there is the one who says of Himself that though He is upon earth, He is still in heaven; there is the one who says, "I and my Father are one" (John 10:30). Why had He any need to pray? Why, before choosing His disciples, did He spend all night in prayer? If you are interested in philosophical problems, answer that. Why was it ever necessary for the Son of God to pray so much while He was here on earth? And yet He did.

In other words, the Scripture teaches that prayer is essential and vital to us, and everywhere we are exhorted to it. Not only that, but if you read the lives of God's greatest saints in the long history of the Church, you will find that they were men and women of prayer. I believe I am right in saying that John Wesley used to say that any Christian worthy of the name should spend at least four hours every day in prayer, and he tended to judge his people by that. There has never been a man or woman of God who has been singularly used of God in this world, but that they spent much time in prayer. The nearer people are to God, the more they pray to Him; so the testimony of the Christian Church supports the teaching of Scripture itself.

Furthermore, we have numerous incidents in Scripture of what God has clearly done by way of answer to prayer, and it seems to me that the explanation ultimately is not really difficult. The God who determines the end determines the means; and if God in His infinite wisdom is determined that He is going to bring certain things to pass as a result of and in answer to the prayers of His people, I ask with reverence, why shouldn't He?

❧ A THOUGHT TO PONDER ❧

The nearer people are to God, the more they pray to Him.

From *Life in God*, pp. 116-117.

PRAY FOR HOLINESS

*And if we know that he hear us, whatsoever we ask, we know that
we have the petitions that we desired of him.*

1 JOHN 5:15

We can pray that all the precepts, all the promises, and all the prophecies in the Bible with respect to ourselves may be fulfilled in us. "For this is the will of God, even your sanctification" (1 Thessalonians 4:3). And if you pray for sanctification, you can be sure that God will sanctify you. It is God's will that we may know His love; ask Him therefore to reveal His love to you by the Holy Spirit, and you can be certain He will do so. And it is the same with all the various other promises that are in the Scriptures: "Ask, and it shall be given you; seek, and ye shall find; knock, and it shall be opened unto you" (Matthew 7:7).

Are you concerned that you do not love as much as you ought? Tell Him about it; ask Him to shed His love abroad in your heart, and He will do so. Are you concerned about some sin that casts you down? Pray a confident prayer. It is the will of God that you should be delivered from sin; so pray for it. Are you concerned that your heart shall be clean? Well, offer David's prayer ("Create within me a clean heart, O God; and renew a right spirit within me," Psalm 51:10), and I assure you, on the basis of the Word of God and His character, that He will answer you, and the blood of Christ will cleanse you from all sin and all unrighteousness. Go through your Bible, and make a list of the promises of God to you; then take them to God, use them in His presence, plead them, and you can be quite certain that you have your petitions. You already possess them, and in His own time and way God will give you a full realization of them and a full enjoyment of them.

✎ A THOUGHT TO PONDER ✐

We can pray that all the precepts, promises, and prophecies in the Bible may be fulfilled in us.

SAFE IN THE ARMS OF JESUS

We know that whosoever is born of God sinneth not;
but he that is begotten of God keepeth himself, and
that wicked one toucheth him not.

1 JOHN 5:18

Jesus prayed, "I pray not that thou shouldest take them out of the world, but that thou shouldest keep them from the evil" (John 17:15)—the very thing John says in this verse. Surely, then, we are confronted here by that statement. It is the same thing of which Jude reminds us: "Now unto him that is able to keep you from falling, and to present you faultless before the presence of his glory with exceeding joy" (24). That is it!

This is the thing we find so constantly in our hymns—the celebration of the fact that the God who has kept and held His people in the past is still our God.

> *Guide me, O Thou great Jehovah,*
> *Pilgrim through this barren land;*
> *I am weak, but Thou art mighty,*
> *Hold me with Thy powerful hand.*
> WILLIAM WILLIAMS

Augustus Toplady's confidence, too, is that Christ is his keeper; He looks after him.

> *A sovereign Protector I have,*
> *Unseen, yet forever at hand,*
> *Unchangeably faithful to save,*
> *Almighty to rule and command.*

> *He smiles, and his comforts abound;*
> *His grace as the dew shall descend,*
> *And walls of salvation surround*
> *The soul He delights to defend.*

❧ A THOUGHT TO PONDER ❧

The God who has kept and held His people in the past is still our God.

From *Life in God*, pp. 149-150.

REPENTANCE

Have mercy upon me, O God, according to thy loving-kindness:
according unto the multitude of thy tender mercies
blot out my transgressions.

PSALM 51:1

Certain things must happen before a man can experience the great salvation that is found in the Christian Gospel. There are certain things that we must realize, we must grasp, we must believe, and the first of these is repentance.

We must be clear about the whole question of repentance. Read the case of any convert you can find in the Bible, and you will always find that this element of repentance comes in. Read the lives of the saints, read the history of men who figure in the church of God in past ages, and you will find that every man who has really known the experience and the power of the grace of God in his life is always a man who gives evidence of repentance. I do not hesitate, therefore, to make the assertion that without repentance there is no salvation. The need for repentance is one of the absolutes about which the Bible does not argue. It just says it. It just postulates it. It is impossible, I say, for a man to be a Christian without repentance; no man can experience salvation unless he knows what it is to repent. Therefore I am emphasizing that this is a very vital matter.

John the Baptist when he began his ministry went out and preached the baptism of repentance for the remission of sins. It was the first message of the first preacher. Our Lord and Savior Jesus Christ, we are told by Mark, went about and preached that men must repent. Repentance is *absolutely* vital. Paul went about and preached repentance toward God and faith in our Lord Jesus Christ. Peter preached on the Day of Pentecost the first sermon under the auspices of the Christian Church, and when he had finished certain people cried out, "What shall we do?" "Repent!" said Peter. Without repentance there is no knowledge of salvation, there is no experience of salvation. It is an essential step. It is the first step.

✍ A THOUGHT TO PONDER ✍
Without repentance there is no salvation.

From *Out of the Depths*, pp. 17-18.

WHAT IS WRONG?

*Wash me thoroughly from mine iniquity, and
cleanse me from my sin.*

PSALM 51:2

Psalm 51 is a classic statement on the whole matter and doctrine of repentance. Because so many people do not realize the biblical teaching concerning sin, they fail to realize so many other things that are contained in the Christian Gospel. So many people today say that they do not see the need of the Incarnation, that they do not understand all this talk about the Son of God having come down to earth, that they do not understand this talk about the miracles and the supernatural, that they cannot follow this idea of the atonement and terms such as *justification* and *sanctification* and *rebirth*. They say that they do not understand why all this seems to be necessary.

They would argue like this: "Isn't it the church that has evolved all these theoretical, purely abstract ideas? Aren't they things that have been conjured up in the minds of theologians? What have they to do with us, and where is their practical relevance?" I would like to point out that people who talk like this do so because they have not realized the full meaning of the biblical teaching about sin. They have not realized that they themselves are sinful. But the Bible, in sharp contrast, constantly insists upon this from the beginning to the end.

Here we are in this modern and perplexing world; we are conscious that something is wrong, and the question is, "What is wrong?" Politicians do not seem to be able to solve our problems. Philosophers are asking questions, but they do not seem to be able to answer them. All our efforts do not seem to put the world right. The Bible says, "You are ignoring the one thing that is the key to the situation! It is sin. Here is the cause of the trouble in individuals, in intimate human relationships, in international relationships everywhere. This is the difficulty."

◈ A THOUGHT TO PONDER ◈
People who talk like this do so because they have not realized the full meaning of the biblical teaching about sin.

From *Out of the Depths*, pp. 18-20.

A Prayer of a Backslider

*For I acknowledge my transgressions: and
my sin is ever before me.*

PSALM 51:3

The fifty-first Psalm is what you might call, if you like, "a prayer of a backslider." Here we are shown the steps through which a man inevitably passes when he becomes convinced and convicted of his sin.

The first is this: *He comes to a knowledge of and an acknowledgment of the fact that he has sinned.* Listen to David: "For I acknowledge my transgressions: and my sin is ever before me." The first thing that happens to a man when he becomes convinced and convicted of sin is that he faces his sin and really looks at what he has done in an honest manner. This whole story [of David and Bathsheba] tells us that was exactly what David had previously not done.

Is there not something almost incredible about this, that a man could do the things that David did and yet really not face them? Surely David must have felt he was doing wrong; yet he did it! But he did not face the fact of wrongdoing, and he went on refusing to face it. And having done these terrible things, David would still not have faced them were it not that God sent the prophet Nathan to him and made him face them by giving him details of the same thing as had happened but in a different form. Thus David saw the truth, and he was humbled to the dust. That is how he came to write this fifty-first Psalm. This is always the first step. We must stop and think; we must pause for a moment and face ourselves and face the life we have lived and what we have done and what we are doing.

Now I know this is very unpleasant, and people dislike a gospel that says a thing like that. But if you want to know God's salvation, you have to repent; and the first step is conviction of sin, and the first way to become convicted of sin is to stop and look at yourself.

✎ A Thought to Ponder ✍

The first step is conviction of sin.

From *Out of the Depths*, pp. 22-23.

TRANSGRESSION AND INIQUITY

*Wash me thoroughly from mine iniquity, and cleanse me
from my sin. For I acknowledge my transgressions: and
my sin is ever before me.*

PSALM 51:2-3

The second step when we become convicted of sin is *a recognition
of the exact character or nature of what we have done.* This is put
here [in Psalm 51] perfectly in three words. The first is the word
"transgressions," the second is "iniquity," and "sin" is the third.

What does "transgression" mean? It means rebellion; it means
the uprising of the will against authority, and especially against a person of authority. "Blot out my transgressions" (verse 1). In other
words, David admits he has transgressed. He has rebelled against
an authority. His own will has risen up within him, and he has
asserted himself. He has been governed by desire and has allowed
himself to be swayed by lust. Transgression means a desire to have
our own way, a desire to do what we want to do.

"Iniquity"—what does that mean? Well, iniquity means that an
act is twisted or that it is bent. It means perversion, and this is obvious in the case of David. "Wash me thoroughly from mine iniquity"—the foul thing, that dastardly thing. "What was it in me that
made me do it? How perverted I must have been to do that!" I ask
you as you examine yourself, do you not see that so many things you
do are twisted and perverted? Jealousy and envy and malice—how
horrible the twist! The desire that evil may come to someone, the dislike of praise of another—evil thoughts, bent, twisted, ugly, foul—
"iniquity"! And we are all guilty of iniquity.

"Sin" means "missing the mark." We are not living as we ought
to be living. A man aims at a target; he shoots, but he misses it.
That is what *sin* always means. A man is not treading the path God
has marked out for him.

✎ A THOUGHT TO PONDER ✎
We are all guilty of iniquity.

From *Out of the Depths*, pp. 25-26.

WHO DO WE SIN AGAINST?

*Against thee, thee only, have I sinned, and
done this evil in thy sight.*

PSALM 51:4

Step number three when a man comes under conviction is that *he
realizes and confesses that all this is done against God and before
God.* "Against thee, thee only, have I sinned, and done this evil in thy
sight."

"Surely," says someone, "that must be wrong. David ought to
have said, 'Against Bathsheba, against Uriah, against men who were
killed in that battle, against Israel and my people have I sinned.'
But he says, 'Against thee, thee only . . .'" Ah, David is quite right!
He does not deny that he has sinned against the others, but here he
is going a step further. He realizes that his actions are not simply
actions in and of themselves. He sees that they not only affect and
involve other people, but their real essence is that he has sinned
against God.

Now that is the essential difference between *remorse* and *repentance.* A man who suffers remorse is one who realizes he has done
wrong, but he has not *repented* until he realizes that he has sinned
against God.

Why should he feel that? Let me try to answer the question in the
following manner. Sin, you see, means a violation of what God has
made and of what God intended man to be. Let me put it, in a preliminary fashion, in this form: When a man sins, he is not only
doing certain things himself that he should not do; he is sinning
against human nature, he is letting it down. He is sinning, therefore, against humanity, and because of that he is sinning against God
who made man. God made man perfect, and God intended man to
live that perfect life. He gave him the possibility of doing so, and
when a man sins he lets God down. "Against *thee, thee only*, have I
sinned." I have violated what God intended man to be. I am twist-
ing and perverting God's creation. Every time I sin, I violate God's
holy law.

❧ A THOUGHT TO PONDER ☙
I have violated what God intended man to be.

From *Out of the Depths*, pp. 28-29.

December 29

MAN HAS NO EXCUSE

Against thee, thee only, have I sinned, and done this evil
in thy sight: that thou mightest be justified when thou speakest,
and be clear when thou judgest.

PSALM 51:4

In the next step a man finds that *he has absolutely no excuse or plea.* David is telling God, "I haven't a single excuse. I have no plea. There is nothing to be said for me. There is no reason for what I have done. The whole thing was the result of utter willfulness. I am altogether wrong. I have nothing to plead in mitigation."

I want to emphasize this. I say that this is an absolutely essential part of repentance and of conviction of sin. I therefore plead with you to examine yourselves and examine your actions. Can you justify all you have done? Can you really put up a plea of mitigation? Let me take up the position of Nathan the prophet. What if I stood in this pulpit and described your love to you in a parable about somebody else? Would you see it? We must examine ourselves in this respect. Let me put it bluntly by putting it to you like this. As long as you are in the position of trying to justify yourself, you have not repented. As long as you are clinging to any attempt at self-justification and self-righteousness, I say you have not repented. Surely the man who is repentant is the man who, like David, says, "There is not a single excuse. I see it clearly. I have no justification. The things that I see in my life—I hate them. I had no business doing them. I did them willfully; I knew it was wrong. I admit it! I frankly confess it—'that thou mightest be justified when thou speakest, and be clear when thou judgest.'"

Do you feel that God is rather hard on you when He condemns you? Do you feel that God would be dealing unfairly with you if you ever found yourself in hell? If you do, you have not repented. I would emphasize that the test of repentance is this—that a man having looked at himself, and at his own heart and life, says to himself, "I deserve nothing but hell, and if God sends me there, I haven't a single complaint to make. I desire nothing better!" That is an essential part of repentance, and without repentance there is no salvation.

❧ A THOUGHT TO PONDER ❧

As long as you are clinging to any attempt at self-justification and self-righteousness, you have not repented.

From *Out of the Depths*, pp. 30-31.

THE DOCTRINE OF REGENERATION

Create in me a clean heart, O God.

PSALM 51:10

Nothing, it seems to me, is quite so strange as the way in which man by nature always objects to the doctrine of regeneration. There is nothing also, I sometimes think, that so demonstrates the depth of sin in the human heart as this objection to the doctrine of the rebirth or being born again. Read the New Testament Scriptures, and you will find that men objected to it in those days. When our Lord and Savior Jesus Christ spoke about it, He was always persecuted. People disliked Him for mentioning it. When He began to expose the depth of iniquity in the human heart and to talk about a rebirth, they invariably misunderstood Him. They disliked it then, and it has always been the same ever since.

When John Wesley was truly converted, he went back to his university at Oxford and preached a sermon on this very subject; and he was hated for it. Those respectable religious people in Oxford disliked this doctrine, and they made it impossible for him to continue preaching there. The natural man, the unregenerate human heart, objected to this great and wondrous biblical doctrine of rebirth and regeneration. And it is equally true today. People sit and listen to an address or sermon on what is called the fatherhood of God or the brotherhood of man and they never object to it. When they are exhorted to live a better life, they never express any objection at all. They say that it is perfectly right, and even though they are reprimanded for not living better lives, they say that it is perfectly true and quite fair and that they could do better. But if a preacher stands before the natural man and says, "You must be born again—you must have a new life from God," they ask, "What is this strange doctrine?"

❧ A THOUGHT TO PONDER ❧

There is nothing that so demonstrates the depth of sin in the human heart as objection to the doctrine of the rebirth.

A STEADFAST SPIRIT

Renew a right spirit within me.

PSALM 51:10

One characteristic of the Christian is always this: *a profound distrust of self and a realization of the power of God.* Listen to David: "Create in me a clean heart . . . and renew a right spirit within me" (Psalm 51:10). The Revised Version margin puts it this way: "Renew a *steadfast* spirit within me."

You see, what he was conscious of was his own unsteadiness. Well might David have felt that. He was a man who had experienced God's blessing, and he had known the joy of the Lord; and yet he had fallen into terrible sins. So he cries out for this renewal and for this reliable spirit within himself. I make bold to say that every Christian knows what this means. A Christian is not a man who relies upon himself. It is only the Christian who knows his own weakness. It takes a Christian to see the darkness of his own heart and the frailty of his own nature. There is a type of Christian, I regret to say, who behaves as if he can do everything. He has had an experience of conversion, and now he is ready to face hell and the devil and everything. Poor fellow, he will not go very far before he loses that sense of confidence. "Let him that thinketh he standeth," said the apostle Paul to such people, "take heed lest he fall" (1 Corinthians 10:12). No; the Christian is a man who knows his own weakness, and he is afraid of it. So he prays for a steady spirit, a reliable spirit. He wants to be a sound man.

❧ A THOUGHT TO PONDER ☙

The Christian is a man who knows his own weakness, and he is afraid of it.

From *Out of the Depths*, pp. 105-106.

SCRIPTURE INDEX

Note: Some references appear more than once on the same page.